EIGHTEENTH-CENTURY MUSIC IN THEORY AND PRACTICE

Essays in Honor of Alfred Mann

Louis Ouzer

Alfred Mann

EIGHTEENTH-CENTURY MUSIC IN THEORY AND PRACTICE

Essays in Honor of Alfred Mann

Edited by
Mary Ann Parker

FESTSCHRIFT SERIES No. 13

PENDRAGON PRESS
STUYVESANT, NY

ML55 .M25 1994
Eighteenth-century music in theory and practice : essays in honor of Alfred Mann

Pendragon Press Musicological Series
Aesthetics in Music
Dance & Music Series
Festschrift Series
Franz Liszt Studies Series
French Opera in the 17th and 18th Centuries
Harmonologia: Studies in Music Theory
The Juilliard Performance Guides
Monographs in Musicology
Musical Life in 19th-Century France
G. B. Pergolesi Complete Works
The Sociology of Music Series
Studies in Central and Eastern European Music
Studies in Czech Music
Thematic Catalogues

Library of Congress Cataloging-in-Publication Data
Eighteenth-century music in theory and practice: essays in honor of Alfred Mann /
　edited by Mary Ann Parker
　　p. cm.—(Festschrift series: no. 13)
　　Includes bibliographical references.
　　ISBN 0-945193-11-4
　　Music—Theory. 2. Music—Performance practice. II. Parker, Mary Ann III.
　　　Series
ML
781—dc20   93-0000
                                                              CIP
                                                               MN

Copyright 1994 Pendragon Press

CONTENTS

Preface	vii
Editor's Introduction	ix
"Et Incarnatus" and "Crucifixus": The Earliest and Latest Settings of Bach's B-Minor Mass *Christoph Wolff*	1
Some Performance Problems of Bach's Unaccompanied Violin and Cello Works *Frederick Neumann*	19
Performing Problems in Handel's Operas *J. Merrill Knapp*	49
Handel: Some Contemporary Performance Parts Considered *Watkins Shaw*	59
Harmonic Patterns in Handel's Operas *Ellen T. Harris*	77
Johann Joseph Fux and Equal Temperament *Hellmut Federhofer*	119
On the History of Musical Instruction in the Austrian Baroque *Eva Badura-Skoda*	131
Towards a Close Reading of Carl Philipp Emanuel Bach *Peter Williams*	143

The Influence of Harmonic Thinking on the Teaching of Simple
Counterpoint in the Latter Half of the Eighteenth Century
David Beach   159

A Bach Borrowing by Gluck: Another Frontier
George J. Buelow   187

Mozart Through His Piano Students
Mario R. Mercado   205

Music as an Analogue of Speech: Musical Syntax in the Writings
of Heinrich Christoph Koch and in the Works of Schubert
Walther Dürr   227

Archaic and Contemporary Aspects of Schubert's *Alfonso und
Estrella*: Issues of Influence, Originality, and Maturation
Thomas A. Denny   241

The Transition from Baroque to Romantic: A Study in English
Provincial Music-Making
Percy M. Young   263

A European at Home Abroad: An Autobiographical Sketch
Alfred Mann   289

An Alfred Mann Bibliography
Michael R. Dodds   329

PREFACE

Although this *Festschrift* was conceived a few years ago, its completion was delayed because of a series of events beyond my control. Its appearance, then, becomes in a way a tribute not only to the remarkable man who inspired it, but also to the patience and persistence of all those involved.

In particular, thanks are due to Robert Freeman, Director of the Eastman School of Music, for his support and advice. Jürgen Thym and Kerala Snyder from time to time generously lent their names and offered their counsel.

Most important, of course, are the authors. I wish to express my gratitude, not only for their fine contributions, but also for the generous and co-operative spirit they brought to the project. Numerous scholars around the world, on hearing about this collection, asked that their names be included as well–wishers. However, it seems that such a list might go on forever, and that it would be too easy to omit valued friends and associates. Suffice it to say, Alfred, that as regards the international network of respect and affection for you, the colleagues whose articles appear here represent only the "tip of the iceberg." And I know it will please you to learn that, a few weeks before he died, I discussed my idea for this book with the beloved Jens Peter Larsen, who was warmly encouraging and became the first to offer a contribution.

I am grateful for the patience and kind co–operation of Robert Kessler and particularly Nanette Maxim at Pendragon. Thanks are also due to John Parsons and Brian Power, who assisted with the preparation of the manuscript.

Mary Ann Parker
Toronto, 1994

INTRODUCTION

A few years ago, when the idea for this book first came to me, I initiated a correspondence on the subject with the late Paul Henry Lang. His letters were warmly enthusiastic and curiously open about his own failing health and his attempts to resume his work. He accepted my invitation to write the introduction to a *Festschrift* for Alfred Mann, remarking that "Alfred was not only my prime disciple; but is a close friend, almost a son, and I would be delighted to pay him tribute." He added that he was glad his deadline was comfortably in the future, because "by that time I will have either recovered or will play pinochle with Handel on the Elysian fields."

Now the writing of the introduction has fallen, not to the senior in a life-long mentor and student relationship, but to the junior. Those who encounter Alfred as a teacher are immensely fortunate. His knowledge extends far beyond the conventional limits of institutional learning, and he dispenses it generously, and with the deep-rooted courtesy that permeates everything he does. I remember the first time I ever submitted a piece of work to Alfred; it was the opening chapter of my dissertation, and I sent it to him in New Jersey shortly before he made the move to Rochester. He returned it almost immediately. Along with a few editorial suggestions and encouraging remarks, he had written "There are a few details that might merit some leisurely discussion." I was thrilled, and so positively disposed to anything he might propose that I actually enjoyed and certainly benefited from what might have been an agonizing process; a few weeks later, the chapter had been cut by two thirds and entirely re-written.

Anyone attempting to characterize Alfred Mann's prolific career as a musical scholar must take into account that his work is still in progress. He brings to it an understanding of music that is uniquely profound; his activities as researcher, writer and editor are informed not only by a rich experience as performer and conductor, but also by a long-standing involvement with music theory. In a way, his own musical education is rooted in the same contrapuntal tradition as the composers he studies. And yet, he is no hidebound conservative: one has only to look at his book *Theory and Practice: the Great Composer as Student and Teacher* to discover a strikingly original creative mind. Alfred's work is timeless; his delicacy of thought and elegance of expression transcend political correctness.

The present volume has been compiled to celebrate Alfred Mann's half century of teaching, music-making and scholarship in America. The essays reflect Alfred's interests in the two broad areas of theory and practice, and particularly in some of his favorite fields of endeavor— Bach, Handel, Mozart, Schubert, and in the history of teaching, learning and understanding.

No one could possibly tell his story better than the dedicatee himself, and that is why, when Alfred confessed to me that he had been sketching an autobiography, I insisted that he allow me to include it in the *Festschrift*. In the end, I had to enlist the aid not only of the publisher, but also of Robert Freeman, Director of the Eastman School of Music, to persuade Alfred that it would not be amiss for him to make this unique and personal contribution to the collection. Those who know him will understand best how this unusual series of events took place; in the end, it is entirely typical of the man that, even while others were striving to offer him a tribute, he presented to them his own distinctive gift.

Christoph Wolff

"ET INCARNATUS" AND "CRUCIFIXUS"
The Earliest and the Latest Settings of Bach's B-Minor Mass

When, in the late 1740s, Johann Sebastian Bach decided to expand to a complete Mass one of the Kyrie-Gloria Masses he had written in the 1730s, he turned to the most ambitious work among the five: the Missa of 1733 which he had dedicated to the Dresden court. This work, BWV 232^I, scored for five rather than four voices and for a particularly large orchestra (including a full brass section and three pairs of woodwinds), represented the type of "missa solemnis," whereas the other pieces, BWV 233–236, fell into the "missa ferialis" category. Naturally, the choice of such a grand-scale work as a point of departure had to have a major impact on the overall plan of the eventual composition.

The Kyrie-Gloria Mass thus determined that the movements to be added had to match the size, format, compositional quality, and general character of the older ones. However, the additions Bach made in the late 1740s for the most part surpassed rather than merely matched the 1733 model. For example, Bach increased the vocal ensemble from five to six and even eight voices, he broadened the stylistic spectrum by introducing forms and techniques previously not employed, and he also

---

Christoph Wolff is William Powell Mason Professor of Music and Dean of the Graduate School of Arts and Sciences at Harvard University. He has published widely on the history of music from the 15th to the 20th centuries, notably on Bach and Mozart.

presented a more refined sense of large-scale musical architecture. Moreover, the degree of compositional elaboration in no way remained below the standards of the earlier work; and this is true especially where the recycling of pre-existing pieces is involved. Whether he incorporated a work such as the Sanctus of 1724 or whether he adapted an aria originally written for a completely different purpose, the process of careful revision permitted Bach, always his own strongest critic, to reshape and reformulate his earlier musical thoughts.[1]

Nowhere do Bach's artistic intentions for the expanded Mass become more evident than in the Credo (*Symbolum Nicenum*), the part of the Mass which—like the Gloria—is based on a particularly large amount of liturgical prose text and, hence, always challenges a composer's organizational skills. Bach had paid considerable attention to the overall form of the 1733 Missa in general and its Gloria in particular. The well-rounded structure of the Gloria was primarily built on the strength of external features, notably on the carefully balanced scoring of the solo pieces by using all five vocal concertists and representatives of all four principal orchestral sections (see Diagram 1).

Diagram 1.

Movement	*Vocal Solo*	*Instr. Obbligato*
Laudamus te	S II	Violino concertato
Domine Deus	S I, T	Flauto traverso
Qui sedes	A	Oboe d'amore
Quoniam	B	Corno da caccia

Compared with the Gloria, the Symbolum Nicenum delineates a much more comprehensive and sophisticated large-scale structure that not only embraces all movements, but also involves detailed and systematic compositional planning. Bach did not arrive at a final solution for the multi-movement structure right away.[2] He originally divided the Credo text into eight sections so that the movements were organized in

---

[1] For a particularly illuminating case see Christoph Wolff, "The Agnus Dei of the B-Minor Mass: Parody and New Composition Reconciled," in *Bach: Essays on His Life and Music* (Cambridge, Mass., 1991), 332–39.

[2] A concise summary of the work's genesis can be found in John Butt, *Bach: Mass in B Minor*, Cambridge Music Handbooks (Cambridge, 1991), chapter 2.

pairs. One pair of solo pieces and three corresponding pairs of choruses (each ending in a virtuosic concertato fugue) together formed a perfectly symmetric layout (see Diagram 2).

Diagram 2.

Chorus	Solo	Feature
Credo		chant, *stile antico*
Patrem		concertato fugue
	Et in unum	vocal duet (S I, A)
Crucifixus		passacaglia
Et resurrexit		concertato fugue
	Et in Spiritum	instrumental duo (2 Ob. d'am.)
Confiteor		chant, *stile antico*
Et expecto		concertato fugue

Bach was ultimately not quite satisfied with this structure of coupled movements, for he changed the central component of the carefully planned formal scheme. He replaced the middle pair of movements by a threefold configuration of choruses:

    Et incarnatus
    Crucifixus
    Et resurrexit

The newly created ninth movement of the Symbolum Nicenum was made possible by a redistribution of the text for the "Et in unum" movement so that the "Et incarnatus" portion of the text became available for a separate setting. This revised final version reflects an even stronger symmetric order and, at the same time, Bach's interpretive goal.[3] By moving the words "Crucifixus etiam pro nobis..." to the centermost point of the composition he makes the musical axis—the only passacaglia movement in the Mass—congruent with the christological core of the liturgical Credo.

---

[3] Cf. Friedrich Smend, "Bachs h–moll–Messe: Entstehung, Überlieferung, Bedeutung," *Bach-Jahrbuch* XXXIV (1937): 51–53; and Christoph Wolff, *Der stile antico in der Musik Johann Sebastian Bachs. Studien zu Bachs Spätwerk* (Wiesbaden, 1968), 131–33.

As a curious result of Bach's extensive structural and compositional manipulations the oldest and the youngest settings of the entire B-Minor Mass are put side by side—the "Crucifixus" representing a parody of the Weimar cantata movement "Weinen, Klagen, Sorgen, Zagen" from 1714; the "Et incarnatus" being newly composed in 1748–49 and as such not only the latest choral setting of the Mass, but in all likelihood Bach's last vocal composition.[4] The way in which these two movements are juxtaposed, however, does not at all appear to be casual or uncontrolled. On the contrary, a closer examination reveals a number of significant details regarding their compositional individuality as well as their intimate musical connection.[5]

CRUCIFIXUS

Text and ostinato structure. The movement is based on the chorus "Weinen, Klagen, Sorgen, Zagen" of cantata BWV 12, composed in Weimar for Jubilate Sunday (April 22), 1714.[6] While the character of the original cantata movement, a highly expressive lament, proved to be most congenial for the Mass setting, there must have been more specific reasons for Bach to turn in 1748–49 to a 35-year-old piece, especially considering the fact that not only the textual contents of the two movements, but also the poetic structure of the cantata text (I)[7] and the prose form of the Mass text (II) are extremely remote from one another:

---

[4]Yoshitake Kobayashi, "Zur Chronologie der Spätwerke Johann Sebastian Bachs. Kompositions- und Aufführungstätigkeit bon 1736 bis 1750," *Bach-Jahrbuch* LXXIV (1988): 61, dates Bach's work on the Symbolum Nicenum after August 1748 and before October 1749. The compositional history of the Symbolum Nicenum, however, is not to be confined to the 1748–49 time span. A newly discovered early version of the Symbolum's first movement, a Credo intonation in G-mixolydian, confirms the hypothesis presented by Wolff (*Der stile antico*: 152–55) that at least the stile antico movements may have an earlier origin, perhaps in the early 1740s; cf. Peter Wollny, "Ein Quellenfund zur Frühgeschichte der h-Moll Messe," *Bach-Jahrbuch* LXXIX (1994) (in press).

[5]The published analyses of the B-Minor Mass have consistently neglected these two movements and their important interrelationship.

[6]One subsequent performance of the piece during Bach's Leipzig years is datable (30 April 1724); cf. Hans-Joachim Schulze and Christoph Wolff, *Bach Compendium*, vol. I/1 (Leipzig, 1985): A 68.

[7]The unnamed librettist is most likely Salomon Franck. A detailed poetic analysis is provided by Z. Philip Ambrose, "'Weinen, Klagen, Sorgen, Zagen' und die antike Redekunst," *Bach-Jahrbuch* LXVI (1980): 35–45.

"ET INCARNATUS" AND "CRUCIFIXUS"

I. A		Weinen, Klagen
		Sorgen, Zagen
		Angst und Not
		sind der Christen Tränenbrot,
B		die das Zeichen Jesu tragen.
A		[da capo]
II.		Crucifixus etiam pro nobis, sub Pontio Pilato, +
		passus et sepultus est.

Bach used for the Mass parody only the A part, that is the passacaglia section of the cantata movement (mm. 1–49: *Lente*), and left out the B section (mm. 49–89: *un poc'allegro*). Nevertheless, the important text reference of the B section to the sign of Jesus ("das Zeichen Jesu") relates directly to the Mass text, for the sign of Jesus—the cross—is indeed its subject matter.

It becomes clear that Bach's choice of a model for the "Crucifixus" movement was not determined by prosodic similarities. Bach actually had to make considerable adjustments in order to make the new text fit the old music. The musically extremely effective vocal entries of the cantata movement, accentuating the four different key words[8] from the opening lines of the poem ("Weinen, Klagen, Sorgen, Zagen") in an anticlimactically descending sequence (Soprano to Bass) corresponding with the passacaglia pattern, could not be reproduced in the Mass movement:

Example 1.

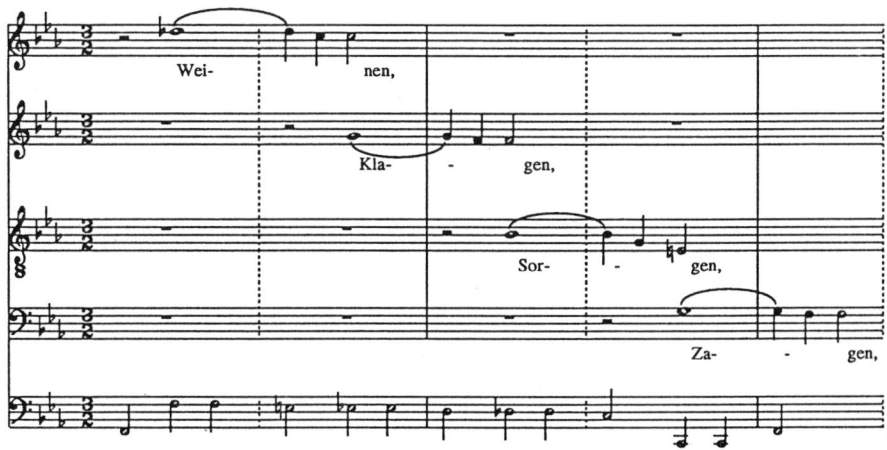

[8]Producing the rhetorical device of *asyndeton* (see Ambrose, note 7).

However, the repeated presentation of the single word "crucifixus" embodied an expressive device in its own right. Bach underscored the intensified declamation by modifying the rhythmic structures. He not only changed the syllabification (the adjustment from "wei-nen..." to "cru-ci-fi-xus" being unavoidable), but also converted the half-note ostinato bass into a quarter-note tremolo pattern:

Example 2.

The declamatory style of the "Crucifixus" thus appears to be actually more emphatic than that of the cantata movement, and its rhetorical vigor is strongly supported by the ostinato technique of the passacaglia. In fact, Bach's application of ostinato technique as a rhetorical device is highly appropriate. The rhetorical figure of *anaphora* or *repetitio* traditionally serves to accentuate and emphasize words of special significance, in this case the word "crucifixus," and with it the central christological message of the Credo.[9]

Compositional changes. A movement that originally functioned as a cantata opening chorus could not simply be transplanted in a larger multi-movement context without changes, be they non-essential (as, for example, the transposition from the original f minor to e minor) or more substantive. In the "Crucifixus," adjustments of the latter variety pertain to the rhythmic modifications already discussed as well as to form and instrumentation.

The orchestral accompaniment of the Weimar cantata movement was scored for five-parts in the French manner, that is with two violas. In the new version Bach modernized the scoring by eliminating viola II. At the same time, he expanded the orchestral accompaniment by integrating flauto traverso I/II and by establishing a complementary pattern of alternating chords in order to underscore the tremolo of the basso continuo (the chordal accompaniment in BWV 12/2 being limited to the first and third beats of each measure):

Example 3.

[9]Cf. Wolff, *Der stile antico*, 106.

Example 3 (continued)

The newly arranged orchestral accompaniment certainly helped to update the movement in stylistic terms and to integrate it with the overall instrumental scoring of the Mass. Moreover, the exposed use of the two flutes in juxtaposition with the strings provides the "Crucifixus" with a distinctive instrumental color that is not used anywhere else, either in the Symbolum Nicenum or any other part of the Mass.

From a performance-practical viewpoint, the use of the bassoon in the instrumentation of this movement is somewhat problematic. Bach's autograph score makes no reference to the bassoon and, regrettably, there exist no original performance parts for the Symbolum Nicenum.[10] All available editions simply let the bassoon play the continuo part. However, a musically much more appropriate solution is found in the original scoring of BWV 12/2, where the bassoon plays along with the upper strings. Correspondingly, the bassoon part in the "Crucifixus" might be arranged as follows:

Example 4.

[10]For a summary of the sources see Schulze and Wolff, *Bach Compendium*, vol. I/4 (Leipzig, 1989), E 1.

Also in line with BWV 12/2 and underscoring the piano dynamics of mm. 49ff., the final measures of the movement require "bassone tacet."[11]

In the "Crucifixus" the first and last four measures are not contained in the parody model BWV 12/2, but newly composed for the B-Minor Mass. The opening ostinato period serves as an instrumental prelude that became necessary only after the "Et incarnatus" movement had been inserted. Otherwise, there would not have been any instrumental transition between the concluding measure of the "Et incarnatus" and the original opening measure (m. 5) of the "Crucifixus." The postlude (m. 49ff.), however, already represented an integral part of the original (prelude-less) version of the movement since it had to provide a modulation to the following D-major movement. But Bach seems to have thought well beyond the merely functional aspects of this quite extraordinary passage.

As for the highly expressive and theologically meaningful setting of the concluding words, "passus et sepultus est" ("he suffered and was buried"), the sudden introduction of the a capella mode in the passage referring to Christ's death is reminiscent of the related recitative passage of Christ's last words, "Eli, Eli lama asabthani?" in the St. Matthew Passion (BWV 244/61a). There, too, Bach suddenly removes the string accompagnato that otherwise serves as a characteristic attribute of the *vox Christi*. But at the point of death, where God becomes man, the distinguishing attribute of the divine is indeed musically illogical and immaterial.

ET INCARNATUS

Text treatment. The third movement of the Symbolum Nicenum, "Et in unum Dominum," exists in two versions with different text underlays. Originally Bach had assigned to it a longer text unit that included the "Et incarnatus" portion which he later extracted in order to set it as a separate movement.[12] It is not entirely clear when Bach made this decision, which had far-reaching implications for the large-

---

[11] Realized in this way in the new Peters critical edition of the B-Minor Mass (ed. Christoph Wolff, Frankfurt–New York, 1993).

[12] Friedrich Smend's 1956 edition (*Neue Bach–Ausgabe*, vol. II/1) contains both versions of this movement. Smend, however, considered the earlier version to have been reinstated by Bach—a view that can no longer be upheld.

scale structure of the Mass, but in the absence of any concrete documentary evidence it seems reasonable to assume that it was made only after the Symbolum Nicenum was completed and the composer had the opportunity to review the whole.

Bach redistributed the text of the "Et in unum Dominum" (see Diagram 3) without making any compositional changes in the piece. The music had, at any rate, been originally conceived for a different purpose and text, although that version remains unknown.[13] Yet, Bach's choice of music for the first major text portion of the second article was anything but arbitrary. The key phrases ("Et in unum . . ., Filium unigeniti . . ., et ex patre . . ., Deum de Deo . . .,")[14] are set in the manner of extremely dense (stretto) imitation, so that the music reflects the symbolism of the text—the second persona or figure derived from, and identical with the first:

Example 5.

In comparison with this primary interpretive focus, all other seeming musical allusions (for example, the passage "descendit de coelis")[15] are secondary and coincidental, if not irrelevant. The new text distribution of the revised version demonstrates that Bach carefully preserved, indeed emphasized the primary interpretative feature of the movement.

---

[13]See Smend, *Kritische Bericht* NBA II/1, 148f.
[14]Mm. 9ff., 17ff., 34ff., 48ff., etc.
[15]Especially the violin passage (mm. 59f.); cf. comments by Smend, *Krit. Bericht* NBA II/1, 160f.

Diagram 3.

S[olo] and C[horal] Movements	original	revised
¶Et in unum Dominum, Jesum Christum, Filium Dei unigenitum ¶Et ex Patre natum, ante omnia secula,	S: mm. 9–28	S: mm. 9–27 mm. 34–42
¶Deum de Deo, lumen de lumine, Deum verum de Deo vero; genitum, non factum, consubstantialem Patri, per quem omnia facta sunt.	mm. 34–42	mm. 48–62
¶Qui propter nos homines et propter nostram salutem descendit de coelis,	mm. 48–62	mm. 64–76
¶Et incarnatus est de Spiritu Sancto, ex Maria virgine, ET HOMO FACTUS EST.	mm. 64–76	C: mm. 4–32 mm. 32–39 mm. 41–49

The extraction of the "Et incarnatus" passage from the solo movement and its conversion into a separate chorus gave considerable weight to the text portion which addresses the incarnation of God's son. What Bach had first set to music in a rather cursory manner, altogether comprising 12 measures (mm. 64–76) and a quasi appendix to the "Et in unum," he now presents in a much more extensive way. In fact, the new movement joins the "Credo," "Confiteor," and "Et resurrexit" movements as the genuine five-voice settings of the Symbolum Nicenum.

The movement contains three choral blocks, two of which are devoted to the first three lines of the text ("Et incarnatus . . ."). The third block then offers, as culmination point of the musical structure, the fourth and theologically most significant line.[16]

"*A la Pergolesi.*" The newly composed movement exhibits a musical character that departs stunningly not only from the styles, techniques, and expressive devices found in the immediately surrounding pieces; it

---

[16]This text line was traditionally highlighted typographically (e.g., also in the Dresden hymnal of 1725, which was used in Leipzig).

also has no parallel in the entire Mass. Moreover, there is simply no piece in Bach's compositional output that would even remotely resemble this movement. What clearly occurred to Bach only after he had, for all practical purposes, finished the Mass turned out to be his most avant garde composition—an extraordinarily forward-looking musical afterthought.

A specific combination of features contributes to the movement's modernity. To enumerate them in summary fashion: (1) in the vocal parts—unadorned (mainly triadic) motifs, generally cantabile declamation, prevailingly chordal harmonic structures with homophonic surface, novel harmonies such as augmented 6/5 chords (for example, in m. 12), unfluctuating rhythmic flow; (2) in the instrumental parts—basically simple and extremely transparent two-part texture, unison violins focusing on a repetitive five-note (triadic) appoggiatura motif, a supporting and contrapuntally not vigorous continuo.

The prototype for this highly unusual kind of musical setting can be found in Giovanni Battista Pergolesi's *Stabat mater* of 1736. Not only did Bach know the piece, he had in fact prepared an elaborate parody arrangement of Pergolesi's last work in 1746–47, which is in very close chronological proximity to the completion of the B-Minor Mass.[17] The model for Bach's "Et incarnatus" is the section "Quis et homo, qui non fleret, Matrem Christi si videret. . ." from the *Stabat mater*, a section whose text not only shares some key words (homo, mater Christi) with the Mass movement, but whose general content is quite similar:

Example 6.

[17]Schulze and Wolff, *Bach Compendium*, vol. I/3 (Leipzig, 1989), B 26.

The Pergolesi model, though considerably shorter and far less sophisticated a structure, presents essentially the same combination of compositional features in both the vocal and instrumental parts of the score. Particularly noticeable are: the steadily repeated five-note appoggiatura motif in the (initially unison) violins, the non-contrapuntal continuo (with opening pedal-point), augmented 6/5 chords (mm. 5–6), subdued vocal texture and cantabile melodic flavor.

At the same time, Bach's setting eclipses its model in many ways. This is especially evident in the unobtrusive, yet exceedingly refined polyphonization of the chordal texture which introduces a most sophisticated crescendo of motivic entries, beginning with a simple descending triad (alto:b, f-sharp, d, b) and ending with a chromatically altered octave leap (bass: b, ... b-sharp):

Example 7.

"ET INCARNATUS" AND "CRUCIFIXUS"

Of particular significance is the final climax of the movement. Bach reverses the previously prevailing descending melodic direction of the vocal parts, culminating in an ascending triad. This presentation of the inverted opening motif of the movement as a canonic stretto gives decisive emphasis to the crucial text phrase "et homo factus est." The passage is further accentuated by an unexpected unfolding of instrumental textures: what had previously been a non-contrapuntal two-part setting slips into a strict three-part canonic counterpoint (divided violins with continuo):

Example 8.

Musical links. This most modern of all of Bach's vocal pieces, apparently his very last choral composition (from 1749),[18] has its place next to what is not only one of the most old-fashioned settings, but the chronologically oldest unit of the entire Mass, the "Crucifixus" (based on a 1714 cantata movement). However, Bach avoided what could have developed into a stylistic and aesthetic clash of incompatible music.

The subtle linking of the two movements seems most ingenious. First, the obviously proportional tempo: eighth notes in the 3/4 notation of the "Et incarnatus" corresponding to quarter notes in the 3/2 notation of the "Crucifixus"; second, the similar chordal qualities of the vocal textures; third, the transparent and stagnant instrumental accompaniment; fourth, the unexpected climactic ending. Finally, and perhaps most importantly, the ostinato principle. What provided the structural underpinning of the "Crucifixus," the four-measure passacaglia bass, has its equivalent in the preceding movement. The element that functions as the decisive unifying device in the "Et incarnatus" is the repetitive, one-measure violin figure. The "Crucifixus" is predicated on the old-fashioned ground bass, whereas the "Et incarnatus" features a treble ostinato—in both instances strategic devices of rhetorical emphasis and intensity.

---

[18]The newly composed sections of the Agnus Dei were probably written later; cf. Wolff, "The Agnus Dei," 332–39.

Bach's virtuoso balancing act in reconciling the two adjacent movements, the earliest and the latest settings of the entire Mass, does not distract from the juxtaposition of contrasting styles, old-fashioned and new, that manifests itself at the center of the Symbolum Nicenum. On the contrary, not just by joining together of the old and new, but generally by embracing a wide spectrum of vocal-instrumental settings and musical styles Bach was able to underscore what he unquestionably perceived as the universality and timeless validity of the liturgical and dogmatic meaning of the ancient Mass text. Hence, the assemblage of multiple compositional styles in the B-Minor Mass can hardly be interpreted as aimless and unplanned, nor reduced to a mere "historical anthology" of exemplary vocal styles. Bach's last and grandest vocal work represents nothing less than the musical legacy of Bach the capellmeister-cantor.[19] Evidently, he had chosen this most historical of all vocal genres to embody the *summa summarum* of his artistry. For the Bach of 1749, the ever self-critical reviser of his own work, the stylistic spectrum of the eight-movement version of the Credo was deficient—lacking a genuine forward-looking dimension. The venerable composer's corrective afterthought then brought about a refocused architectonic center as well as an unprecedented pinnacle of cultivated musical modernity.

---

[19]Cf. Christoph Wolff, "Bach the Cantor, the Capellmeister, and the Musical Scholar: Aspects of the B-Minor Mass," *The Universal Bach* (Philadelphia, 1986), 39–49.

Frederick Neumann

SOME PERFORMANCE PROBLEMS OF BACH'S UNACCOMPANIED VIOLIN AND CELLO WORKS

Bach's "Sei Solo [sic] à Violino senza Basso accompagnato," consisting of three Sonatas and three Partitas, occupy a unique place in the very center of the repertory, as do the six Suites for cello solo. Both sets owe their eminent station to the unflaggingly exalted quality of their music. At the same time they present the performers with problems that are unique in character and complexity. They are unique owing to the fact that Bach wrote contrapuntal music for two purely melodic instruments that can form pitches on only four strings with only four fingers (the thumb was not yet in use for cello fingerings). As a consequence the demands of these works by far exceed the inherent potential of the instruments and indeed do violence to their nature. That is true of the cello which is more mercifully treated, but more so of the violin which Bach charges with stupendous polyphonic feats in three fugues and several other movements of similar textural complexity. To force works that would have been appropriate for an organ or an orchestra into the narrow confines of an unaccompanied string instrument was indeed an unheard-of *tour de force*. That Bach succeeded in extracting such

---

Frederick Neumann, author of a number of works on performance practice which have accorded him a foremost place in the field, served as both Concertmaster and Professor of Musicology in Richmond, Virginia.

glorious music from such self-imposed adverse circumstances is one of the greatest miracles of Bach's miraculous oeuvre.[1]

The purpose of this essay is to discuss a few of the performance problems of these compositions, with a chief focus on the works for the violin and an occasional reference to those for the cello. An attempt to discuss all their problems would fill a book for each instrument. Here the space is limited and I shall simply stake out a few problem areas and discuss them briefly as they occur in selected passages. I shall address first matters of general interest and leave to the end such problems as are posed by the anti-violinistic polyphonic texture.

TEXTUAL PROBLEMS

The violin works have been preserved in one of Bach's most beautiful and careful autographs (Staatsbibliothek Kulturbesitz, West Berlin, Mus. ms. Bach P 967). It is available in several facsimile prints, the finest of which was published by Bärenreiter in 1950.[2] The chief source for the cello Suites is a not overly careful copy by Anna Magdalena, also available in facsimile editions.

The occasional oversight with regard to actual pitch crept into the violin manuscript, and indeed, there are spots where Bach is assumed by most editors to have made mistakes. Furthermore, there are cases of actual misreading by the editors.

A certain oversight occurs in the first movement of the G minor Sonata, measure 3, third quarter (Example 1a). Here the written E should almost certainly be an E flat and is normally so interpreted. Bach wrote the piece in the "Dorian" signature of one instead of two flats for G minor and had to enter all the E flats individually; here, he apparently forgot to do so.

In the Siciliano of the same Sonata in measure 9, eighth eighth-note, Bach wrote an F natural which is widely believed to have been intended as F sharp (Example 1b). The F sharp sounds smoother to our ears, but is not necessarily what Bach had in mind. The F natural is by

---

[1] Bach had predecessors in writing for unaccompanied violin, among them H. I. F. von Biber, J. P. von Westhoff and his contemporary J. G. Pisendel (who wrote an unaccompanied sonata in 1716, four years before Bach), but none approached Bach's complexity and difficulty nor, needless to say, the height of his inspiration.

[2] A brief survey of eleven of the violin editions can be found in Robin Stowell, "Bach's Violin Sonatas and Partitas," *Musical Times* cxxviii (1987): 250–56.

no means incongruous: smoothness is no decisive criterion for authenticity. Bach's harmonies often have a bittersweet pungency and the F natural, of the melodic or natural minor, was probably intended. Had Bach meant F sharp, he probably would have added a cautionary natural sign to the last note F in the measure. The *Neue Bach-Ausgabe* has the F natural.

Example 1.

a)

b)

Very interesting and very important is the case of the Sarabanda of the D minor Suite. In measure 10, second quarter, Bach wrote a clear flat sign before the B (Example 2a). In her copy of the volume, Anna Magdalena either forgot it or misread it as a natural sign. Her manuscript was for a long time mistaken for another autograph and as such accorded equal authority with the genuine autograph. Since the B natural sounded smoother to nineteenth- and even twentieth-century ears, it became firmly ensconced in all editions and performances. Yet the B flat has great musical assets. It may be less smooth, but it is richer and more colorful and provides a perfect counterpart to the similarly chromatic, and similarly piquant progressions of measures 18–19 (Example 2b) which too would sound more euphonious, if far less characteristic, if the chromatic alterations were omitted. That the flat sign was intended seems most likely. Bach wrote the sign, as can be seen in the key signature and on every occurrence, in one motion starting from above, whereas he had to make two motions for a natural sign. There is a slight smudge, like a slip of the pen to the right below the flat sign, but it can hardly be interpreted as an attempted correction; when Bach corrected a mistake, as he did on the next line just below our measure (see Example 2a), he took great pains to clarify the change, here from G–F to A–G, not only by a graphic change that is clear in itself, but also by writing the letters "a g" below the notes. In our case an attempted correction would have had to be much clearer, would have had to touch the flat sign distinctly, and Bach, unless the correction was graphically unequivocal, would have had to write the German "h" above the note. I believe the B flat was intended, in which case a wrong note has been printed and played all along. (Surprisingly, the *Kritische Bericht* of the *Neue Bach Ausgabe* does not even mention the questionable note.)

Professor Christoph Wolff pointed out to me that another early source, a partial copy of Bach's violin solo works made in 1726 by Johann Peter Kellner (1705–1772) has the note in question, like Anna Magdalena's, as B natural. In addition to being incomplete, Kellner's copy shows many vast divergences from Bach's fair copy of 1720. It contains variants, some of them drastic, of some of the best-known movements. It is conceivable that Kellner's copy goes back to an earlier lost source. Furthermore, Kellner was highly unreliable. As Russell Stinson has suggested, Kellner was "an exceedingly careless scribe . . . whose numerous errors range from incorrect notation of pitch and rhythm to inaccuracy of phrasing and the omission of duplication of whole bars."[3] Kellner committed similar scribal transgressions in copying other Bach works, where divergences can be clearly ascribed to Kellner's own arbitrary manipulations. In view of these circumstances, and in view of Bach's clear flat sign before the note, Kellner's B natural cannot be given much weight.

Another misinterpretation, of far lesser musical consequence, but a misinterpretation nonetheless, concerns the first movement of the G minor Sonata, at the first note of measure 18 (Example 2c). Here what is unmistakably the second flag of the sixteenth note A has been widely mistaken as the note head of a D. It happens to make musical sense and therefore was not questioned, but Bach did not write it; his note heads are invariably round, never wedge-shaped as is the flag. The note should be eliminated.

[3] "J. O. Kellner's Copy of Bach's Sonatas and Partitas for Violin Solo," *Early Music* xiv (1985): 200.

Example 2.
a)

b)

c)

TWO WIDELY MISUNDERSTOOD MOVEMENTS

The slow introductory movements of the Sonatas in G minor and A minor are widely misinterpreted. Both are in the style of Italian church sonatas, like those of Corelli. The Italians wrote such adagio movements in an austere, skeletal, or semi-skeletal form with mainly quarter- and eighth-notes, rare sixteenths, and no thirty-seconds or shorter values. They were not meant to be played as written but were meant to be embellished by the performer with florid figurations. Bach, to our good fortune, did not entrust such embellishments to the performers but wrote them out. For this procedure, to which he adhered consistently in all of his works, he was severely chided by a contemporary critic for impinging upon the performer's traditional privilege of improvisation.

This circumstance has an important bearing on interpretation. We have to realize that all those thirty-seconds and sixty-fourths are not of the melodic essence and should not be played as if they were, that is, slowly and with deep feeling. They are purely decorative and should be rendered with lightness, elegance, and a certain improvisatory freedom. They should sound as if an inspired performer devised them on the spur of the moment. The opening passage of the G minor Sonata (Example 3a), written by an Italian, or for that matter by Telemann or Handel, might have looked as given in Example 3b. This is important to realize because it places the coloraturas in better perspective. An editor of this Sonata would be well advised to use small note heads for the coloraturas, just as Beethoven did with similar florid figurations in the slow movement of his Violin Concerto. As a rule of thumb for both the G minor and the A minor Preludes, the sixteenth-notes are structural and should be played expressively, the thirty-seconds are ornamental and should be played accordingly and not so as to present a deeply-felt melody. In order to give an appropriate accounting, the tempo must not be taken too slowly. One should count in slow four to allow for rhythmic freedom within the four regular beats; one should not subdivide into eight, which is rhythmically too confining for the coloraturas and would tend to slow down the tempo inordinately.

Not only performers but also editors share this misunderstanding; this can be seen from many ill-advised suggestions of subdivided bowstrokes in the middle of coloraturas.

Example 3.

a)

b)

BACH'S UNACCOMPANIED VIOLIN AND CELLO WORKS   25

What has been said about these two movements applies equally to the Allemande of the Cello Suite in D major, which should be counted in moderate four and not in eight. Its many thirty-seconds and shorter notes are similarly ornamental and should be rendered accordingly.

PROBLEMS OF RHYTHM

The dotted notes in the Corrente of the D minor Partita. The symbol: ♩³♪ which indicates a ternary rhythm within a binary meter is relatively modern. Brahms may have been the first major composer to have used it systematically. It was not available to Beethoven, Schubert, or Chopin, let alone to Bach. All these masters had to use the dotted note as a makeshift by giving it a 2:1 ternary, instead of its literal 3:1 binary, interpretation. As a consequence the meaning of the dotted note prior to the mid-nineteenth century is ambiguous. Only a consideration of the context can help us decide the intended ratio in a given situation. The Corrente in question (see Example 4), though like most Italian Correntes written in three-four meter, is characterized by a pervasive triplet motion from beginning to end. The consistency of ternary rhythm in this movement with its unflagging *Fortspinnung* makes the ternary interpretation of the dotted notes as good as mandatory. The insertion of binary sections within the torrential flow of triplets would destroy the unity of the movement and sound like the incongruous intrusion it would in fact represent.

Example 4.

Given this ternary meaning, these "dotted" figures need not be played with the modern bowing: that is convenient for fast 3:1 dotted notes, but can be comfortably and to very good advantage played as written:

Rhythmic alterations. A purely mechanical, machine-like rhythm is inappropriate for just about any music, and Bach's rhythms certainly have to pulsate with life, to breathe and be flexible—in some pieces or some spots more than others. On the other hand there is no justification in some editors' and commentators' ideas that all evenly written notes should be played with decisive unevenness, either long-short or short-long. These ideas are linked with the French convention of the *notes inégales* which called for a long-short rendition of evenly written pairs of specific note values in specific meters. Though Bach was acquainted with French performance manners, the available evidence speaks overwhelmingly against his use of the convention.[4]

Some rhythmic freedom was suggested above for the written-out coloraturas. In addition to these figurations, we find other passages that call for rhythmic flexibility scattered throughout the two volumes. Often at or near the ends of movements, there are phrases which invite a touch of improvisatory freedom. Of the four last measures of the G minor fugue, the first two seem to call for a distinct rubato of accelerating and retarding (suggested by several editions). We also find in some, mostly slow, movements after a deceptive final cadence some meditative perorations that sound like organ improvisations and call for imaginative rhythmic pliancy. Among the most magnificent examples are the last five measures of the D minor Sarabande, the last three measures of the C major Adagio, and the last four measures of the C major Largo.

In the cello suites there may be even more such occasions of indicated freedom from metrical precision, since every single suite opens with a prelude, and preludes by their very nature have improvisatory traits. Certain rhapsodic characteristics are usually most pronounced in their final measures, most obviously perhaps in the C major Prelude. The end of the D minor Prelude (Example 5) too calls for rhythmic flexibility; the dotted half notes need not be held for their full value, but can be played with the kind of free rhythm suggested by individual fermatas over shorter note values, such as, say, dotted quarter-notes: ♩· ♩· ♩· ♩· .

On the other hand it is a mistake, widespread in both editions and performances, to transform those dotted half notes into arpeggiated figures loosely patterned after the preceding measure. If, and only if,

---

[4]On this matter see my *Essays in Performance Practice* (Ann Arbor, 1982), chaps. 3–5, and *New Essays on Performance Practice* (Ann Arbor, 1989), chap. 5.

that last measure had contained an obvious arpeggio formula, a case might be made for its continuing application to the chords, except that Bach invariably writes "arpeggio" or "arp" when he wants chords to be so treated. However, the melody in that last measure does not even resemble an arpeggio and, as it stands, is not readily applicable to the following chords. For these reasons it is quite certain that the chords were meant to be played as chords. In their majesty they seem to evoke the emptying of a mighty stream into the ocean, but a pedantic sustaining for three beats will, on the cello, diminish their majesty (whereas on an organ their full value would be impressive).

Example 5.

PROBLEMS OF ORNAMENTATION

Symbolized ornaments. Only four *Vorschläge* are marked in the violin works, none in the cello suites. We find one vibrato symbol each in the violin and cello works. There are a number of arpeggiated passages, some quite extensive, that offer performance problems (arpeggiation of chords that is not ornamental in nature, but necessitated by the technical limitation of the instruments, will be discussed later). By and large the ornament problem is the trill.

One *Vorschlag* occurs in the opening movement of the G minor Sonata (given in Example 6a) and would perhaps best be rendered as the brief appoggiatura suggested in Example 6b. The three others are all in the same Menuet movement of the E major Partita. The first of these (Example 6c) is very likely a brief appoggiatura to be played approximately as given in Example 6d. The occasionally heard and occasionally editorially suggested rendition as overlong appoggiatura (Example 6e) follows the designs of the galant masters, especially C. P.

E. Bach, but is not applicable to Johann Sebastian, as I trust I have shown in my extensive study of Bach ornamentation.[5] J. S. Bach's symbol-indicated *Vorschläge* are basically short. An unaccented, pre-beat rendition (as "grace notes") is possible but seems less appropriate in this vigorous dance movement.

The second and third of these graces occur in the second Menuet in the parallel passages of Example 6f in measures 2 and 10. Here, in this contrasting legato gentleness and smoothness, an accented appoggiatura seems out of place and an unaccented brief inflection, preferably before the beat, more fitting.

Example 6.

---

[5]*Ornamentation in Baroque and Post-Baroque Music: with special Emphasis on J. S. Bach* (Princeton, 1978), hereafter *Ornamentation*.

The vibrato as ornament for the violin occurs in the penultimate measure of the A minor *Grave* as shown in Example 7a. This spot has puzzled performers and editors alike and given rise to the most varied misinterpretations. Mostly the wavy line is understood to mark a trill, which on several counts makes no sense. First, a trill in sixths with two whole notes was not in the vocabulary of pre-Paganinian violin technique;[6] second, the clear trill symbol over the quarter-note would make no sense if the preceding notes were already trilled; third, the wavy line was a trill symbol only for the keyboard, not for strings; fourth, Bach used the wavy line repeatedly for voices, and occasionally for strings, clearly to mean vibrato, and did so invariably in chromatic progressions, with their intensely emotional overtones.[7] In Bach, we find the vibrato symbol on words with a strong affect such as fear or sorrow, such as "tot" (dead), whose nature precludes embellishment with trills. Moreover, there are French, Italian and German antecedents for the vibrato meaning of the wavy line other than for the keyboard.[8] The vibrato meaning is unquestionable. Since notably in the Italo-German tradition vibrato was often done by bow pulsations instead of, or in addition to, left hand pulsations, the spot in question was mostly likely intended to be played as shown in Example 7b along with a left hand vibrato.

It is significant that the indispensable chromatic progression necessitates a main note start of the tril (as indicated in the suggested execution of Example 7b).

A similar bow vibrato might have been intended for the single vibrato symbol in the Gigue of the C minor Cello Suite (Example 7c).

---

[6] Bach shunned it even on the cello where a similar trill would be technically simpler, yet near the end of the C major Prelude, after the slow preparation of a gradually accelerating trill in sixths, he gives up with rising speed on the lower sixth and continues the trill only with the upper note. Since it is quite obvious that Bach would have liked for the trill to continue also with the lower note, cellists would do well to play a gradually accelerating trill in sixths throughout.

[7] For many illustrations and a more detailed discussion, see *Ornamentation*, 519–20.

[8] See *Ornamentation*, 514–16.

Example 7.

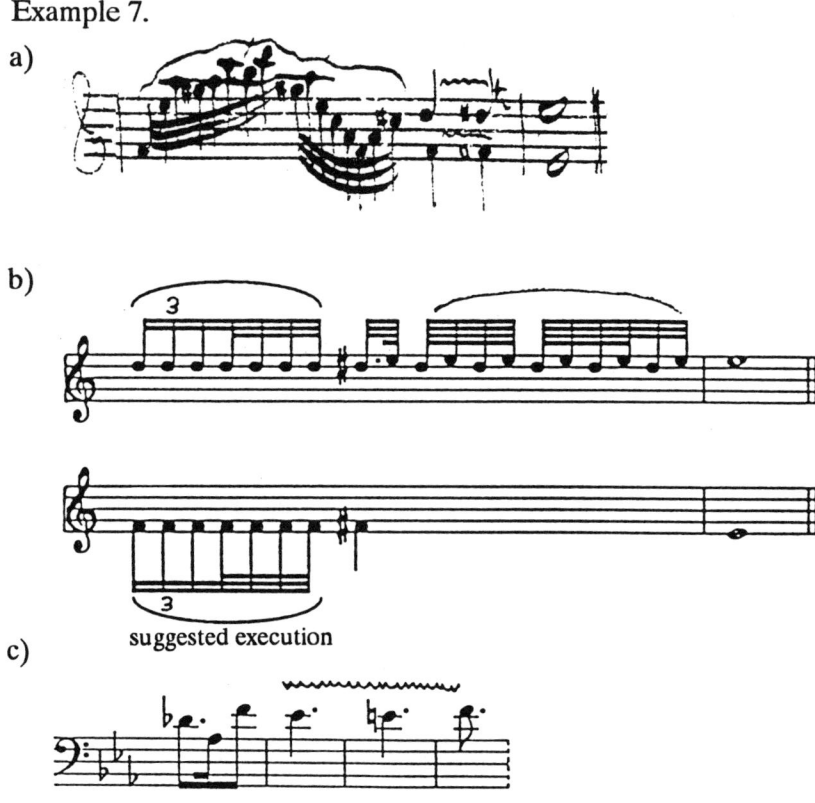

The trill. According to a widespread belief, Bach's trills as well as those of all of his contemporaries have to start with the auxiliary on the beat. As I have demonstrated elsewhere, this is not so.[9] The upper-note start of the trill was common for French keyboard players, yet was often done before rather than on the beat, while French singers and players of melody instruments used the main-note along with the upper-note start; Bach's Italian and German predecessors overwhelmingly used the main-note start.

Bach, who was acquainted with all these precedents, used the trill in all its possible designs: start with the main note, with the upper note,

[9]*Ornamentation*, chap. 29.

on or before the beat, or with full or partial anticipation of the trill itself. There is no rule that determines the shape of individual Bach trills. But as a help in making a sensible choice about the design best suited to a specific situation it is advisable first to leave out the trill and consider whether the addition of a brief (on-beat) appoggiatura, or a (pre-beat) grace note would be desirable; if so, then the start of the trill with the auxiliary in the respective rhythmic placement (in either of the two manners) would be indicated. If no such addition seems to suggest itself, then the start with the main note will be the proper choice. As a rough rule of thumb, a trill on the pitch of its preceding note will mostly suggest an upper-note start and so will one that follows a falling third; a trill slurred to its preceding upper neighbor will always start on the main note. When the preceding upper note is a long written-out appoggiatura, the repercussion can often start in anticipation; appoggiatura and trill form in such combination a single ornament in which the two constituent parts can rhythmically adjust to best musical advantage. For an illustration, see Example 8a from the D minor Sarabande, where the trill's repercussions might anticipate the beat and give the trill some breathing space before the fast *tirata* in thirty-second notes, and yet provide good rhythmic definition as sketched in Example 8b.

On several occasions, technical considerations alone call for a main-note start without resorting to anachronistic contortions, as shown for instance near the start of Example 2a from the D minor Sarabande, with the suggested approximate execution of Example 8c.

Example 8.

a)

b)

possible execution

Example 8 (continued)
c)

approximate execution

On other occasions where, be it after the fall of a third as in Example 9a from the Loure of the E major Partita, or on a tone repetition as in Example 9b from the third movement of the A minor Sonata, a start with the upper note might suggest itself, our above mentioned test will often favor a pre-beat placement of the auxiliary. In the first example a pre-beat connective note in the manner of a *tierce coulée* will produce a leaner, more elegant melodic line whereas the insertion of an appoggiatura G sharp on the weakest beat of the measure would disturb the dynamic direction of the phrase that leads to the following structural quarter-note G sharp as its climax; not to speak of the redundancy of three accented G sharps following one another within the small space of four beats. The pre-beat style seems almost mandatory here.

In the second example, the trill is prepared and *de facto* started with the written-out appoggiatura C on the preceding beat. The introduction of a second appoggiatura on the third beat that carries the trill symbol would be redundant and disturb the unity of the compound ornament: the three thirty-second notes that follow the appoggiatura are a trill prefix that must flow into, and merge immediately with the trill's repercussions. The auxiliary could be appended as a fourth note to the three-note prefix and sounded before the beat (Example 9c). The above proposed test for the desirable trill start definitely favors such a solution.

Certainly there are other contexts where an on-beat, appoggiatura start of the trill is either preferable or is a reasonable option. In Example 9d from the B minor Allemande, an on-beat start of what is an unmarked but understood cadential trill seems the preferable solution (Example 9e).

Occasionally tone repetition on a trill can be thematically important, as for instance in Example 9f from the Gavotte en Rondeau of the E major Suite. Here an accented upper note start would disturb the melodic line by blurring the important tone repetition; the trill will best start with the main note, though a very brief unaccented grace note that would still preserve the sense of tone repetition on the G sharp would be an acceptable option.

Example 9.

a)

b)

c)

possible execution

d)

Example 9 (continued)
e)

possible execution

f)

Unmarked ornaments. In cadences, the dominant preceding the final resolution into the tonic routinely received a trill. This was so widely understood that Bach, along with most other contemporary composers, often failed to specify it. One such case was shown in Example 9d, and there are many others of which only one more is shown in Example 10a from the end of the Chaconne.

Bach frequently wrote out the common two-note suffix to the trill and did so invariably with regular notes, not with the two little unmetrical notes that many other masters, Couperin among them, used for that purpose. While Bach marked the suffix often, he did not do so always, and the failure to write it out does not mean that he did not wish it to be added. When the trill is short, and especially when it is slurred within the same beat to its lower neighbor, a suffix is usually not proper, as the slurred note functions as *Nachschlag,* hence as suffix. But a trill of some length will mostly call for the suffix, especially if the following note is on a separate beat and is detached. In the Loure of the E major Partita the trills in both the first and second measures (see Example 9a) call for a suffix, whereas the trill in m. 12 of the same piece (see Example 10b) can easily forego one, being followed on the same beat by the lower neighbor. Exact rules do not exist and it is for musical intelligence to decide in individual cases. C. P. E. Bach has a point when he says that even a "mediocre ear will always sense where the suffix may be made and where not."[10] What we have to remember is that J. S. Bach was inconsistent in the notation of minor matters. Hence his failure to write out a suffix does not mean that he did not want one.

Example 10.

a)

b)

Ornamenting the repeats. I mentioned above Bach's felicitous habit of writing out the florid embellishments of adagios that were a hallmark of the style, and that cause us great headaches in the performance of the music of Handel, Telemann, Vivaldi and others who mostly used skeletal notation for their slow movements. Yet there is another aspect of free ornamentation that Bach performers have to face—varying the repeats. In a time in which performers were given wider, often much wider, latitude in interpreting a score than we grant them today, one of these freedoms arose from a widespread dislike of literal repeats. In da capo arias the varying of the da capo was a stylistic requirement. C. P. E. Bach gave us instructive examples of how to vary repeats in sonatas. Though his style was vastly different from his father's, we are dealing here with a practice of long standing, not one that was new to the galant period. Though we have no documentary evidence about the father's

---

[10]*Versuch über die wahre Art das Clavier zu spielen* (Berlin, 1753), chap. 3, par. 17.

handling of repeats in soloistic performance, we have no reason to believe that he would have frowned on the introduction of some variants on repeats, provided they were discreet and in good taste.

Whether it was a matter of musical ethics to make every marked repeat we do not know, but I rather doubt it in view of the performer's great discretionary powers. But when we do make the repeats, a measure of variation is generally desirable. Often a change of dynamics will be sufficient to break the monotony of an exact replica; or a change in articulation: what was played on the string could on repeat be played off the string, with a change from the more serious to the more light-hearted; or by introducing a few slurs where there were none at first (for instance in the Double of the B minor Sarabande); maybe even (maybe not) a slight varying of the tempo; and finally, more in slow than fast movements, the adding of new ornamental pitches. Here the greatest discretion will be in order. Not as a model to emulate, but rather as a rough indication of what might be done, Example 11 shows such variants for the opening measures of the E major Loure.

Example 11.

PROBLEMS OF ARTICULATION

Though Bach used staccato dots and strokes from time to time, there are none in the works under consideration, where articulation signs are limited to slurs. The slurs in the violin works are carefully marked and are in themselves a feat of genius in their imaginativeness, appropriateness, and ideal adaptation to idiomatic bowing; by and large they are designed to favor the downbow on the strong beat, which is the most natural bowing pattern for the violin.

Problems arise for two reasons. First, there are cases where the exact start or, more frequently, the end is uncertain. While Bach rarely overdraws a slur, he occasionally falls short. In many such instances the alternative that leads to the downbow on the downbeat will have the presumption of correctness. In Example 12a at measure 102 the slur mark does seem to end at the fifth note A, whereas the slur in measure 104 is more vague; the bowing idiom, which in this particular movement is unusually consistent and clear, speaks for detachment of the B flat in measure 102, and for the slurring of the whole measure in measure 104.

A far greater problem is Bach's frequent failure to mark bowings that were most likely intended. We find that he marked slurs carefully and completely in homophonic movements (like the just-quoted Presto from the G minor Sonata), where slurring patterns are mostly of the musical essence. That they are is apparent from their consistent sameness in both sequences or parallel spots (see for instance in Example 12a, mm. 105–109 or Example 12b, mm. 12–16). Georg von Dadelsen, using this same movement as illustration, distinguishes "essential" affect-bound articulation, which is a composer's choice, from the articulation as "minor matter" that falls into the competence of the performer.[11] Here he would seem to refer to many works (like most keyboard compositions) that have no or only very sparing articulation marks but were not meant to be played with unremitting detachment.

Example 12.

[11]"Die Crux der Nebensache; Editorische und praktische Bemerkungen zu Bach's Artikulation," *Bach-Jahrbuch* lxiv (1978): 95–112.

Example 12 (continued)
b)

Where the texture is more complicated, and especially in polyphonic movements, articulation easily becomes a "minor matter" in von Dadelsen's sense, and there Bach is often much less careful in writing desirable slurs, and counts on the performer's intelligence in supplying them. As a consequence we face the problem of deciding whether an unslurred passage was meant to be detached, or whether slurs ought to be added. It is here that some modern editors who try hard to be faithful to the text, let down the practical performer whom they address, by calling for detachment when for various reasons such detachment is inappropriate. They should suggest desirable slurs, in a manner of course that clarifies the editorial nature of such suggestions.

Sometimes the lack of a slur is a clear oversight in an environment of carefully marked bowings. A case in point is Example 13a from the first movement of the G minor Sonata. Here a slur over at least the first two notes is necessary for two reasons: first, it is an appoggiatura and as such must be slurred to its resolution; second, one of the few certainties of Bach articulation is a required slur for the Lombard rhythm pattern. For the following three notes a slur may not be as certain but is extremely probable: as I pointed out before, all thirty-second notes in this movement "and in most others" are ornamental in nature and as such need to be slurred. That Bach did not encompass these three notes under the following slur is easily explained by the superior bowing pattern achieved by taking a separate up bow for the three notes that leads to perfect downbows for all the following first beats.

BACH'S UNACCOMPANIED VIOLIN AND CELLO WORKS 39

Similarly ornamental and similarly in need of slurs is Example 13b at the end of the A minor Fugue, as suggested with dots for the first beat.

Example 13.

a)

b)

There are many other instances where the ornamental nature of notes or note groups suggests or even demands the addition of slurs. In Example 14a from the Allemande of the B minor Suite the two thirty-seconds at the end of the second beat are a suffix to the trill and as such have to be slurred to the latter. The two thirty-seconds in the following beat also constitute a *Nachschlag*, which again calls for a slur to its preceding parent note, and the same applies to the first beat of the second measure. That the four notes following the dotted D at the start of measure 3 need to be slurred becomes clear from Example 14b in measure 14 where the same phrase is explicitly slurred. Similarly, the need to slur the figure of measure 11 (Example 12c) is clarified by the slur in the parallel spot of measure 18 (Example 14d).

Often the basic affection of a piece will suggest that slurs be supplied. In the Siciliano of the G minor Sonata the basic affection of tenderness and warmth is underlined in the first measure by the slurs in the second, third and fourth beats (Example 15a). To remain true to this feeling, the addition of many other slurs seems desirable in this movement, for instance in the second measure for the quasi-appoggiatura of

Example 14.

a)

b)   c)

d)

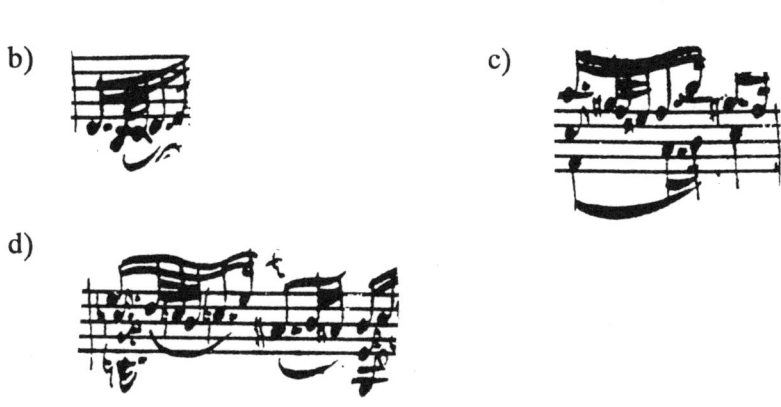

the first, the two sixteenth notes of the second, and the four sixteenths of the third beat. The slur over the anapestic figure of this second beat is vindicated by similar written-out slurs in measure 6 (Example 15b) and measure 17 (Example 15c).

Example 15.

a)

b)   c)

In the A minor Fugue, articulation is again a "minor matter" and it is likely that the theme itself (Example 16a) need not be entirely detached. The frequently heard and editorially suggested slurring of the second measure by twos is not un-Bachian and finds a good measure of justification in the slurs written when the theme occurs in its inversion in measures 156 and 158 (Example 16b).

Example 16.

The last movement of the A minor Sonata features problems not offered by the score but created by editors and performers. As in any of the homophonous movements, articulation is a major, not a minor matter, and Bach consequently marked it with great care and total consistency. For this reason the presumption is strong that here an absence of slurs does call for detachment and we ought to think twice before introducing unmarked slurs; yet most editors and performers do so in measure 3 and its various parallel spots (Example 17a). I believe this to be a mistake. First, in the fiery, aggressive piece the detached rendition of measures 3, 4, 17, 27, 28, 42, 43, and so on creates much more energy and excitement than does their slurred version, especially if, as is so often done, the slurs are done by anapests across the beats ♫♫♫ . Slurring by dactyls on the beat would be a lesser mistake, but a mistake nevertheless. The detached reading finds strong support in measures 27 and 28 (Example 17b) where the agitated figure, repeated three times, is followed on the fourth quarter by a contrasting, calming figure that is appropriately slurred (the detachment of its last note F sharp assures the downbow start on the following downbeat). An identical articulation pattern is found in measure 28. This repeated pattern of the slur on the last quarter and the absence of slurs on the preceding figurations—an absence totally consistent in all the eight appearances of this theme—is a study in contrast, and as such weighty evidence for the intention of detachment. Also, Bach's downbeat slur on the last quarter is incompatible with the anapestic slurs and thereby exposes the latter as spurious.

Example 17.

If it is risky to add slurs in movements where articulation is of the musical essence, it is outright unconscionable to tamper with Bach's bowings where they are clear and perfectly playable. Such offense is frequently perpetrated in measures 48–49 of the same movement (Example 18). In this memorable passage, which with the help of Bach's slurs seems to evoke ill-natured stubbornness, many editors and performers shift the slurs by a note to the right to make them cross the beats ♪♪♪♪♪♪♪♪♪♪♪♪♪. When this is done, stubborn anger turns to shallow frivolity and the affection is falsified.

Example 18.

THE VIOLINISTIC PROBLEMS OF POLYPHONY

As pointed out at the outset, polyphony runs counter to the nature of the instrument, and by exceeding its potential adds a new dimension to the difficulties of execution. The resulting problems also make special demands on the listeners who have to carry in their memory pitches only briefly sounded, and supplement in their imagination others that are missing altogether. It is the player's task to ease the burden on the listeners by helping them with the perception of the musical structure, with its often very complex counterpoint and very rich harmony.

The greatest difficulty lies in the execution of polyphonically created three- and four-part chords in a manner that not only sounds the chords in their verticality, but clarifies the horizontal strands of melody passing through them. Here we have to keep in mind that a violin (and cello) can sound simultaneously three pitches only in *forte* and only for a brief time span. Other than in *forte* and for notes of a certain length, arpeggiation is necessary. The "baroque" violin has here an advantage because the flatter bridge and the lower tension of both strings and bow hair make it somewhat easier to play triple chords. Quadruple chords must be arpeggiated under any circumstances.

Performers and editors vary a great deal in their approach to these problems. The thorniest challenge is a main melody in the bass, or, on quadruple chords, in bass or tenor, and we frequently encounter two different methods both of which are questionable. One is arpeggiation from above and the other is a kind of ricocheting, of arpeggiating first upward, then immediately turning around and moving downward to the melody note.

Downward arpeggiation was an occasional French practice, mainly of clavecinists but also of violinists (for example, Leclair) and was either written out or indicated by a special symbol. For the keyboard Bach had only a single arpeggio symbol (the wavy line) and a study of his usage in various contexts strongly indicates that for single chords he used only the upward, not the downward type. (Naturally for sustained chords that are kept alive by arpeggiation one has to alternate up and down movements.) Also, on stringed instruments the arpeggio that is used not as ornament but as technical makeshift, is invariably done upwards only. It so happens that the trickiest problems of polyphonic chords can be reasonably solved by upward arpeggiation in connection with nuances of rhythm and dynamics.

It seems advisable to avoid downward arpeggiation for the sake of clarifying voice-leading. As to the ricocheting type, it forbids itself by its ungainliness, reminiscent as it is of nothing more than a musical hiccup.

Space allows only very few characteristic illustrations. In Example 19a from the Siciliano of the G minor Sonata we have the problem of a phrase ending overlapping with a phrase beginning. The frequently heard and suggested downward arpeggiation (Example 19b) fails to do justice to the phrase ending which is skimmed over. A good way to avoid such one-sided neglect as well as the dubious downward arpeggio, is ever so slightly to anticipate *forte* the low B flat, followed *piano* by the two eighth-notes D and B flat that can now be held *quasi tenuto* to clarify the end of the phrase, as intimated in Example 19c. The strongly articulated phrase beginning on the low B flat will be easily carried by the ear and connected with the continuation of the phrase. The dynamics play a decisive role, and it may be worth noting that to bring out the contrast of *forte* and *piano* in the way suggested here is technically quite simple and certainly within the capability of any competent player; furthermore, the perception of continuity across the gap after the first note of the new phrase is within the capability of any competent listener. It makes no greater, and maybe lesser, demands on the aural imagination of the listener than does, in a similar polyphonic setting, the need to connect mentally the notes of a slow melody on the harpsichord and to disassociate them from a simultaneous counter-melody.

Example 19.

a)

b) c)

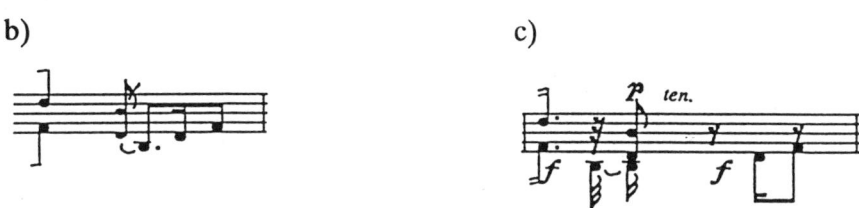

A similar procedure will achieve good results (the best, I believe, that can be achieved) in spots like those of Example 20a from the A minor Fugue or of Example 20b from the C major Fugue, as sketched in Example 20c: here, again, one should strongly announce with slight anticipation the melody note in the lowest part and then, after upward rolling, sustain the upper voices softly long enough to clarify their counterpoint.

The same procedure is advisable also in the homophonic texture of Example 20d, which is almost always done with downward arpeggiation. The procedure recommended here has the advantage of preserving the sense of the thematically important, heavily striding quarter-notes, which can be sustained for more than an eighth-note length, while the listener should have no problem in perceiving the melody in the bass; whereas, with downward arpeggiation the three quarter-notes disappear.

Example 20.

a)

Example 20 (continued)
b)

c)

d)

A special problem, one of the toughest of all, is presented in the first variation of the Chaconne as shown in Example 21. Here, too, we have at the start of measure 9 an overlap of phrase ending and phrase beginning. Downward arpeggiation is again inadvisable. The solution suggested for Example 19 is a possible option here, too. Another option would seem to be, where instrument, bow and technique allow it, to sustain the dotted eighth-note of the tenor, while simultaneously sounding the two top notes, if ever so briefly. This would be a nearly literal rendition of the notation. Where the lower note cannot be sustained with desirable tone quality, the first option would be far superior to the often heard ugly ricocheting style of rolling upward, then downward again, sounding the D twice.

Example 21.

For final chords of three or four notes, like those of the G minor Adagio, the B minor Sarabande, the A minor Fugue, or the C major Largo, it is not advisable to sustain the pitch of the alto part for its full value, because to do so leaves the listener with the impression of an inversion of the chord rather than its root position. The alto may be held for a while but in the end the soprano should be sounded alone, as sketched in Example 22.

Example 22.

approximate execution

A WORD ON FINGERING

It is not appropriate to go mountain-climbing on the fingerboard for the sake of richer sonorities or more unified timbres. In his C minor Cello Suite Bach gave us clear proof that he expected position playing solely for the sake of reaching the proper pitches and not for any other reason. This Suite is written in *scordatura*, with the A string tuned down to G. For the convenience of the player Bach wrote all the pitches for the A string one whole tone higher, as if writing for a transposing instrument in B flat. From this notation we can gather that, whenever possible, he took for granted first position playing with frequent use of the open string. There is no reason to assume that his ideas should have differed for the violin. One or the other recent edition is commendably discreet in the use of positions without having made so far a noticeable dent in the "mainstream" performances of these works.

By way of an epilogue, while speaking of fingering, I would like to show one that strikingly facilitates the execution of a notoriously difficult passage, one so difficult that some editors have re-designed the spacing of the chords. The passage in question is at the end of the B minor "Tempo di Borea" (Example 23a). If at the start of measure 66 the necessary first finger on G is kept down while pivoting to second position (Example 23b), the troublesome chord at the end of the measure lies, as if by magic, ready-made in the hand.

Example 23.
a)

b)

J. Merrill Knapp

PERFORMING PROBLEMS IN HANDEL'S OPERAS

Dear Alfred,

I am writing this in the form of an open letter to you. Since you and I unite in being both conductors and editors—a somewhat rare combination if I may say so—I feel it would be interesting to put knowledge of performance and *Urtext* into the written word. Even though much of what I shall touch on is quite familiar to you, I hope it may be a good summary of problems and their possible solutions that are not entirely known to the public.

Aside from Handel editions, of which we have both been editors, it is good to recall as evidence of practice that you were among the first in this country to investigate authentic performing traditions with Handel oratorios and his Chandos anthems and to conduct them with resulting recordings.[1] I had the honor of giving the first performances in the United States of two Handel operas. These were *Imeneo* and *Amadigi*: the first, in a staged version, the second, in a concert version.[2] So we both talk with some experience of what it is to make the music

---

[1] Issued by *Cantate*, *Vanguard*, and *Bärenreiter*.
[2] Princeton, N.J.: *Imeneo* (1964); *Amadigi* (1969).

J. Merrill Knapp was Professor in the Department of Music at Princeton University from 1960 to 1982 and Dean of the College from 1961 to 1966. A widely recognized Handel scholar, he was a founding member of the American Handel Society and Vice-President of the Georg-Friedrich-Händel-Gesellschaft.

come alive. There are also written articles which bear out our ideas.[3] Mine mostly concern the operas; yours, Handel's oratorios, anthems, and instrumental music.

Now that I have finished blowing our mutual horns, which is solely for the purpose of proving that we are not just that favorite target of some critics—button-pushing musicologists—or merely an inflator of respective egos, let me partly pretend that I am something of a musical neophyte conductor thinking of a Handel opera performance. Yet I wish to be both as reliable and authentic as possible without sacrificing musical vividness and integrity.

The thought of a performance immediately brings to mind an edition. Where shall one find it? What should it be? Only three operas (*Amadigi*, *Orlando*, and *Serse*) out of 39 (counting *Muzio Scevola*) have been issued in full score critical editions by Halle and one of them, *Serse*, is not a critical one. Chrysander (or its Gregg reprint) needs to be handled with care. Although Chrysander did remarkable work in his nineteenth-century edition, he never quite made up his mind whether he was printing Handel's original autograph, a first performing edition, or a revival. Also, unfortunately, he left very little explanation of what he was including and why, so the conscientious preparer of a full score must do considerable sorting out to arrive at a good and accurate result—presumably a first performing edition with possible additions. Aids in this process without access to the manuscripts themselves can be found in several volumes.[4] Then, having gone this far, the conductor and the stage manager have an important task: they must thoroughly read the original librettos, either early Italian or London ones, always keeping in mind that the librettist-arranger for Handel was generally the stage director of the opera and he often included directions in the libretto that may not be found elsewhere. Happily there is now a modern

---

[3]For you, Nos. 774, 775, 776, 777 in *G. F. Handel: A Guide to Research* by Mary Ann Parker-Hale (New York, 1988), and for me in the same volume, No's. 312, 433, 763, 764.

[4]*Catalogue of the King's Music Library, Part I, the Handel Manuscripts* by William Barclay Squire (London, 1927); *Händel-Handbuch, Band I: Bühnenwerke* by Bernd Baselt (Leipzig and Kassel, 1978); *Handel's Operas, 1704-1726* by Winton Dean and John Merrill Knapp (Oxford, 1987); *Händels Direktions-Partituren* (Hamburg, 1972). There are other sources, but these are the most important.

facsimile reprint[5] of all the librettos and their revivals which makes the former onerous task of searching libraries everywhere for them no longer necessary. The "little book" is also a key to what was actually first performed with dates and casts. Ideally, the preparer should also look over the source libretto[6] to see what Handel and his adaptors omitted or compressed. Further background on the older plot and its staging can yield valuable insights.

Next comes the copying of instrumental parts. Before doing this, the conductor must decide what he is adding to the main score in the way of dynamics (crescendo and diminuendo are necessary as well as piano and forte), tempo indications (Handel often omits them), trills, appoggiaturas, and other performing symbols that become a necessity for the modern performer. The twentieth-century musician, even the most experienced early instrumental player, is not generally conversant with all eighteenth-century style and practice. He or she needs guidance to make for ensemble uniformity, particularly with the problem of limited rehearsal time. It is not a matter of "improving" Handel or adapting his music for modern ears but merely achieving a balanced result, tempered by the conductor's taste, his or her knowledge of performing practice and careful preparation.

To be more specific, double dots, if desired, may have to be inserted for the overture Grave section and elsewhere. If dotted notes appear in conjunction with triplets, should the dotted rhythm be modified into a triplet rhythm or kept separate as written? By now it is generally conceded that shortened cadences, not only in *secco* recitative but many times in *accompagnato*, were the rule for Handel. These are not indicated in Chrysander, and alterations in the score and parts must be made. If the conductor and stage manager decide there should be cuts—and the three to four hour length of most Handel operas in their entirety makes some cuts almost imperative for a modern audience, except under festival conditions—then adjustments have to be made in recitative endings so that the progression fits harmonically from recitative to aria, dominant to tonic or mediant to tonic being the most

---

[5]*The Librettos of Handel's Operas*, 13 vols. ed. Ellen T. Harris (New York and London, 1989).
[6]Reinhard Strohm, "Handel and his Italian opera texts" in *Essays on Handel and Italian Opera* (Cambridge, 1985), 34–79.

common. With cuts, the sometimes barbarous habit of only performing the A section of an aria or going back on the da capo to the opening ritornello and stopping is now regarded as poor musical judgment. It is much better to omit a complete aria or scene than chop it into pieces.

The reduction of the string ensemble for vocal portions of most arias is another delicate adjustment. The so-called Tutti and Soli string sections are not always carefully indicated by Handel (sometimes there is only a forte followed by a piano to show it). The conductor-editor must decide what the make-up of his or her string Soli section should be, generally determined by the size of the ensemble. The same kind of adjustment has to be made for oboes and bassoons in wind doubling. If called for by Tutti, do the winds automatically drop out when the soloist sings and only reenter on ritornellos (many times not shown in the score)? Should both Oboe 1 and 2 double Violin 1 and not Violin 1 and 2 if there are two separate violin parts? What do the oboes do if the instrumental line on the low end exceeds their range (below c' or b flat)? Handel's directions for these matters are not always clear, either because such things were self-evident at the time or because oral directions were given by the composer who was directing his own performance from the harpsichord or the string section.

Regarding instruments, it is now felt that they should ornament as well as the voices. But should this be written out, or left to the discretion of a few soloists who know how to perform the ornamentation without disrupting the ensemble?

Phrasing (bowing) and articulation marks cannot be taken for granted. Often Handel would indicate what he wanted in bowing for a measure or two, leaving the rest blank. The same is true for a Violin 1 part in distinction to the Violin 2 and Viola below. Uniformity becomes obviously necessary for the modern player who cannot be expected to guess what should be done or merely follow the first chair with a pencil in hand for clarification.

Having constructed a score and parts as close to the original as possible, we come to thoughts about the actual performance itself. One of the most gratifying and interesting developments of around the last fifteen years or so has been the rise of early instrumental ensembles, comprising orchestras of original eighteenth-century instruments or modern authentic reproductions of them. The clear, subdued, but elegant sound heard at a' = 415 pitch (half-tone lower than modern 440, although there was no prevailing pitch in Handel's and Bach's time) has been a revelation in works by these composers and other contemporaries, particularly in recordings. As techniques and styles have developed, the old "sewing machine" approach (little expressivity or dynamic change, too rapid tempos) has given way to *affektvoll* playing and stylistic nicety. The ability of the smaller musical organization, however, to gather together such an ensemble is limited outside of professional centers in large cities or bigger music departments. A modern instrumental orchestra will probably be the norm. Yet this group must be coached in baroque practice: little or no vibrato, less bow, *detaché* passages, clean attacks, trills beginning on the upper note, avoidance of portamento, and so on. Such coaching eats up time and makes for great rehearsal pressure, but it has to be done if the performance is to have validity.

Then there comes the matter of vocal casting. The demands of Handel's music almost always require professional voices or expert conservatory singers. Happily, the old procedure of putting castrato roles down an octave or less in pitch for tenors and basses in order to create a male Giulio Cesare or another male hero has virtually disappeared. Women in male parts or counter-tenors singing at Handel's original pitch have become almost the rule. Yes, Handel did make transpositions for new singers in operatic revivals but almost never of the octave variety which often puts the vocal line below that of the *basso continuo*, creating awkward intervals. Conductors should study the tessitura of the original part, keeping in mind that castratos were generally mezzo-sopranos or altos, and select a female singer for a male role (costumed carefully for not too overt a female contour) with this range in mind. Counter-tenors may not vocally fill a large opera house, but they are male and they sing at pitch.

Ornamentation for the repeat in the da capo aria is now almost a requisite, but the conductor and singer must approach it with care. The few examples we have directly from Handel's hand[7] show a conservative,

---

[7]"O caro mio tesor" in *Amadigi* (*Hallische Händel-Ausgabe, Serie II: Opern*, Band 8), ed. J. Merrill Knapp; G. F. Handel, *Three Ornamented Arias*, ed. Winton Dean (Oxford, 1976). See also Robert Donington, *A Performer's Guide to Baroque Music* (London, 1973), 165–66.

tasteful approach (most appoggiaturas and filling-in of intervals) and not a wild, fanciful outpouring. One of the most egregious procedures is with cadenzas where some singers suddenly leave the eighteenth century for the nineteenth (Rossini and Bellini) and give forth several big octave jumps to high notes that are exaggerated. Ideally, singers should devise their own ornamentation in the proper style and invent a line with which they feel comfortable. The ornamentation should always give a feeling of improvisation and not be stereotyped and rigid.

Singers have now been told and taught often enough about the proper declamation and free interpretation of Italian recitative. They know it is declamatory speech with the customary appoggiaturas. But this is one of the most difficult areas to master, particularly with the English-speaking singer for whom the language is not native. He or she can be helped by a good continuo group who lightly touch the chords and bass line (harpsichord plus cello or bass), giving a bounce to the singer's delivery. Inexperienced cello or bass performers often forget that the held half or whole notes in the continuo line were only a convention and should be treated as quarter or eighth notes with rests in between and not as a steady drone as written. The continuo sound can also be varied from time to time by the use of lutes and guitar for chordal accompaniment instead of the harpsichord.

It goes without saying that one of the chief aims of early eighteenth-century practice was to delineate an expressive, melodic line, both in the voice and in the orchestra. Nuances (flexibility of rhythm and note coloring) make a great difference, and they must be assiduously cultivated in order to avoid mechanical divisions and vapid *passaggi*. There is also the *messa di voce* (gradual diminuendo and crescendo on a sustained note) that was highly cultivated by such singers as Senesino. Just a held note without this coloring goes against the grain of what was expected.

Tempos will always be a personal matter for the conductor, determined by taste, the size of the hall, its acoustics, and the make-up of the ensemble. Tempo indications are quite often mood suggestions with Handel and not strictly time patterns. Andante Allegro or similar terms are not contradictory but qualifications of the main speed. In general, Allegros should be quite brisk, and 3/8 meter is almost always one beat to the measure unless indicated slower. Modern musicians want to make a distinct difference between cut time and common time, but often this does not exist in baroque music. Cut time does not automatically mean *alla breve*: the character of the music is the determining factor. Cadential rallentandos are certainly in order as long as they are not overused or carried to excess. Largo and Adagio are not generally distinct from one another in tempo. Again the music itself will dictate the proper tempo when it is analysed carefully. Since so many of Handel's arias are stylized dances, the designation minuet, gavotte, or rondo should demonstrate the proper dance-like gait in the music. Sicilianos in compound meter are often in flat, minor keys and indicate reflection or moods of grief which can *ipso facto* determine the proper tempo.

One of the iron performance rules is not to let gaps or pauses take place between recitative and aria, so that the connection of plot and musical comment on it is lost. Sometimes special effects of interruption are necessary when a sudden stage event occurs. But rapid movement avoids a stop-and-go effect which is inherent in much of the musical texture.

The direction of the performance from the harpsichord had certain practical advantages. The conductor-harpsichordist could control the pace of the recitative, determine his continuo realization, and keep his ensemble together. If there were two harpsichords, the conductor could be more vigorous with his arms on tutti passages and get shading from the orchestra not otherwise possible with his head alone. Today a number of early ensemble conductors with only one harpsichord at their disposal operate this very way and can be seen rising from the harpsichord bench when a fuller orchestral sound is demanded and the orchestra has to be more closely controlled.

Continuo realization brings to mind the desirability of having the harpsichordist tastefully inject little solo or quasi-solo passages (runs or ornamentation that sounds through the orchestra) to brighten up and give variety to the chordal structure. This "something extra" gives a delightful lift to the performance and avoids a continual plunking accompaniment.

While the discussion so far has emphasized the musical part of Handelian opera, it should never be forgotten that opera in any age is music, drama, and stage spectacle. The conductor and stage director must work hand-in-hand if the performance is to surpass routine. Like the growth of the early instrument orchestra, there has been knowledge and sophistication acquired in recent years about baroque staging. Seldom does one find anymore the closing of the curtain to indicate separate scenes in an act while the audience and orchestra sit in silence—a common practice not so long ago in certain German theatres. Stage personnel now have learned about baroque flats changed in sight of the audience by way of grooves extending in series to the back of the stage; of action and singing carried on under the proscenium or in front of it; of the so-called obligatory exits after an aria; of the placing of singers onstage in relation to each other according to their prominence; of the curtain drawn and closed only at the beginning and end of the opera. All these practices cannot be exactly duplicated on the modern stage, but they must be kept in mind as once-contemporary practice. Modern lighting helps to alleviate static positions, and so do other technical devices that create variety when movement on stage is lacking.

Yet modern stage directors with the best of intentions still have difficulty adjusting to the musical demands of a da capo aria. They want movement during a long ritornello and with the repeat of the A section they are sometimes driven crazy by the necessity of music becoming central to the action and not subsidiary to it. In their minds the tableau seems to freeze itself and it becomes a concert in costume. Obviously there are ways of lessening this effect by compromise between music and action on stage. Stage spectacle and music must work in harness for the desired realization.

Handelian opera has many more purely instrumental movements than is generally supposed. These come at the beginning of acts or at moments of striking action on stage (storms, battles, fires, a character falling asleep, a sudden change in location, magic visitations, even the *deus ex machina* in a cloud machine). All of them must be carefully cued in by music and stage action, so that the effects do not become ludicrous or distracting. The plot and character portrayal are still essential elements in the opera, portrayed by a series of moods and pictures in scenes and music that have a cumulative force and only occasionally in a mixed psychological one as found in the modern theatre.

The dance also has an important role to play, especially in the Covent Garden operas for which Handel had a dance troupe at his disposal, or in an opera like *Admeto* where Admeto is tortured in his sleep at the beginning by evil spirits who dance around his bed of pain. Directions may not always specify dance movement, but the presence of specific dance music indicates it was expected in some form or another.

Since so many Handel operas deal with kings, queens, ceremony, and courts, the representation of these noble figures by postures and gestures becomes a vital component for the opera singer. A recent book on practices and principles of eighteenth-century acting[8] is a valuable guide to what was expected on stage during this period and can be referred to for telling assistance in older acting styles. It deals not only with plays but also with opera in passing, albeit largely of the French theatre. Much of this may seem stilted to the naturalistic playgoer of today, but these various components must jell if they are to bring out the best of each unit in the production. Acting techniques, particularly for the recitative with changes in delivery, can be as articulate and graceful as the words and music they illustrate. Singing, acting, gesture, and rhetoric are all means to the desired end.

There are many more details, my dear colleague and old friend, on which I could elaborate. But these thoughts may help the editor, conductor, and stage director to coordinate their efforts and bring to vivid realization the operatic works of one of the world's great composers. These works are not dead, stiff, and boring. They come to life when given the proper treatment, and they can claim the highest artistic verity in the field of opera. Comparisons with later or earlier ages are invidious. Handel's operas can stand on their own feet. They may not be a regular part of the operatic repertory, but they fulfill their earlier function of being an aesthetic enterprise that can be exciting, entertaining, and eminently satisfying on the operatic stage.

---

[8]Dene Barrnett with the assistance of Jeanette Masy-Westropp, *The Art of Gesture: The practices and principles of 18th-century acting* (Heidelberg, 1987). Even more specific for Handelian opera is Joachim Eisenschmidt, *Die szenische Darstellung der Opern Georg Friedrich Händels auf der Londoner Bühne seiner Zeit* (Berlin, 1940–41; R Karlsruhe, 1987), Part II.

Watkins Shaw

HANDEL: SOME CONTEMPORARY PERFORMANCE PARTS CONSIDERED

To what extent Handel, as a composer, may have concerned himself with thoughts of posterity we cannot tell. Certainly he envisaged performances of *Messiah* at the Foundling Hospital in London after his death, but this arose from a unique charitable impulse. His careful preservation of all save a very few of his autograph scores—and those mainly early—was probably at least as much for practical, professional reasons as for any regard for his future repute.

However, by passing them, together with his large supplementary collection of so-called conducting scores, to J. C. Smith the elder, he did ensure that they were not disregarded at his death; and if he thought of posterity at all, he would certainly consider that what he had put on paper in his scores contained all he needed to indicate. His purpose in bequeathing not only a score, but a set of vocal and instrumental parts of *Messiah* to the Foundling Hospital was to facilitate future performances, not to amplify or clarify his text.

Be that as it may, when those parts re-emerged at the end of the nineteenth century it became clear, to the surprise of nearly all the few who were then interested in such things, that they did indeed indicate

---

Watkins Shaw has edited several choral works by Handel, and his Textual and Historical Companion to Handel's "Messiah" *is a standard work on the subject.*

something more than the score and that any other such material would be worth examination in supplementation of the autograph scores. The following observations do not arise out of any deliberately undertaken or comprehensive investigation of the field. They are simply, so to speak, chippings remaining on a workbench after other tasks, and relate only to a few works. Yet when brought into synthesis and focus they offer sufficient points of interest to merit report.

For the Utrecht Te Deum, *Deborah*, and *Samson*, I shall refer to parts made during Handel's lifetime to the order of Charles Jennens (d 1773). Hereinafter called the Flower parts (or "Flower"), from a former owner whose name has become attached to them, they now belong to the collective holding MS 130 Hd4 in GB Mp.[1] They were not, however, used by Jennens or anyone else in performance, and why he should have troubled to acquire such material is unknown. But the fact that they were not so used only marginally minimizes their value. For they were drawn out by the group of copyists presided over by J. C. Smith the elder (in fact mainly by S2 in Larsen's classification),[2] responsible for transcribing for the composer himself, men familiar with his work and the conventions which he took for granted.

The parts of *Messiah* bequeathed to the Foundling Hospital (hereinafter FH)[3] were similarly not performed from, but were copied to fulfil the terms of Handel's will. They, too, are the work of his own circle of copyists, with this additional feature, namely that they appear to have been copied directly from the set of parts (no longer extant) actually played and sung from at the Foundling Hospital performance of 1754.[4]

Far more fascinating are the rare though incomplete survivals of performing material for six of his early works in Italy. It is worthwhile

---

[1]For fuller details and reference numbers, see Arthur D. Walker, *George Frideric Handel: The Newman Flower Collection in the Henry Watson Music Library* (Manchester, 1972).

[2]J. P. Larsen, *Handel's Messiah: Origins—Composition—Sources* (New York/London: Norton, 1957), chapter 4.

[3]Now in the possession of the succession body, the Thomas Coram Foundation. Performances at the Hospital after the composer's death must have used parts supplied by J. C. Smith the younger, who directed them.

[4]See my detailed account in *A Textual and Historical Companion to Handel's Messiah* (London: Novello, 1965), chapter IV.

to set out the original designation of each part as follows, together with present library references ("Violetta" is simply the contemporary Italian usage for viola, and "alto" and "tenore" applied to them merely indicates the C clefs employed):

1.*Salve Regina*: Concertino; Canto solo. (D-brd B, Mus. MSS 9036/1, 9036/2). 2.*Nisi Dominus*: Concertino. (US NYpm, MS MA845). 3.*Laudate pueri Dominum* (D major): Concertino Ouboé Primo; Ouboé Secondo; Violino Primo; Violino Secondo; Alto Violetta; Tenore Violetta; Canto Primo; Soprano Secondo Concertato; Alto Primo Choro; Tenore Primo Choro; Basso Primo Choro; Continuo Organo Primo Choro; Soprano Secondo Ripieno; Alto Secondo Choro; Tenore Ripieno Secondo Choro; Basso Secondo Choro; Continuo Organo Secondo Choro [title corrected from "Violone"]. (US NYpm, Koch Deposit 1085.) 4.*Haec est Regina*: Concertino; Violino Primo Concerto Grosso (2 copies); Violino Secondo Concerto Grosso; Violino Secondo; Viola; Contrabasso; Canto solo; Organo. (US NYpm, Koch Deposit 1085.) 5.*Te decus virgineum*: Concertino; Violino Primo Concerto Grosso (2 copies); Violino Secondo Concerto Grosso (2 copies); Violone; Contrabassi; Alto solo; Organo. (US NYpm, Koch Deposit 1085.) 6.*Saeviat tellus*: Concertino; Canto solo (not headed). (US NYpm, Koch Deposit 1085).

The story surrounding the provenance of the parts now in New York is a fascinating one in its own right;[5] but here it is sufficient to say that, together with those for *Salve Regina*, they were transcribed by, or under the direction of, the copyist G. A. Angelini, and that they were used for performance under the composer himself in 1707, *Salve Regina* at Vignanello, the others in Rome (hereinafter the Vignanello and Rome parts).

It is manifest that these parts are incomplete. Did common sense not suggest missing violoncello parts, that would be made explicit (1) by Handel's own instruction in his autograph score (GB Lbm1, R.M. 20.f.1) that one of the movements in *Laudate pueri* was to be for "due Violoncelli e Contra Basso"; (2) by the word "violoncelli" in both Organo parts (general bass) of "Excelsus super omnes" of the same work; and (3) by the direction "violoncello solo" over certain bars of the general bass in

---

[5]See my own papers, "Some original performing material for Handel's Latin church music," *Göttinger Händel-Beiträge* II (1986): 226; "Handel's Vesper Music 1: Some MS sources recently discovered," *The Musical Times* CXXVI (1985): 392.

the Concertino and Organo parts of *Te decus virgineum*. (Thus, by the way, text of the missing part can be recovered.) When the parts for *Laudate pueri* are assembled it becomes evident either that the Soprano Primo ripieno part is not represented, or that the solo soprano was regarded as sufficient to deal with the first soprano part in the five-part choruses "A solis ortu" and "Quis sicut Dominus?". In the light of parts extant for other works, one must ask whether bassoon parts, sharing in the general bass, may not also be missing. But this is unlikely in a Roman work of this date, and need hardly be taken into account.[6] As we have reason to think that all the works except *Salve Regina* were performed on one and the same occasion, it is evident that three types of stringed instruments took part in the general bass: violoncello, violone, contrabass; but we have no means of telling whether the violone was of 8 ft or 16 ft pitch.

When assembled, the instrumental text of *Te decus virgineum* is convincingly complete for unison violins and general bass, so that any lack of violetta parts does not preclude complete reconstruction of the score. But it would be interesting to know whether such parts were drawn out following the track of the bass (see the discussion below of brief non-obbligato parts for violettas supplied by the copyist of *Laudate, pueri*). Unfortunately, as we have no means of knowing what, if any, duplicate ripieno (or concerto grosso) parts are now missing, or whether performers shared copies, an attempted estimate of the vocal and instrumental forces employed for these works would be too speculative to be useful. No importance should be attached to the nominal labels "Primo Choro" and "Secondo Choro" found in *Laudate pueri*. The score calls for no such division, and there is no difference in the text. But, as the work was performed on the same occasion as Handel's *Nisi Dominus*, the "Gloria Patri" of which is written for double chorus, doubtless this labelling of chorus parts was carried over from that.

Evidently the organs used in the church of the Madonna di Monte Santo in 1707 were of lower pitch than the oboes, whose parts for *Laudate pueri* are transcribed a tone lower than the notational pitch of the work. All the surviving Concertino parts (as also that of *Salve*

---

[6]H. J. Marx, "Die Instrumentation in Händels frühen italienischen Werken," *Göttinger Händel- Beiträge* II (1986): 86–87.

Regina, performed a few weeks earlier at Vignanello) show that the leading first and second violinists shared a desk. Where the other parts are upright, these are oblong in format, and have violins 1 and 2 set out in score together with the general bass (or sometimes a voice part) for guidance to the players in their responsibilities as leaders. To us, apart from revealing an interesting detail of orchestral dispositions at that date and place, this has the incidental advantage of telling us something about the general bass part where that is missing from the parts.

When the FH material first came to light late in the nineteenth century, its inclusion of oboe and bassoon parts of a non-obbligato nature came as an astonishing disclosure. Since then, increased understanding of early eighteenth-century practice in this respect enables us to take such things for granted. The bassoon parts will be discussed presently in relation to other material. But the oboe parts are elemental in the extreme. It will be recalled that the score of *Messiah* contained no hint of the presence of oboes until the chorus setting of "Their sound is gone out," with obbligato oboes in its instrumentation, was introduced some years after its inception. Essentially, in all other choruses save one, the FH scribe treats oboes 1 and 2 in unison with the soprano voice. The exception is "The Lord gave the word," in which a certain amount of ingenuity has been applied to contriving an oboe 2 part as follows:

measures 1–4:	with alto voice.
measures 5–6:	with violin 2.
measures 7–2nd beat, measure 9:	with alto voice.
2nd beat, measure 9–measure 10:	rests.
measure 11–2nd beat, measure 13:	with alto.
3rd beat, measure 13–end:	with soprano.

It is hard to see why in this movement rather than in any other an attempt should have been made to provide a second oboe part; yet, if the effort was to be made, only a very little more ingenuity would have been needed to continue to do this from measure 13 onwards. It is curious to find rests in measure 9–10.

Six choruses have introductory instrumental ritornellos. In three of them the scribe uses oboes merely to double the sopranos. In three others ("And the glory of the Lord," "For unto us a child is born," and "Lift up your heads") he uses them to double violin 1 and violin 2 in the introduction before combining them to double the sopranos. "For unto us" has a concluding instrumental ritornello, but oboes are not included in it.

The primary, and very simple aim, then, apart from the odd treatment of "The Lord gave us the word," and the inconsistent treatment of instrumental ritornellos, was nothing but to strengthen the choral soprano line. As for the overture, both oboes double violin 1 in the Grave (thus avoiding any trouble about compass or awkward notes in violin 2), but divide to double violins 1 and 2 respectively in the Allegro, the scribe forgetting to make allowance for the troublesome sharp c' in bars 36 and 39. (It is worth noting in passing that whoever constructed the text of the overture for *Handel's Six Overtures. . . the Eighth Collection* published in parts by Walsh in 1743 took a slightly different line in the Grave, making a second oboe part doubling violin 2, dodging to violin 1 where necessary.)

When all is said and done, however, *Messiah* is a special case of a complete work without any obbligato oboe parts in the score. But it is interesting to look at a short example of non-obbligato oboe parts, not explicit in the score, supplied by the Rome parts to the chorus "A solis ortu" in *Laudate pueri*. Broadly speaking, the instrumental parts (unlabelled but primarily for strings) to this five-part chorus in Handel's score simply double the voice parts; but there are important divergences of disposition (without including any note independent of the voices) which enrich the sonority. Thus, violin 1, having at first doubled the tenor voice an octave higher, proceeds to double the first soprano either at the unison or at the octave, also taking one alto passage an octave higher. Violin 2 begins by doubling the alto voice and then switches to second soprano at the unison. In supplying oboes to Handel's score perhaps we might assume that, as in *Messiah*, they should strengthen sopranos at the unison. If so, we should be wrong, for the Rome transcriber causes them to double violins 1 and 2.

In further connection with the provision of what may be termed non-explicit oboe parts, an apparently regular convention can be deduced about the interpretation of Handel's direction "Tutti" when applied to the top instrumental line of his scores. By this, as Winton Dean has already pointed out, he

> intended all the oboes to double the first violins, even when the second violins have a part below. This is. . . confirmed by the contem-

porary Flower parts. With very few exceptions (coro movements are the most notable) [the scribe] interpreted the Tutti indications ... in the above sense, supplying two identical oboe parts.[7]

Turning now to non-explicit bassoon parts, we find that the Rome sets, as already explained, can offer nothing. However, in addition to FH, the Flower sets provide illustration in abundance from which clear ruling principles emerge. Bassoons, if having no obbligato part, share the general bass in both arias and choruses, even if the stave does not explicitly name them (their inclusion not depending on the presence of oboes). Significant confirmation of this is plainly seen in "Glorious hero" (*Samson*). Here, for measures 1–9, Handel writes an obbligato part for bassoons 1 and 2, after which mention of them in his score vanishes. But from measure 10 to the end of the movement, "Flower" allots them to the general bass, though respecting, of course, the phrases marked 'Violoncelli con Organo'—which was evidently not regarded as implying simply that double basses alone would otherwise share the part.

It was apparently the general rule that in arias bassoons did not play when the soloist was singing, even though the upper instruments were accompanying. But a salient exception to this standard treatment seems to apply to *arie all'unisono*. In FH, bassoons play throughout the general bass of "The people that walked in darkness" (*Messiah*), coinciding, of course, with the solo voice except for a few notes which it would be ridiculous to cut out of the bassoon part.

Some exceptions to the otherwise standard treatment catch the eye, for example in *Samson*. In both "Just are the ways" and "How willing my paternal love" 'Flower' has bassoons playing throughout, whether or not the voice is singing. Can this be by design, or is it carelessness? In "Go, baffl'd coward" there is a certain inconsistency. As far as measure 28, and again from measure 38, it follows standard practice (bassoons silent in vocal passages); but for no apparent good reason bassoons are allowed to play beneath the voice in measures 28–38. In "Honour and arms" these parts again maintain bassoons throughout. Presumably this arises from the *all'unisono* character of most of this aria, although there are considerably longer stretches departing from it than are found in "The people that walked in darkness" (notably measures 22–31, and 43–48). But perhaps it was judged

---

[7] Winton Dean and J. Merrill Knapp, *Handel's Operas: 1704–1726* (Oxford: Clarendon Press, 1987), 34.

unduly fussy to view these as *fagotti tacent*, even though such treatments would have corresponded to the changes of texture.

In thus constructing a part for bassoons, the copyist frequently had to use his discretion about the precise point of a phrase at which they dropped out or re-entered. This can sometimes be questionable. Numerous examples in FH are listed in my *Textual companion to Messiah*, and in a single instance from "Rejoice greatly" is all that need be cited here. In measures 75–76 the bassoons drop out after the third beat of measure 76, rather than more suitably after the first. In "Our fears are now for ever fled" (*Deborah*), the re-entry of the bassoon is allotted by 'Flower' to the sixth eighth-note value of the measure, where one might have been disposed to take the eighth. In "At my feet extended low" (*Deborah*) the brief re-entry at measure 14 is treated as extending to the fourth quarter note of measure 15, not just to the third. In measures 69–76 of "In the battle fame pursuing" a bassoon part is extracted from the general bass as shown in Example 1, when one might have reserved its entry until measure 71, marked by Handel "Tutti forte" (the dove-tailing of measures 74–75 is a nice touch).

Example 1.

But that anticipatory entry in measure 70 is not alone. At measures 22–23 of "Thus when the sun" (*Samson*), 'Flower' brings in the bassoons three eighth notes before the upper strings enter with the ritornello on the first beat of measure 23; and one cannot but feel the effectiveness of this. A striking example of the same feature is the entry of the bassoons with the rising scale at the end of measure 39 of "Choirs of angels" (*Deborah*) on the last note of the solo phrase and before the ritornello on the first beat of the next measure. Here the copyist was watchful enough to take a hint from Handel's own "forte" mark in the general bass.

So far as the overt evidence of the FH parts takes us, it does not appear that bassoons were reduced in number when accompanying an aria, for both bassoon copies contain the text.

Certain techniques of composition in Handel's day conveniently lent themselves to abbreviated notation. But this involved reliance on the transcriber of the performance parts, putting him somewhat into the position of an amanuensis rather than a mere copyist. A famous aria illustrating this is "The people that walked in darkness" (*Messiah*). Here Handel labelled the highest stave of his three-stave MS score "V. unis e Viola," and marked the part "all ottava coll Basso" without completing the notation. A quick glance might suggest that this covered all that was necessary. But this is not an *aria all'unisono* in its entirety. From time to time on his otherwise empty top stave Handel wrote passages which at times create two-part texture, and at others, when the vocal bass diverges from the general bass, three-part texture, yet did not deem any further direction necessary for drawing out the parts.

The FH scribe, having looked at the score, perceived this feature, and concluded that Handel's general direction was not free from ambiguity as to the violas. The first instance occurs at the end of measure 14, and here, in a passage well within viola compass, the scribe simply doubled the violins. Then, in measures 17–19, follows a passage in which the part on the top stave exceeds the then customary viola compass, and could only be reinforced in the violas by unsuitably adjusting their contour. So the transcriber here made them double the general bass an octave higher, doing so also for a similar reason in measures 31–33 and 48–49. Meanwhile, at measures 29–31 a passage of three-part texture occurred; but as the highest part lies low, there is no problem in having violins doubled by viola. Looking now at measures 38–40, 44–46, and 53–54, we find passages similar to each other in phraseology and texture in which the bass voice solemnly sustains the word "death" and the highest instrumental part exceeds the old normal viola compass. In treating these the scribe was inconsistent. At measures 38–40 he attempted to allow violas to double the violins by making an adjustment as in Example 2. Had he wished, he could have treated measures 44–46 and 53–54 in corresponding fashion; but there he made the violas double the general bass at the octave.[8]

Example 2.

Finally he had to deal with the concluding instrumental measures. He might (just conceivably) have treated the first two bars as viola in octaves with violins, the last two in unison with them. Without Handel's direction, yet more in accord with what we should expect, he doubled the general bass by violas an octave higher.

This is a good example of the work of a scribe who, presumably guided by known principles, made a sensible job of things, but who may be thought to have misjudged things slightly at measures 38–40. It is, by the way, interesting to reflect that none of these decisions was taken by the scribe of the conducting score, who might have been thought in such respects to stand between the composer's autograph manuscript and the scribe of the parts.

The decision from time to time to move the viola to the general bass, where, if not attempting to make it follow the violins in some adjusted fashion, he might simply have silenced it, perhaps rests on an elastic interpretation of Handel's "all ottava coll Basso." But it does not surprise us. There is indeed a supposed usage of the late seventeenth century and early eighteenth century whereby violas, if not explicitly named in the score, did as best they could to join in the general bass, with any necessary octave adjustment. Such procedure is very likely in, for example, the final chorus of Purcell's ode *Welcome to all the*

---

[8]In the instrumental parts to my own edition (miniature score, Novello and Co., Ltd., n.d.) I have adjusted the viola at this point to conform to measures 44–46 and 53–54 by doubling the general bass.

HANDEL: CONTEMPORARY PERFORMANCE PARTS 69

pleasures. Now and again, Handel actually scored for violas in this way, one example being "Excelsus super omnes gentes" in *Laudate pueri*, where, pressed for time though we have reason to think he was, he goes to the extraordinary trouble of writing out the part in full instead of giving directions to the copyist. But neither FH nor "Flower" gives any sign whatever—so far as my knowledge goes—that violas were supplementarily employed in this way; and surely players could not be expected to crane their necks to get sight of a cello part. But there is one tiny and interesting instance in *Laudate pueri* in which the copyist decided to treat violas thus. Almost to the end, the aria "Suscitans a terra inopem" is scored for basso continuo accompaniment only, for which Handel specified organ, two cellos, and a double bass. Then, by way of a 12–measure conclusion, he introduced violins 1 and 2, marking the instrumental bass at this point 'Tutti'. By this one might have supposed that the introduction of all the F clef bass instruments was indicated, and no more. But the copyist went further, and applied violas to reinforce the bass. Having divided violas at his disposal, he exercised modest ingenuity as shown in Example 3. One notes how at measure 91 he carefully avoided taking viola 1 above the violins.

Example 3.

But there is a discrepancy between these parts and Handel's autograph directions for rendering the instrumental bass of that very movement. He prescribed, somewhat precisely, "primo Organo solo con due Violoncelli e Contra Basso." Yet this movement is entered, not in one, but in both organ copies. However, what is called the second organ part may have been intended (as at first labelled) for violone; but in that alternative case this movement should not have been included either. Was this a nicety of his own scoring to which Handel was indifferent, or was it dealt with at performance without putting a mark on the copy as a reminder? One recalls that though the Pastoral Symphony and "All they that see him" (*Messiah*) include a part for violin 3, that is ignored in the FH parts.

Momentary slips of the pen apart, Handel's autograph scores rarely leave room for doubt about the essentials of the musical text in the sense of the primary pitch and note values. But his was not the sort of mind which delighted to take precise care in dry details, so that there are not a few instances of omission, inconsistency, and anomaly in connection with his instructions which today a publisher's reader would pick up and refer back to the composer. With Handel's music it fell to the lot of the transcriber of the parts to deal with these (and we assume he was not encouraged to go running back to bother the composer). Some examples from the Utrecht Te Deum and *Laudate pueri* constitute brief case studies of this point.

In the Utrecht Te Deum's opening chorus "We praise thee, O God," at measure 43 the highest instrumental part (violin 1 doubled by oboe 1) goes up to e'''. Although in earlier similar passages (measures 13–15, 20–21) Handel has acted to modify oboe 1, he does not do so here. When transcribing the oboe part, "Flower," having got as far as writing the eighth-note rest at the beginning of the measure, realized what lay ahead, and, scratching this out, substituted a whole measure rest, bringing the oboe in again on the sixth eighth note of measure 44—a reasonable treatment.

In "The glorious company of the Apostles" at measure 134, Handel silences both oboes after the first beat, and neglects to mark any re-entry. "Flower" sensibly brings them back at measure 141, doubling violins 1 and 2 respectively. (One may think it perhaps curious that he did not reintroduce them earlier, to strengthen the powerful adagio at measures 137–40).

At the chorus entry in "When thou took'st upon thee" (measure 20) the highest instrumental line in Handel's score is marked "Tutti," and, as expected (see principle adduced by Dean, mentioned above), "Flower" doubles this by oboes 1 and 2 in unison. But though Handel gives no further direction, "Flower" then causes the oboes to continue divisi at measure 26 (triple time), allotting oboe 1 to the highest stave (violin 1), oboe 2 to the next below (violin 2), so departing from that principle.

Example 4 is taken from the first movement of *Laudate pueri*. Handel, writing oboes 1 and 2 with violins 1 and 2 respectively, marks his score as in the example. Modern copyists might well make the oboes drop out after only an eighth note at the third beat. Not so the Rome copyist who turned that eighth note into a quarter note for the oboes before completing the measure with a quarter-note rest (simile in measures 7, 31, 41, 45). It may be noted, too, that the Flower copyist generally did the same when "signing off" a bassoon phrase if the general bass proceeded in eighth-note movement.

Example 4.

In measures 15–16 of the same movement a problem arises about doubling violin 2 by oboe 2. In the original notation there is the awkward sharp *c*'; in the transposed notation, *b* is too low for the instrument. The copyist dealt with this by carrying oboe 2 up an octave, momentarily taking it above violin 1/oboe 1 (Example 5).

Example 5.

At measure 59 of the opening movement the copyist has failed to grapple with a problem comprehensively. At this point there is clearly an instrumental tutti entry, but with no guidance from Handel's full score as to instrumentation, though the general style of the movement suggests oboes 1 and 2 doubling violins 1 and 2 respectively. But, presumably because Handel, unlike elsewhere, gave no direction to this effect, the scribe, when writing out his oboe 1 part, entered rests until reaching the final D major ritornello of the last four measures. And yet, when he then addressed himself to drawing out the part for oboe 2 he doubled violin 2 from measure 59. There seems no good reason for this treatment, and it is obvious enough that he should also have doubled violin 1 by oboe 1. This is a striking demonstration of the danger that could lurk if Handel left too much for his copyists to tidy up.

A much more significant instance calling for a copyist's knowledge and judgment is the "Gloria patri" of *Laudate pueri*. Here oboe 1 plays a soloistic role, but Handel's full score is by no means explicit about oboe 2. Though most (but perhaps not all) of the solutions of the Rome parts would be arrived at by a modern editor, it is satisfactory to see how they are treated by a copyist working for the composer.

In measures 9–16, for example, which are marked "Tutti" should oboe 2 join oboe 1 on the top stave with violin 1, as one might imagine? The Rome parts make oboe 2 run with violin 2. At measures 33–42, and again at 100–108 the top stave of the score is allotted to oboe 1 (solo), and the stave below is marked "Tutti violini." The Rome parts add oboe

HANDEL: CONTEMPORARY PERFORMANCE PARTS 73

2 to the violins (so also measures 53–60, not marked in any way by the composer). An interesting touch of detail occurs at measure 103 where, in doubling violin 1, oboe 2 is slightly modified by the copyist as in Example 6. And where, from measure 108 the unison violins which oboe 2 have been doubling now divide for a passage of thirds in sixteenth notes, the transcriber decides to allow the oboes to drop out.

Example 6.

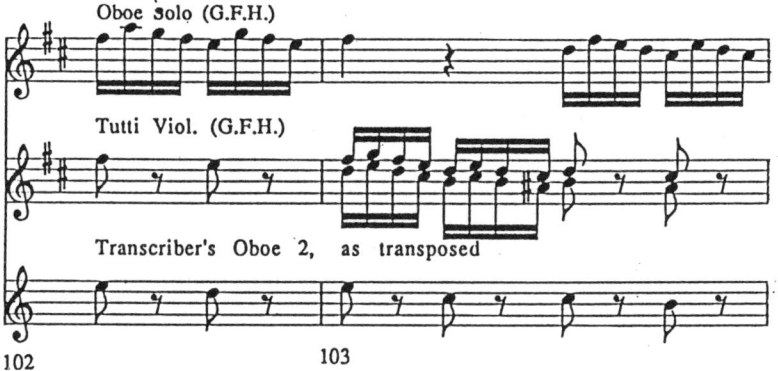

The Rome, Flower, and FH parts are at one in their testimony to the practice whereby vocal soloists sang in chorus movements, presumably as leaders. Another feature finding explicit confirmation in "Flower" is that any small part for transverse flute was undertaken by an oboist, in whose copy it was entered.

If we can turn with undoubted profit to the transcribers of all these various parts for guidance in many aspects of bringing Handel's scores to life, it is unreasonable to turn to them for alternative readings of his explicit text. Like all copyists they were capable of errors in transcription. Solemn collation of their innumerable slips with Handel's autographs would be ridiculous. And this leads to a concluding reflection about standards of performance.

What one expects is that parts used in performance, even if not scrutinized beforehand, would be marked with corrections arising in rehearsal. This cannot apply to the Flower parts, of course. Nor, strictly, can it apply to the FH parts, which contain mistakes in plenty, bad enough to mar a performance seriously. And yet one cannot but think that not all those errors are original to those copies: that there is at least a possibility that some were already in the set of parts being copied, and which had been used in performance. At any rate, they were handed over to the Foundling Hospital without being checked.

However, let our present comments be confined to the firm testimony of the Rome and Vignanello parts. They do in fact bear a few—a very few—traces of having been corrected. The Canto Solo parts of *Haec est Regina* and *Saeviat tellus* have small amendments (which might, of course, be second thoughts) in what seems to be Handel's writing; and in the Ouboé Primo of *Laudate pueri* it appears to be he who has usefully introduced two dynamic marks not found in the score. But that is all. Thus, one of Handel's own rare slips goes forward unremarked in *Laudate pueri* ("A solis ortu," measure 16, violin 2, oboe 2). In his autograph of *Salve Regina* (D-ddr Bds, Mus. MS. autogr. Händel 2) measures 44–45 of the adagio "Ad te clamamus" are difficult to decipher, partly because he wrote crossing violin parts on a single stave and partly because he made alterations to them. When copying the Concertino part for the leading players, Angelini misunderstood this; but the copy bears no sign that Handel detected the mistake when the passage was played through. Even that very sheet which carries the aforesaid extra dynamics in *Laudate pueri* (oboe 1, "Gloria patri") includes two uncorrected erroneously copied groups of sixteenth notes; and it also carries a very insecurely noted whole measure rest (barline omitted; no figure '1' as regularly elsewhere) which might have caused a stumble in reading. No modern player would pass this without adding a warning mark.

These instances are but specimens. Beside them must be placed a casual attitude to accidentals. They omit some that Handel gives, while rarely supplying the many which he takes for granted in relation to the key in his mind. Example 7 gives an exact rendering of (a) measures 25–26 and (b) measures 29–34 of the Rome Concertino part (unison violins) of the opening movement of *Nisi Dominus*.

Example 7.

However much at home with a familiar idiom the players may have been, however promptly responsive their ears to what they heard around them, such passages cannot have been straightforward to negotiate at the points now noted by asterisks. The first beat of measure 26 is a decided trap, no tonal inkling of the required sharp to C having occurred until the tenor part on the first eighth note of the measure. (The last sixteenth note, by the way, is C natural in the modern convention.) And if the players were skilled enough to dispense with accidentals, then the pedantic form of measure 32 is unnecessary. On the testimony of these parts in general one hardly feels confident that performances were impeccable.

Ellen T. Harris

HARMONIC PATTERNS IN HANDEL'S OPERAS

Opera seria adheres to a chain-like pattern of construction in both text and music. That is, individual segments of an opera seria tend to be related only to their neighbors and not, through a series of formal relations, to segments far distant.[1] The links in the chain are not, however, arbitrarily placed. Nor does the completed chain lack structural integrity. Only by pointing to the worst examples of revisions and pasticcios can contemporary scholars, editors, and performers justify

---

[1]There are, of course, exceptions to this generalization. One obvious instance in Handel's operas occurs in *Poro*. In Act I, v, Poro swears to his wife, Cleofide, that he will control his jealousy, "Se mal più sarò geloso." In I, vi, Cleofide sings an aria attesting to her fidelity, "Se mai turbo il tuo riposo," in which the three-verse, A section parallels in meter and rhyme scheme the text previously sung by Poro. At the end of the first act (scene xii), Poro and Cleofide renew their vows in a duet that combines the music and texts from both arias. See Ellen T. Harris, ed., *The Librettos of Handel's Operas*, (New York, 1989), vol. 6, 171–238, for a facsimile of the original libretto (London, 1731). See also Graham H. Cummings, "Reminiscence and Recall in Three Early Settings of Metastasio's *Alessandro nell'Indie,*" *Proceedings of the Royal Musical Association*, CIX (1982–83): 80–104.

Ellen T. Harris is Professor of Music and Associate Provost for the Arts at the Massachusetts Institute of Technology. She has written extensively on Handel, Purcell, and performance practice and has edited Purcell's Dido and Aeneas *and the thirteen-volume facsimile edition of Handel's opera librettos. Her edition of sixteen alto cantatas by Handel from a Bodleian Library manuscript is due shortly.*

cutting recitatives, arias, and scenes, shifting sections from one part of the opera to another, and adding material at whim.[2]

In the operas of Handel, the musical structure is closely tied to the text. By re-examining the formal patterns underlying the construction of an opera seria libretto, including the nature of scenic continuity and the relation of the exit aria convention to the use of the da capo form, it is possible to show how Handel's harmonic patterns in his operas parallel the textual patterns found in librettos.

The scenes in opera seria are constructed around the entrances and exits of the characters—a new scene occurring at the entrance of one or more characters, a scene ending at the exit of one or more characters.[3] Groups of such scenes are linked together by the *liaison de scène*, or the maintenance of at least one character on stage over the scene break. Generally these scenes are bounded by a set change, at which point the stage is momentarily without any characters. The group of scenes occurring within one scenic backdrop thereby becomes a unit in itself. Throughout this paper I will refer to this unit as a set to distinguish it from the scenes of which it is made.[4] Various patterns of

---

[2]Perhaps the best, which is to say the worst, example of this occurred in the 1966 performance and 1967 recording of *Giulio Cesare* by the New York City Opera under the direction of Julius Rudel, who explains his alterations in the notes to the recording (RCA LSC-6182): "Recent approaches to Handel all too often combine equal parts of reverence and trepidation with a zealous search for literalness. I doubt that this would have pleased Handel . . . In the spirit of baroque writing, Handel did not fix the content of his works, often interchanging parts, never finding it necessary to dot every musical 'i' or cross every dramatic 't.'" In this spirit, therefore, Rudel explains that they "had to cut some of the arias" and "transfer others into different places." "For the sake of continuity and contrast we added one chorus and several brief orchestral interludes from Handel's cantata *Parnasso in Festa*." Also, "we changed the role of Caesar from castrato to bass-baritone, which seemed somehow more suitable than a female alto for the role of hero-warrior." And finally, "I should like to reiterate that we sought authenticity for this production in spirit and intent rather than in literalness." One wonders what spiritual authenticity would do for other composers such as Mozart and Verdi.

[3]My discussion of librettos is indebted to the work of Robert Freeman, especially: "Opera without Drama: Currents of Change in Italian Opera, 1675 to 1725, and the Roles played therein by Zeno, Caldara, and Others," 2 vols. (Ph.D. dissertation, Princeton University, 1967; rev. ed. Ann Arbor, 1981) and "The Travels of *Partenope*" in *Studies in Music History: Essays for Oliver Strunk*, ed. Harold Powers (Princeton, 1968), 356–85. For a more detailed discussion of Handel's librettos than is possible here, see Harris, *The Librettos of Handel's Operas*, "Introductions," vols. 1–13.

[4]This word was coined in a seminar at the University of Chicago on Handel's harmonic patterns to designate a group of scenes played against a single scenic backdrop. In later drama this unit is simply named a scene, but in early eighteenth-century librettos the

HARMONIC PATTERNS IN HANDEL'S OPERAS 79

entrances and exits are possible within one set; using letters arbitrarily to represent characters it is possible to visualize these.

In one such pattern, many characters can enter at the beginning of the set and then exit one by one. This situation is most likely to occur at the beginning of the opera, when a multitude of characters may be "discovered" on stage at the raising of the curtain, the curtain thereafter not being lowered until the end of the opera. Assuming a set of four scenes, this pattern might look as follows: ABCD ABC AB A. In this example, character A is given precedence by remaining on stage throughout the set. Secondary characters are not given this privilege, nor are they generally allotted the final solo scene that normally occurs at the end of the set.

In addition to the possibility of using a gradually diminishing number of characters, sets can be constructed with a recurrent series of entrances and exits. These may give a single character precedence: AB AC AD . . . A. That is, two characters enter at the beginning of the set, one (B) exiting at the end of the first scene. A new character (C) then enters at the beginning of the second scene and exits at its end. This continues until a scene is reached where no new character enters. Thereupon the dominant character (A) has a solo scene at the end of the set.

Of course, it is possible, using this same pattern, to construct a set where no one character has dominance, such as: AB BC CD . . . D. In this case, two characters enter at the beginning of the set, and one (A) exits. In scene ii, a new character (C) enters, and the liaison character (B) exits. This pattern, as before, can continue indefinitely until no new character enters and the remaining single character takes the ending solo scene.

By mixing these three patterns in various permutations, a large variety of set constructions becomes possible. The first set of Handel's

---

scene is still defined not by the backdrop but by the entrances and exits of the characters. The shift toward naming scenes by location can be seen occurring in Handel's late operas, *Serse*, *Imeneo*, and *Deidamia*, as well as in some late revisions, especially *Rossane* (1743), an adaptation of *Alessandro* (see Harris, *The Librettos of Handel's Operas*, "Introductions", vols. 8 and 13), but in discussing Handel's librettos throughout his career, it is useful to have a single word identifying the text occurring within one scenic location. In Handel's early operas the "sets" encompass many scenes; in the late operas mentioned above, the sets frequently become synonymous with scenes.

Rodelinda (1725), for example, is constructed as follows: ABC AB ABD AD A. This generally follows the first pattern above, with A given precedence, although the pattern is expanded with a new entrance in scene iii. In the second set of Handel's *Scipione* (1726), the pattern is basically: AB AC AD DE DBE E. This follows the second pattern above, although the dominance of A is replaced in scene iv by the dominance of E. In the short opening sets of the first two acts of *Tamerlano* (1724), the second pattern is followed exactly, with the same character allotted the solo scene in both cases: AB AC A and AC AD A, and, finally in the third set of Act I in *Sosarme* (1732), the third pattern can be found: AB BC CD D.

These patterns serve as the background convention against which the libretto is written, and they provide the normal means of dramatic continuity. Their disruption increases the tension and underscores the dramatic conflicts of the libretto. The placement of the aria at the end of the scene, which offers the singer a dramatic exit, also serves as an aid in the perception of normal scenic continuity. Entrance arias and medial arias usually illustrate a heightened dramatic moment, and scenes without arias usually result from an increased speed in the dramatic actions.

In the same way that the convention of the exit aria highlights the patterns of scenic construction, the convention of the da capo emphasizes the use of the exit aria. The vast majority of all arias in opera seria are da capo. In Handel's operas the percentage varies from a low of 59% in the late opera *Imeneo* (1740) to 96 or 97% in many of his earlier operas, including *Rodrigo* (1707), *Teseo* (1713), *Ottone* (1723), and *Siroe* (1728). Handel uses the da capo predominantly as an exit aria; entrance arias and medial arias without exit, which are frequently remarkable but few in number, are typically in cavatina form (the A section only of the da capo), binary dance form, or through-composed.[5] Thus, the da capo became practically synonymous with the exit aria, and,

---

[5] The cavatina is an aria "carved out" from a da capo, that is, it is equivalent in text and music to the A section of a da capo aria. This term, or the non-diminutive "cavata," is used by many composers throughout the eighteenth century to define such movements. Although not used by Handel, it identifies the textual and musical form of a specific type of eighteenth-century aria. The term "arioso," which is sometimes used for such movements, is better reserved for movements in which the text is structured like recitative and the music follows no conventional repetitive scheme. See Harris, *The Librettos of Handel's Operas*, vol. 4 and elsewhere.

like the convention of scenic succession, was part of the normative procedure of opera seria.

Disrupting the da capo process was undoubtedly the most audible procedure available to the librettist and composer to indicate surprise, emotional tension, or dramatic conflict. Sometimes, the da capo is cut off in mid-word, as occurs in "Prendo/Prendi da questa mano" from *Ariodante* I, vi (1734), when the father of one of the young lovers enters the stage in the middle of their declaration of love. Sometimes, as happens in "V'adoro pupille" from *Giulio Cesare* II, ii (1725), the da capo is interrupted by another character's comments, but resumes normally. Interrupted da capos also highlight abnormal scene endings that lack exits. Most obvious, however, is when the da capo is eliminated altogether, as in the death scene of Bajazet from *Tamerlano*, III, x (1724) and the mad scenes of *Orlando*, xi, and III, viii (1732); the dying Bajazet and the mad Orlando do not sing in the normal form because they are no longer normal.

Handel not only knew and understood these conventions governing the construction of the opera seria libretto, but in some cases it is clear that he participated in the preparation of his own librettos. Two operas stand out in this regard. In *Tamerlano* Handel at one stage in the compositional process included two full da capos, one a solo and one a duet, after Bajazet's death scene and before the closing ensemble. Before opening night and before the libretto for this performance was printed, Handel altered the ending to eliminate both da capos and moved the action directly from the death scene to the ensemble without any intervening closed forms.[6] This is infinitely better theatre, avoiding anti-climax and leaving the characters and audience with the full impact of the self-sacrificing suicide. Normalcy, represented by the da capo, cannot return easily after such an event. This situation is similar to that

---

[6]The text "figlia mia" is set as an extremely condensed da capo, but it is embedded in accompanied recitative and does not "function" as a da capo in terms of libretto structure, exit aria convention, or, presumably, ornamentation. The genesis of *Tamerlano* has been discussed by J. Merrill Knapp, "Handel's *Tamerlano*: the Creation of an Opera," *The Musical Quarterly* LVI (1970): 405–30, and in Winton Dean and J. Merrill Knapp, *Handel's Operas 1704–1726* (Oxford, 1987), 527–71. Recently C. Steven LaRue has re-evaluated the significance of the first (pre-performance) version of *Tamerlano* in "The Composer's Choice: Aspects of Handel's Compositional Process in the Royal Academy Operas" (Ph.D. dissertation, The University of Chicago, 1990, forthcoming from Oxford University Press).

in *Acis and Galatea* (1718), where the trio "The flocks shall leave the mountain" is interrupted by Acis's death. After this event there are no further da capos in the masque. To take a somewhat different case, in the mad scene at the end of Act II of *Orlando*, three separate texts ("Amor, caro Amore," scene x; "Già latra Cerbero," scene xi; and "Vaghe pupille," xi) appear in the printed libretto as da capo arias. In the score, without any omission of text, they become part of the fabric of a sustained musical *scena* representing Orlando's insanity. Again, the appearance of normalcy through the use of the da capo would be dramatically unsupportable in this scene, and Handel makes the necessary alterations. In *Orlando* overall, Handel ignores eight da capo indications for similar, dramatic reasons.[7]

If Handel was aware of textual patterns in the construction of his librettos and sometimes participated in their creation, it should come as no surprise that patterns also played a large role in his compositional practices. This seems to be particularly true of his large-scale harmonic practices.[8] The da capo itself provides the first and clearest example. Most of these arias are in what is called "five-part da capo aria form." That is, the aria opens with an instrumental ritornello, the A text is sung completely once (A1), the ritornello returns in abbreviated form, the A text is repeated in a varied and extended musical setting (A2), and finally the opening ritornello returns in full. The B section is usually much shorter, with no formal demarcations, regardless of whether the B text is sung only once or twice. Then A1 and A2 are repeated in full. This formal pattern elicits from Handel a normal harmonic pattern as well. Arias in major keys modulate at the end of A1 to the major dominant and return to the tonic by the end of A2. The B section usually begins in the relative minor and cadences to the minor mediant key. Arias in minor keys modulate to the relative major at the end of A1, and the B section cadences to the minor dominant. In general, minor-key arias are

---

[7]See Ellen T. Harris, "Eighteenth-Century Orlando: Hero, Satyr, and Fool," in *Opera and Vivaldi*, ed. Michael Collins and Elise K. Kirk (Austin, Texas, 1984), 105–28, for a discussion of these changes. A comparative edition by Lorenzo Bianconi of Handel's libretto and the source libretto by Capeci was printed in the Program booklet for the 1985 performance of *Orlando* at La Fenice, Venice. See Harris, *The Librettos of Handel's Operas*, vol. 7, xv–xvi, for an extensive bibliography on *Orlando*.

[8]The harmonic practices of Handel in terms of specific progressions, juxtapositions, and modulations within arias and recitatives are not discussed in this paper.

not as predictable as arias in major keys; for example, minor arias offer no typical key for the opening of the B section, although the relative major (repeated from the A section) appears frequently. To give examples of these patterns, an aria in C major will typically cadence to G major at the end of A1 before returning to C by the end of A2, will move to A minor at the opening of the B section, and at the end of the B section will cadence to E minor. An aria in C minor will typically modulate to E-flat major at the end of A1 before returning to C minor, will perhaps also begin the B section in E-flat major, and at the end of the B section will cadence to G minor.

An important and regular part of these patterns concerns the relation of the tonic key of the aria to the B section cadence. This may be called the normal A/B pattern, which in major key arias may be schematized I(iii); in minor i(v). After examining twenty-eight of Handel's forty-two operas in detail (choosing one opera from every year in which Handel composed opera), it can be shown that Handel strongly favored this pattern above all others. The statistics are given in Chart I, with the number of arias in each opera given in column 1, the number and percent of arias in da capo form in column 2, and the number and percent of da capo arias with the normal A/B harmonic pattern in column 3.[9]

A number of things are apparent from these figures. First of all, the da capo form may be found on average in 85% of the arias in any one opera, and on average 76% of da capos per opera use one of the two A/B patterns. The two figures are frequently at odds, however, as in *Alcina*, where 81% of the arias are da capo, but only 54% of these have the A/B pattern, and in *Imeneo*, where only 59% of the arias are da capo, but 94% of these have the A/B pattern. *Imeneo* (1740) represents the most extreme case in a general trend after 1728 for Handel to use fewer da capos.

---

[9]The statistics gathered in Chart I are based largely on Chrysander's edition of Handel's operas with corrections made from a study of the autographs. For each opera, there has been an attempt to represent the state of the first performance. Although this goal has surely not been achieved in every case, the evidence as to Handel's common practice is without doubt accurate. That is, the evidence of 711 arias (preceded by recitative) provides sufficient basis for this discussion without the necessity of providing for each of the 28 operas the exact version first performed.

Chart I. Arias, Da capos, A/B Harmonic Relation and Recitative Link in Handel

Year	Opera	Arias	Da capos*		Normal A/B pattern		Da capos with preceding recitatives	Recitative link		Recitative link with normal A/B pattern	
			#	%	#	%		#	%	#	%
1704	*Almira*	55	46	83	27	58	35	15	43	11	73
1707	*Rodrigo*†	33	32	97	24	75	30	9	30	7	78
1709	*Agrippina*	46	38	83	28	74	35	16	46	12	75
1711	*Rinaldo*	35	33	94	25	76	31	16	52	13	81
1712	*Il pastor fido*	25	22	88	14	64	19	11	58	9	82
1713	*Silla*	24	21	88	18	86	19	13	68	13	100
1713	*Teseo*	35	34	97	25	73	31	13	42	13	100
1715	*Amadigi*	27	24	88	18	75	24	17	71	15	88
1720	*Radamisto*	31	26	83	20	77	26	12	46	10	83
1721	*Floridante*	31	27	87	25	93	27	16	59	14	88

*d.c. or ABA written out
†incomplete score

1723	Ottone	30	29	97	24	83	27	14	52	13	93
1724	Tamerlano	29	25	86	24	96	25	16	64	16	100
1725	Rodelinda	31	27	87	24	89	27	12	44	12	100
1726	Alessandro	31	26	84	21	81	26	11	42	11	100
1727	Admeto	31	28	90	21	75	27	16	59	15	94
1728	Siroe	26	25	96	20	80	25	12	48	12	100
1729	Lotario	30	27	90	18	67	26	12	46	11	92
1730	Partenope	38	29	76	26	90	28	15	54	15	100
1731	Poro	26	22	85	19	86	22	14	64	14	100
1732	Orlando	29	20	69	17	85	20	13	65	13	100
1733	Arianna	28	26	93	19	73	26	15	58	13	87
1734	Ariodante	34	26	76	21	81	25	11	44	11	100
1735	Alcina	32	26	81	14	54	26	11	42	9	81
1736	Atalanta	23	18	78	13	72	18	6	33	6	100
1737	Arminio	30	25	83	16	64	24	13	54	11	85
1738	Faramondo	27	23	85	15	65	23	11	48	10	91
1740	Imeneo	27	16	59	15	94	16	11	69	11	100
1741	Deidamia	35	26	74	18	69	23	7	30	6	86

Possibly Handel compensated for the formal irregularity of *Imeneo* by keeping the da capos themselves very regular. Or else the increased flexibility of form eliminated the necessity, or even the underlying *raison d'être*, for irregular da capo patterns, the irregularity being provided by the larger number of non-da capos. For whatever reason, however, one sees this pattern repeated; the fewer da capos in an opera, the more regular they are harmonically. Only somewhat less striking than *Imeneo* in this regard is *Orlando*. In *Alcina*, where Handel's concern for balancing irregularity with normative patterns may be even clearer, the reverse pattern occurs. A comparison of *Ottone* and *Tamerlano*, composed in consecutive years, offers a less extreme example of this balancing process.

Handel's use of a harmonic convention in the da capo parallels the use of the da capo form in the text. In both cases, disruption is dramatically significant. The depiction of the sorceress Alcina in the opera of the same name offers an example of Handel's use of this convention. In her six arias, she sings of her love sickness, jealousy, heartbreak, impotence, revenge, and desolation; in each, her emotion is stretched to the limit. It is no surprise, then, that of these arias only one follows the normal A/B pattern and that in Act II Alcina's arias are the only ones not to follow this pattern. The growing tension in her role is illustrated in part by the growing tension of the A/B relation, which becomes more and more unusual (see Chart II for a survey of these relations in the twenty-eight operas listed in Chart I): I(vi), i(v), i(III), i(III), I(v), and i(ii), or, by key, B-flat(g), a(e), c(E-flat), e(G), F(c), and f-sharp(g-sharp). The A/B relations in Alcina's arias, therefore, pass from very common [i(v)] and relatively common [I(vi) and i(III), using the relative major/minor relation], in the first two acts, to very uncommon [I(v)] and unique [i(ii)] in the last act. On single occasions other characters also use patterns other than the normative two, but never ones as unusual as those given to Alcina in Act III. In Act I Oronte uses I(vi) and Ruggiero uses I(IV), and in Act III Ruggiero and Oberto both use I(vi) and Morgana in confessing her foolishness uses i(vi). Just as the patterns of libretto construction are used for dramatic purpose and the irregular patterns carefully placed within a normative convention, so too is the A/B harmonic pattern turned to dramatic purpose in Handel's hands. Irregular harmonic patterns reflect tensions and conflicts in the libretto and aid in characterization; they serve the purpose of a disrupted da capo in places where the da capo form remains intact. That is, where Bajazet and Orlando give up the da capo form at moments of great dramatic tension, Alcina maintains the form but with more and more harmonic conflict.

Chart II. A/B relations in Handel's operas

pattern	#	%
Major		
I (iii)	330	76
I (vi)	52	12
I (V)	25	6
I (IV/iv)	12	3
I (ii)	10	2
I (v)	7	1
Minor		
i (v)	221	80
i (III)	44	16
i (iv)	5	2
i (VII♭)	3	1
i (ii)	1	0.5
i (i)	1	0.5

Handel extends his use of harmonic patterns beyond the aria to the level of the scene by linking the aria harmonically to the preceding recitative. In his normal procedure, the preceding recitative cadences to the same key as the following B section, creating the patterns iii–I(iii) and v–i(v). Thus, the A section of the aria is typically prepared harmonically in the same way for both of its occurrences. In determining these patterns two factors must be taken into account. First, it is possible for an aria, its B section, or preceding recitative to be in minor but cadence to a major triad. Thus, the final chord is less a determinant of mode than the preceding phrase. Secondly, Handel sometimes cadences to the dominant, especially by means of a Phrygian cadence. In such cases, the final chord, even though a dominant, is related as a tonic would be to the A and B section cadences of the aria. In all cases, therefore, an attempt has been made to compare the relation of the root of the recitative cadence to the principal tonalities of the following aria. An aria in C major, following the normative pattern, will have a B section that cadences to E minor and a preceding recitative that does likewise, although one or both of the minor mode cadences may use a Picardy third, and the recitative cadence may be a Phrygian cadence effectively in A minor. With the same caveats, an aria in C minor is normally preceded by a recitative cadence to G minor and contains a B section with a cadence to the same key. The idea of linking the recitative cadence to the cadence of the following B section of the da capo not only allows the identical harmonic preparation of the A section both times, but it presents an ingenious solution to the integration of the da capo into the harmonic fabric of the longer composition.

In order for the linking process to work, it is obviously not necessary for the da capo to adhere to the A/B harmonic pattern. That is, V–I(V) is as much a recitative link as iii–I(iii). However, the normal A/B pattern appears to be strongly connected to the link, which occurs overwhelmingly in connection with it. Chart I offers in column 4 the number of da capos in each opera that have preceding recitative. This excludes, for example, arias that begin an act and those preceded by choruses, sinfonias or other arias. Column 5 offers the number and percent of arias with preceding recitative that use the link, and column 6 offers the number and percent of linked arias that use the normative A/B harmonic pattern.

It is easy to see from Chart I, cols. 4–6, that Handel favors the A/B relation in the recitative link by an overwhelming margin. Indeed, arias without the recitative link are more prevalent than arias using a different harmonic pattern with the link. Chart III lists the patterns used by Handel in the twenty-eight operas I have examined and the frequency with which they occur.

In the first Academy period (1720–28), Handel begins to treat the recitative link as another harmonic pattern with dramatic potential. *Tamerlano* provides an example, and in Chart IV the harmonic continuity of the opera is laid out in abbreviated, graphic form. Each scene is identified by a lower-case Roman numeral; scenes are separated by single diagonal lines; set changes are indicated with double diagonal lines. The beginning and ending keys of recitatives are given in parentheses; the primary key of *da capo* arias is given alone, immediately followed by the B section cadence, also in parentheses. Arias and recitatives are separated with dashes. Major keys are indicated by upper-case letters, minor keys by lower-case letters. Relationships between the previous recitative cadence and the following B section are indicated with slurs. The characters' names (in abbreviated form) appear underneath the arias they sing; in addition, exits without arias have been indicated. The chart illustrates the version of *Tamerlano* performed in 1724.

Chart III. Recitative Linking Patterns in Handel's Operas

major keys		*minor keys*	
pattern	frequency	pattern	frequency
	recitative link with A/B pattern		
iii – I (iii)	175	v – i (v)	151
	A/B pattern without link		
V/v – I (iii)	113	III – i (v)	50
vi – I (iii)	23	iv/IV – i(v)	10
IV/iv – I (iii)	10	VI/vi – i(v)	3
ii – I (iii)	5	VII♭ – i(v)	2
I – I (iii)	2	i – i(v)	3
VI♭ – I (iii)	1	ii – i(v)	1
vii – I (iii)	1		
	A/B pattern in recitative cadence only		
iii – I (vi)	23	v – i(III)	29
iii – I (V)	9	v – i(iv)	4
iii – I (ii)	8	v – i(VII♭)	2
iii – I (iv/IV)	5	v – i (ii)	1
iii – I (v)	4	v – i (i)	1
iii – I (I)	1		
	alternative recitative links		
V – I (V)	11	III – i (III)	11
vi – I (vi)	8		
IV – I (IV)	2		
	other patterns		
V – I (vi)	18	VI – i (III)	1
vi – I (V)	5	iv – i (III)	1
V – I (IV/iv)	5	IV – i (III)	1
V – I (ii)	2	i – i (III)	1
IV – I (vi)	2	III – i (iv)	1
iv – I (v)	1	III – i (VII♭)	1
I – I (v)	1	ii – I (v)	1
I – I (vi)	1		

Chart IV. Harmonic Patterns in *Tamerlano* (1741)

Act I
Overture i   ii   iii
   c /   (c–g–a)–C(e) /   (D–a)–F(a)   /   (D–f♯)–D(f♯)   //
            Baj   Tam   And

iv   v   vi   vii
(B♭–d)–g(d) / (A–B)–e(b) / (A–f♯)–D(f♯) / (c♯–D)–b(f♯) //
   Tam   Ast   Baj   Ast

viii   ix
(G–b)–G(b) / (c–G)–E♭(g) //
  Ire   (acc) And

Act II
i   ii   iii
(B♭–F)–B♭(d) / (D–e)–A(c♯) / (g–g)–E♭(g) //
  Tam   Ast   (acc) And

iv   v   vi   vii   viii
(C–C) / (E–A♭) / (e°–b)–G(b) (g–D)–g(d) / (c–C)–a(e) / (D–a)–F(a) /
Tam   Ast   Ire   Leo   Baj   And

ix   x
(D–f♯–/–A) (d–a) (–f♯) –D– (B) –e– (G♯) –E– (G) –G– (E♭–d)–B♭(d) //
   (acc)   trio   Baj   And   Ire   Ast
            (Tam exit)

Act III
i   ii   iii   iv   v
(f–F)–g(d) / (F–/–E–G)–D(f♯) / (D–b) / (B–B)–e(b) //
   Ast   Tam   Baj   And/Ast

vi   vii   viii
(A–A)–F(a) / (D–a)–F(a) / (d–D) (c–D) (B♭) (B♭) (g–d)–g(d) /
   Ire   And   (acc) (acc) And (acc) Baj
                                       Ast

HARMONIC PATTERNS IN HANDEL'S OPERAS 91

ix   x
(E♭–D) / (g–d) (B♭–A) (F♭ –f–e) (–C) (–B♭) –f(c̑) (B♭–d) (B♭–g)/
              (acc)   (acc) Baj (acc) (acc)
                                        (no exit)   (Baj exit)

ultima
(E♭–b)   –e(G) //
(Ast exit) coro

In Act I, all nine scenes are regularly organized with recitative leading to a *da capo* exit aria. Each of the nine arias uses the common A/B harmonic pattern, and seven use the recitative link as well. In this act, then, the regularity of the tonal construction parallels the regularity of the scenic construction. That is, at the same time as the basic outlines of the plot are laid and the situations of the various characters are explained, the textual and musical norm is also set forth.

In the second act the dramatic tension rises, misunderstandings occur, and a crisis is reached. The scenic patterning begins to disintegrate, and the tonal patterning also starts to give way. Although all of the *da capo* arias retain the normal A/B harmonic relation, only a little more than half (five of eight) use the recitative link.

In the third act the situation worsens, culminating in Bajazet's suicide. Here only five of the eleven scenes follow the normal pattern. Of the eight da capos, however, seven, including the written out "Figlia mia" in scene x, maintain the A/B relation, but again only five of the eight include the recitative link.

Like the A/B pattern, the recitative link is closely connected to the drama and the scenic construction. Regular scenic continuity and harmonic patterning describe the norm. Disruptions in harmonic patterning frequently precede a breakdown in scenic continuity. And scenic discontinuity can be emphasized and placed in relief by normal harmonic patterns.

Although every opera is unique in regard to its harmonic scheme, and a few seem not to attempt this kind of tonal patterning within scenes, the vast majority of scenes not only contain the recitative harmonic link, but also maintain the relation between scenic construction and the link. The pattern found in *Tamerlano*, where the first act depicts a musical norm which crumbles in the later acts as intrigues increase, is typical of Baroque opera and can be quickly identified by the number of the A/B patterns and recitative links in successive acts. For example, in *Lotario* (1729), the first act has nine da capos, eight of which use the normal A/B pattern and the link. In the second act there are nine da capos, six of which use the A/B pattern, two of these with the link. In Act III, of nine da capos, only four use the A/B pattern and two use the link, only one of these, however, in the normal A/B pattern. Similar situations occur in many operas, notably *Radamisto* (1720) and *Alcina*.

In *Orlando* the pattern is reversed. The disruption, or Orlando's decision to follow love rather than duty, occurs immediately, and the opera traces his further disintegration and return to the right path. Thus, the first three scenes are unusual in construction, but the first da capo, sung by the magician Zoroastro, urging Orlando to follow the course of reason, follows the conventional A/B pattern and uses the recitative link. When, at the end of the third scene, which is the end of the first set, Orlando chooses to follow love instead of reason, his da capo breaks all of the conventional harmonic patterns, and it uses a specific harmonic scheme found in only eight arias among these twenty-eight operas: iii–I(ii). Once Orlando reaches the pastoral landscape, beginning in scene iv, set 2, the remaining scenes of the act follow a normal constructive pattern, but the harmonic patterns of the arias illustrate the tension caused by Orlando's arrival. Of the seven da capos in these scenes, only the first and last use both the common A/B pattern and the recitative link, three others use only the A/B pattern, and two use neither pattern. Of these last, one is sung by the shepherdess Dorinda when she realizes that Medoro does not return her love; the other is sung by Angelica after her first confrontation with Orlando. Neither, however, presents as unusual a harmonic scheme as Orlando's aria in scene iii, both following the familiar alternative of iii–I(vi). Thus, Orlando's aria choosing love over reason contains the most atypical harmonic pattern of the act. The lesser harmonic disruptions of the first act prepare for the large scenic disruptions in Acts II and III, and in the later acts, to balance the scenic discontinuity that represents Orlando's madness, the only aria not to use both the typical A/B pattern and the recitative link is the only da capo sung by Orlando during his insanity, "Già lo stringo" (III, iii). As in *Tamerlano*, Handel complements and balances the elements of scenic patterning with his harmonic patterning.

Handel's normal compositional practice indicates the deliberateness with which he forged the harmonic recitative link. That is, when composing an opera, Handel commonly set the arias first, leaving space for the recitative by writing out the text. Only when the arias were completed did he return to compose the recitatives. This practice demonstrates that Handel commonly chose his recitative keys after completing the arias, giving him the opportunity to link the recitative cadence with the following aria or not. Not only does it illustrate, therefore, the compositional importance of the link, but it indicates similarly the importance of consecutive aria keys to Handel's harmonic planning. Indeed, past writers, especially Rudolf Steglich and Hugo Leichtentritt, have examined Handel's aria keys in order to uncover large-scale harmonic plans.[10] But despite the inherent value of their research, such conclusions have been largely discredited, as, for example, by Manfred Bukofzer.

> Of late it has become fashionable in German musicology to discover key architectures in Handel's operas and the Bach Passions, but these rationalizations try to establish relations that cannot exactly be called convincing. It goes without saying that among the hundreds of acts from Handel's operas a few can be found that display, at least in certain scenes, the key architecture of a cantata, but the great majority of the acts begin and end in different keys....[11]

Apparently Bukofzer did not realize that the vast majority of Handel's cantatas, unlike those of his Italian contemporaries, also begin and end in different keys. Handel's large-scale harmonic organization is not regularly governed by the use of a single tonic in the cantatas or the

---

[10]Rudolf Steglich, "Händels Oper *Rodelinda* und ihre neue Göttingen Bühnenfassung," *Zeitschrift für Musikwissenschaft* III (1920–21): 518–34; and Hugo Leichtentritt, "Handel's Harmonic Art," *The Musical Quarterly*, XXI (1953): 214, gives an harmonic analysis of the first act of *Amadigi*.

[11]Manfred Bukofzer, *Music in the Baroque Era* (New York, 1947), 367.

operas, nor is it determined by the pervasive use of symmetrical schemes, although both situations do sometimes occur.[12]

Recently, Eric Chafe has reopened the question of tonal architecture in Bach's passions. He sees these works as divided into scenes that are composed within a single group of sharp, flat or natural keys, and he emphasizes the importance of the contrast between sharp and flat keys in the works of contemporary theorists:

> In the writings of Werckmeister, Scheibe and others we find references to modulations made by means of cross relations, enharmonic changes, and so forth, described as the confrontation between sharps and flats or the transformation of the one sphere into the other.... As will be shown below, it is the idea of separation, and even opposition between sharp and flat keys that Bach makes into his main allegorical structural principle in the two passions.[13]

Chafe, however, argues against the existence of similar harmonic patterns in Handel's operas, stating that whereas Bach's passions are clear in the delineation of key areas, Handel's operas frequently "have arias in unrelated keys within the same scene."[14]

Although Handel's operas do not regularly exhibit stable harmonic patterns in a single key, or even in a group of related keys, they, like Bach's passions, often focus on the conflict between flat and sharp keys to illustrate the dramatic tension and conflict in the libretto. Each set change or break in the *liaison de scène* determines a group of arias. That is, the exit of all the characters from the stage delimits the arias that

---

[12]Robin Fenton has recently discussed Handel's choice of aria keys at length in "Handel's *Almira* (1705): a study of Handel's first opera and its relationship with the opera *Cleopatra* (1704) by Johann Mattheson," (M. M. thesis: University of Queensland, 1985). There is much of value in his discussion, but Fenton argues (incorrectly, I believe) that Handel's choice of aria keys is ultimately "analogous to a progression of chords" (p. 35). For example, Fenton interprets the aria keys of *Almira*, Act I, set 1 (with the chorus and ensuing dances given in brackets: B-flat [D g g] d g F c) as a progression in B-flat with a deceptive cadence from the dominant (F Major) to the supertonic, thus setting off the last aria as interruptive: "The shift in *Almira*, from the dominant to the supertonic, is a dark, heavy change creating the effect of profound meditation" (p. 36). In terms of simple juxtaposition, however, this key is not disruptive at all. (See below Charts V and VI and the relevant discussion.)

[13]Eric Chafe, "Key Structure and Tonal Allegory in the Passions of J. S. Bach: An Introduction," *Current Musicology*, XXXI (1981): 40–41.

[14]Eric Chafe, "J. S. Bach's *St. Matthew Passion*: Aspects of Planning, Structure, and Chronology," *Journal of the American Musicological Society*, XXXV (1982): 55 and 58.

HARMONIC PATTERNS IN HANDEL'S OPERAS   95

belong to a set. Sometimes these sets are harmonically closed; sometimes they are symmetrical. The first set from *Rodelinda*, for example, shown in example 1 of Chart V, is both. It is also stable within the flat-key area. In other cases, however, sets are built around a strong tonal conflict representing the tension in the drama. For example, in the first set in Act II of *Alcina*, shown in example 2 of Chart V, the arias of Melisso and Bradamante, who have come to rescue Ruggiero from Alcina's magical spell, are tonally separated from the enchanted knight; their arias are in sharp keys, whereas Ruggiero's are exclusively in flat keys.

Chart V. Sample sets from Handel's operas

Example 1: *Rodelinda*, Act I, set 1

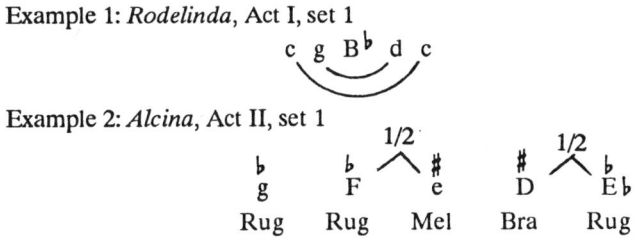

Example 2: *Alcina*, Act II, set 1

In this case, as in many others, the strong dramatic conflict is indicated by placing consecutive arias in keys a half-step apart. In other cases, to be discussed below, the tritone relationship replaces the half-step, for these two intervals create the strongest possible shifts around the circle of fifths from flat to sharp key areas or vice versa.

In these sets, as on lower harmonic levels, Handel shows a predilection for certain patterns that recur with some frequency. He will often maintain continuity between movements by using dominant (often in minor) or relative major/minor relations. These close harmonic links serve as the normative background to the harmonic conflicts. Example 1 of Chart VI offers a number of variations on this pattern with the harmonic conflict in the middle. In *Rodelinda* I, 2, the initial fifth motion and the closing relative relation are linked by the use of B minor in both cases. The conflicted key of F major is therefore not only a half-step from E major, but a tritone from B minor. The first set of the second act is similar, but with the relative motion at the beginning and the dominant relation at the end. *Agrippina* III, 1 follows the same pattern as *Rodelin-*

da II, 1, but with the use of the weaker parallel major/minor relation in place of fifth motion at the end, and *Agrippina* III, 2 only fails to fulfill

Chart VI. Harmonically conflicted sets from Handel's operas

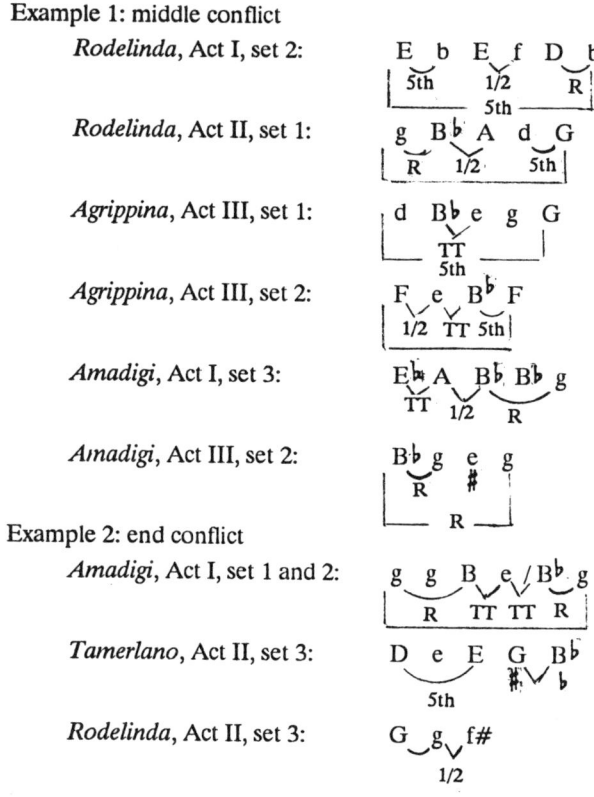

this same pattern by the lack of a D minor aria to precede the F major aria. The use of an unpaired initial aria is found in *Amadigi* I, 3, where the final fifth motion is replaced by relative motion. In *Amadigi* III, 2, the unpaired aria comes at the end rather than the beginning.

The dramatic situation in each of these sets motivates the harmonic pattern. In *Rodelinda* I, 2, Bertarido, who is thought to be dead by most of the other characters, muses over his tomb and yearns to be returned to his wife Rodelinda [da capo: E(g-sharp)]. Bertarido and his friend, Unulfo, hide when Rodelinda enters with their son and weeps over Bertarido's funeral urn [written out ABA: b(f-sharp)]. Garibaldo, a friend of the usurping tyrant, Grimoaldo, enters to tell Rodelinda that she must marry Grimoaldo or see her son killed. Rodelinda pretends to she must marry Grimoaldo or see her son killed. Rodelinda pretends to comply, but reveals that she plans to kill Grimoaldo on the throne [da capo: E(g-sharp)]. Grimoaldo enters to tell Garibaldo that there is nothing to fear [da capo: F(a)]. Meanwhile, Unulfo and Bertarido have only heard Rodelinda's compliance, not her secret plan, and Unulfo tries to encourage Bertarido to bear the pain [da capo: D(f-sharp)]. Left alone, Bertarido expresses his anger and hurt [da capo: b(f-sharp)].

This set follows many normative patterns. First, as in many of Handel's operas, the key areas are directly related to the characters. That is, victims of love and politics tend to express their agony in sharp keys, whereas the tyrant reveals his power and apparent control in flat keys. Thus Bertarido and Rodelinda sing in sharp keys and Grimoaldo sings in a flat key. This demarcation obtains also, for example, in *Tamerlano*, where Asteria and Bajazet are depicted mainly in sharp keys, and Tamerlano sings in flat keys. In the set from *Rodelinda* this conflict is emphasized by the use of only one flat aria surrounded by sharp arias. Moreover, the specific key relations describe the tension of the set. In the first three arias, the emotional tie between Bertarido and Rodelinda is emphasized in fifth relations, and in the last two arias, Bertarido's and Unulfo's friendship is described by the relative major and minor. The conflict between Rodelinda and Grimoaldo can be felt by the half-step, sharp/flat, shift in their consecutive arias. Finally, just as Rodelinda repeats Bertarido's key when she vows to avenge him, he repeats her key of mourning when he thinks he has lost her love.

The other sets are similar. In *Rodelinda* II, 1, Eduige, Grimoaldo's first betrothed, and Rodelinda speak about Grimoaldo's intentions. Eduige sings of her love turning to hate [g(F)]. Rodelinda takes charge and tells Grimoaldo that she will marry him only if he kills her son in front of her; she moves into a flat key [B-flat(d)]. Grimoaldo cannot agree and realizes he is a prisoner of love, moving for the first time into a sharp key [A(c-sharp)]. Garibaldo reveals to Unulfo his belief that a ruler cannot show pity [d(a)]. Unulfo realizes that Rodelinda is faithful and that Garibaldo is treacherous; he praises fidelity [G(b)]. As in *Rodelinda* I, 2, the central conflict concerns Rodelinda and Grimoaldo. Again, it is demonstrated by a half-step shift, but the use of sharp and flat keys illustrates that the power has changed hands. The tonal relations at the beginning and end of the set show the common goal of

Eduige and Rodelinda, and the privileged information shared by Garibaldo and Unulfo, although in the latter case, the sharp/flat contrast illustrates that the singers belong to different sides of the question.

In *Agrippina* III, 1, the central conflict occurs between Nerone, Claudio's step-son and heir to the throne, who sings to Poppea of his love, and Claudio, who defensively sings "I am the Jove of Rome" after arriving for an assignation with Poppea only to find that Nerone is hiding behind a curtain (as is Ottone, but Claudio does not discover this) and that Poppea fears the vengeance of his wife (Nerone's mother), Agrippina. These revelations precipitate the successful resolution of the plot, although Agrippina's continued deceitfulness is nicely depicted by Handel in III, 2, where her placating aria to Claudio asking him to trust her love and faithfulness is the only sharp aria (E minor) in a stable, flat set. In *Amadigi* I, 3, Amadigi and Oriana are separated by means of Melissa's magic; the estrangement is evidenced in the music just before the action, when Amadigi's A major aria is set off from Oriana's preceding aria in E-flat major and her following aria in B-flat major by a tritone and half-step respectively. In the preceding sets of this act Amadigi's estrangement from Melissa has been similarly illustrated in a group of three arias: B-flat major (Amadigi), E minor (Melissa), and B-flat major (Amadigi). Melissa's E minor aria and Amadigi's A major aria are the only sharp arias in the entire first act. In *Amadigi* III, 2, Dardano's arioso as a ghost is the only movement in the first two sets of this act in a sharp key.

The use of tonal conflict in the middle of a set is common in Handel's operas. A less frequent pattern, shown in example 2 of Chart VI, places the conflict at the end. Indeed, this effect is sometimes mitigated by the tonal pattern of the following set, as in *Amadigi* I, 1, discussed above, where the following set provides the relative relation and tonal closure. On the other hand, *Tamerlano*, II, 3 ends the act, and the tonal shift illustrates Asteria's triumph after all the other characters leave the stage angry or contrite. The conflict at the end of *Rodelinda*, Act II, 3, also occurs at the end of an act and separates Grimoaldo's threat of death to Bertarido (G minor) from Rodelinda and Bertarido's farewell duet before Bertarido is taken off to prison (F-sharp minor).

At three different levels, therefore, Handel's harmonic plans parallel patterns of libretto construction. First, the harmonic construction of sets emphasizes this structural unit, which in the libretto is indicated by a single scenic backdrop and usually the maintaining of the *liaison de scène*. The juxtaposition of related or strongly opposed keys similarly underscores the dramatic relationships within the set. Second, the recitative link relates to the construction of the single scene and, like the typical scene with recitative leading to exit aria, has a normative function. Finally, the normal A/B harmonic pattern parallels the structural use of the da capo itself; disruption can be indicated by the interruption or omission of the da capo, but tension and conflict can also be depicted by the use of a da capo with an irregular harmonic pattern.

Just as Handel's librettos illustrate the development of normative patterns and a growing sense of their dramatic potential,[15] the large-scale harmonic patterns of Handel's operas depict chronological changes in Handel's conception of musical-dramatic structure. First, in Handel's two earliest extant operas, and to a certain extent in *Agrippina* also, there is a strong preponderance of flat keys. Of fifty-two pieces in *Almira*, only ten are in sharp keys; in *Rodrigo* only nine of thirty-three pieces are in sharp keys. In Handel's later works flat and sharp keys are well-balanced. Second, in all of Handel's operas before 1720, there is a distinct tendency to repeat keys in consecutive arias or to use a single key repeatedly. For example, in Act II from the 1711 *Rinaldo*, the keys of consecutive movements are: e e d c g / F d B-flat G g G: and, in the second act of *Amadigi* : F f f c B-flat / d d A A D. After 1720, Handel avoids the redundant use of single keys. Third, the use of half-step and tritone relations is only perfected after 1720. Except for *Agrippina* (1709), the use of flat-sharp contrast is not an important part of Handel's harmonic planning until *Teseo* and *Amadigi* (1713 and 1715). After 1720, it is a regular part of his operatic composition.

The key relationships which Handel used in his operas are, of course, somewhat typical of the late Baroque period in general, although the harmonic planning relating to three levels of libretto construction may be unique. Although it is impossible to survey the entire

---

[15]The development of conventional patterns and the dramatic use of these in Handel's librettos is discussed in Harris, *The Librettos of Handel's Operas*, "Introductions," vols 1–13.

repertory of dramatic vocal music from the first half of the eighteenth century, and difficult to know whether any chosen sampling is representative, it nevertheless remains valuable to attempt some comparisons. Having looked at some of the chronological trends in Handel's use of aria keys, it is useful to examine operas of an important predecessor to discern whether similar trends exist and whether Handel may have modeled his harmonic planning on a common, or at least previous, practice.

Chart VII offers statistics on six of Alessandro Scarlatti's operas dating from his first in 1679 to his last in 1721. Not surprisingly, *Gli equivoci nel sembiante* (1679) shows little adherence to the da capo. None of the arias is literally in that form, but seven of eighteen are in written-out ABA form; three of these seven follow the A/B pattern, one using the recitative link. In *Massimo Puppieno* (1695), the number of arias has increased enormously, as has the proportion of da capos, but the percentage of arias with the recitative link remains low. Strikingly, only one of six arias with the recitative link uses the A/B pattern. Two years later, however, in *La caduta de'Decemviri* (1697), the percentage of recitative links has almost doubled, and the percentage of those that use the A/B harmonic relationship typical of Handel's operas has almost tripled. This difference between the 1695 and 1697 operas represents the biggest change within these six operas in Scarlatti's use of these harmonic patterns, underscoring, perhaps, Malcolm Boyd's conclusion that the biggest shift in Scarlatti's style occurs around 1695.[16] Even after this date, however, the percentage of links continues to rise, and the connection between the linking process and a specific harmonic relationship is ever more strongly confirmed.

Handel's operas also show a developmental process in regard to harmonic relationships and the recitative link (see Chart I), but in his very first opera, *Almira* (1704), Handel already uses the linking process more than Scarlatti does in operas written as late as 1721—43% in *Almira* as compared to 37% in *Griselda*—and it nearly equals the highest percentage found in any of these six operas: 44% in *Marco Attilio Regolo*

---

[16]"Form and Style in Scarlatti's Chamber Cantatas," *Music Review*, XXV (1964): 17–26.

Chart VII. A/B relation and link in Scarlatti

Year	Opera	Arias #	Da capos #	Da capos %	A/B pattern #	A/B pattern %	Da capos with preceding recitative #	Links #	Links %	A/B Links #	A/B Links %	Tonic preparation
Scarlatti												
1679	Gli equivoci nel sembiante	18	7*	38	3	43	5	1	20	1	100	6
1695	Massimo puppieno	62	42	68	21	50	33	6	18	1	17	3
1697	La caduta de'decemviri	62	50	81	24	48	47	15	32	7	47	8
1710	La principessa fedele	50	46	92	37	80	42	15	36	12	80	1
1719	Marco Attilio Regolo	52	40	77	34	85	39	17	44	14	82	2
1721	Griselda	41	41	100	30	73	38	14	37	13	93	1

*written out ABA

(1719). On the basis of these figures, therefore, it would be difficult to argue an influence from Scarlatti in terms of this compositional practice.

A comparison of Handel's harmonic patterns with those of his exact contemporary, J. S. Bach, also proves interesting. According to Robert Marshall in *The Compositional Process of J. S. Bach*, Bach's preferred recitative cadence was to the tonic of the following aria. In the eleven autograph instances of an altered harmonic closure of a recitative, nine were changed "to conclude on the tonic of the following movement." Marshall continues, "Since this is by far the most frequent relationship between the final chord of a recitative and the tonality of the following movement, these corrections suggest that Bach, unlike Handel, wrote the recitatives, at least in these instances, before he had composed the succeeding formal movements, or was even certain of their tonality."[17] By favoring tonic preparation for his arias, Bach ensured that his A section would be entered from a different tonal position for each occurrence. In the *Christmas Oratorio*, for example, there are twelve arias; eight are preceded by tonic recitative cadences; none of the *da capos* uses the recitative link.

Although Bach relies more on tonic preparation than many of his contemporaries, he is not alone in his use of this static link. In fact, it seems to be a Pre-Classical trait, for by eliminating the recitative tonic chord, the first chord of the aria then resolves the tonal sequence of the recitative (the typical Classical pattern). However, even Reinhold Keiser uses tonic preparation of arias—of the forty-seven numbers preceded by recitatives in *Octavia* (1705) there are twelve tonic preparations. On the other hand, Handel typically avoids this relation in favor of the pattern of the recitative link. For example, tonic preparation never occurs in *Orlando*; in its one occurrence in *Tamerlano* (Act II, ix, Irene's aria), the aria was originally in a different key; and the one time it appears in *Rodelinda*, Handel later rewrote the recitative to make it adhere to his favored linking process. Among the 711 da capo arias with receding recitative examined for this paper, the tonic link occurs only eight times.

---

[17]Robert Lewis Marshall, *The Compositional Process of J. S. Bach: A Study of the Autograph Scores of the Vocal Works* I (Princeton, 1972): 96, where he also cites Hermann Melchert, *Das Rezitative der Kirchenkantaten Joh. Seb. Bachs* (Frankfurt am Main, 1958), 86, on Bach's preference for tonic preparation.

The recitative link is important to recognize, for by offering an identical harmonic preparation of the A section both times, it presents one solution to the integration of the da capo into the harmonic fabric of the longer composition. However, the link seems not to be used by many of Handel's contemporaries—partly because the repetition of harmonic preparation was not favored (as seems to be the case with Bach, who uses the A/B pattern in his arias but avoids the link), but also because the linking process itself was identified with harmonic relationships that were out-of-date. The linking process does not demand that major tonics be related to minor mediants or that minor tonics be related to minor dominants, but even as late as 1742, five of the six linked arias in Leonardo Leo's *Andromaca* follow the typical A/B patterns.

Antonio Vivaldi and Leonardo Leo are the two Italian composers whose periods of operatic composition coincide most closely with Handel's. Handel wrote forty-two operas between 1704 and 1741; Leo wrote thirty-one operas between 1714 and 1744; and Vivaldi wrote forty-five operas between 1713 and 1739. Each of these composers, moreover, wrote predominantly for a single city: Handel for London, Leo for Naples, and Vivaldi for Venice. The demands and traditions of these different geographical locations undoubtedly affected the style of the operas composed for them, as much as Handel's German heritage assuredly separates him from the Italian-born, but the contemporaneity of these composers' operatic careers and the similarity of their association each with a single city, allowing for more stylistic stability than exists, for example, in the operas of J. C. Bach, makes comparisons both alluring and valuable.

I have examined four operatic works by each composer: by Vivaldi, *Orlando* (1727), *La fida ninfa* (1732), *Griselda* (1735), and *Mio cor, povero cor* (a serenata with no date) and by Leo, *Catone in Utica* (1729), *Demofoonte* (1735), *L'Olimpiade* (1737), and *Andromaca* (1742). (See Chart VIII). Although both Leo and Vivaldi favor the typical A/B harmonic pattern in these works, and more of the recitative links in their operas use these third-related or minor dominant relations than any other pattern (40% in Vivaldi and 72% in Leo), neither composer employs the recitative link frequently (see Chart VIII). Indeed, as a comparison of Charts III and IX illustrates, Handel uses the recitative link, even with alternative A/B harmonic patters, significantly more than

Chart VIII. A/B relation and link in Leo and Vivaldi

Year	Opera	Arias	Da capos		A/B pattern		Links		A/B Links		Tonic preparation
		#	#	%	#	%	#	%	#	%	#
Vivaldi											
1727	Orlando (ms. I: Tn)	24	23	96	12	52	5	22	2	40	1
1732	La fida ninfa (ed. Monteroso)	28	22	79	11	50	2	9	1	50	0
1735	Griselda (Garland)	21	21	100	11	52	3	14	1	33	2
n.d.	Mio cor povero cor (ed. Bettarini)	16	16	100	5	31	1	6	0	–	0
	Totals	89	82	92	39	48	11	13	4	40	3 4%

Leo										
1729	Catone in Utica (Garland)	26	25	96	11	44	6	24	3	50	4
1735	Demofoonte (ms. GB: Lbm)	24	24	100	19	79	12	50	9	75	2
1737	L'Olimpiade (Garland)	22	22	100	17	77	5	25	4	80	3
1742	Andromaca (Garland)	23	23	100	17	74	6	26	5	83	6
	Totals	95	94	99	64	68	29	31	21	72	15 16%

Chart IX. Recitative linking patterns in Vivaldi's and Leo's operas

	Leo	Vivaldi
recitative link with A/B pattern		
iii – I (iii)	13	2
v – i (v)	8	2
alternative linking patterns		
vi – I (vi)	3	3
IV – I (IV)	1	0
V – I (V)	1	0
V – I (v)	2	0
ii – I (ii)	0	1
i – i (i)	1	0
IV – i (IV)	0	1
III – i (III)	0	1
VII – i (VII)	0	1
A/B pattern without link		
V/V – I (iii)	18	11
vi – I (iii)	10	8
i/I – I (iii)	9	1
ii – I (iii)	1	6
IV/iv – I (iii)	0	4
VII♭ – I (iii)	1	0
vii – I (iii)	1	0
i – i (v)	2	1
iv/IV – i (v)	0	2
III – i (v)	0	2
other tonic preparations (see also above)		
I – I (V)	1	0
I – i (ii)	1	0
i – i (VI)	0	1
other dominant preparations (see also above)		
V/v – I (vi)	2	4
V – I (ii)	1	4
V – I (IV)	0	1
v – I (i)	1	0
other A/B pattern preparations (see also above)		
iii – I (vi)	3	4
iii – I (v)	2	0
iii – I (V)	1	0
iii – I (vii)	1	0
iii – I (ii)	0	1
v/V – i (III)	2	2
v – i (iv)	2	0
other relative preparations (see also above)		
vi – I (ii)	0	3

Chart IX (continued)

other supertonic and sub-
dominant prepara-
tions (see also above)

ii – I (vi)	2	4
IV – I (vi)	0	2
ii – I (v/V)	2	1
IV – I (V)	1	0
ii – I (IV)	0	1

other seventh degree preparations (see also above)

vii – I (vi)	0	1
VII – i (III)	0	1

arias without recitative

        0   6

his Italian contemporaries. On the other hand, Leo and Vivaldi prefer dominant or relative preparation of the aria, as in the patterns V–I(iii) and vi–I(iii), to links of any kind. Leo also favors tonic preparation, found in fifteen of his arias (see "tonic preparation" in Chart VIII), while Vivaldi frequently uses supertonic preparation, found in thirteen of his arias. In these operas of Leo and Vivaldi no one pattern of recitative cadence, aria key, and B section cadence predominates. The lack of an established normative procedure makes the dramatic use of these patterns impossible.

The greater variety of harmonic patterns, however, masks a more limited set of harmonic goals and keys. Leo uses fewer keys overall than Vivaldi, and he limits himself more rigidly to major keys. The patterns of six arias taken only from the second act of Leo's *Catone* (see Chart X) illustrate not only the predominance of major keys, but a redundancy of harmonic goals, including tonic preparation, the repetition of cadential goals in A1 and B, the repetition of cadential goals in the recitative and A1, and in one case the repetition of the same cadence in the recitative, A1, and B. This combination of patterns is rarely if ever found in Handel's operas.

Chart X. Six arias from Leo's *Catone*, Act II

(G) – G [D (D)]   (D) – G [D (a)]   (B) – F [C (B♭)]   (d) – g [d (d)]

       (B) – E[B (B)]   (a) – D[A (d)]

Leo's and Vivaldi's preference for major keys differs from Handel's early bias towards flat (not minor) keys, but even Handel's operas show a growing preference for major, especially after 1726. Only in the last two operas, however, is the major mode favored by more than a two to one ratio. Generally, Handel uses major and minor in relatively equal amounts as primary keys even when he favors flat keys, and Leo and Vivaldi use flat and sharp keys in relatively equal amounts even when they favor major. This difference represents an important shift in the concept of tonality, which was caused at least in part by changes in the tuning system. In modern equal temperament the difference between major and minor is the most clearly heard tonal contrast, whereas in the earlier mean-tone tuning the importance of circle-of-fifths motion (emphasizing the contrast between distant keys in sharps and flats) was greater. It does not matter for this comparison that Handel, Vivaldi, and Leo were contemporaries in terms of their operatic compositions, nor is it necessary to know what tuning system each composer used. The evidence of the scores illustrates that Handel was conceptually (even if not aurally) tied to an older tuning system that was closer to modal practice, as is obvious in his use of third relations and minor dominants as well as in the sharp/flat tonal conflicts, whereas Leo and Vivaldi conceived their music following newer conventions of tonality and tuning.

It should be no surprise, therefore, that the use of sharp-flat tonal conflict discussed by Werckmeister and Scheibe and favored by Handel as well as Bach is not found in the works of Vivaldi and Leo; the tonal practice of the so-called "Pre-Classical" style, in emphasizing dominant-tonic relations, limiting the number of keys, and using major overwhelmingly, turns away from abrupt shifts of tonality. It should also be no surprise to find aspects of the Pre-Classical style in the Italian composers, as the style originated contemporaneously in Italy in the works of such composers as Tartini, Sammartini and Pergolesi. Germany and England were slower to follow this lead. Thus in England, as late as 1753, Charles Avison in his *Essay on Musical Expression* discusses the expressive effect of sharp and flat keys, concluding that "changing the Key of separate Movements, whether from Flat to Sharp, or vice versa will still, in a higher Degree, afford Relief and Pleasure to the Hearer."[18]

---

[18]Charles Avison, *Essay on Musical Expression* (London, 1753), 79.

HARMONIC PATTERNS IN HANDEL'S OPERAS

Leo's bias towards major keys has already been illustrated in Chart X. This trend toward major keys, and also the use of only a few related keys, is even more obvious, however, in the sets of Leo's operas. For example, Act II, 1 of *Catone* contains six arias that use only three keys, all major, as follows: G, B-flat, D, G, D, B-flat. Not surprisingly, because of the reduction in the number of keys, many more of the sets in Leo's operas are closed than in Handel's. Chart XI gives some of these, including the entire second act of *Demofoonte*.

Chart XI. Closed sets and acts in Leo's operas

Catone, Act II, set 2:   D G d E D

Demofoonte, Act II, set 1: G B♭ G

Demofoonte, Act II, set 3: G G

Demofoonte, Act II: G B G/d B♭D F/G G

L'Olimpiade, Act I, set 1: G D G

L'Olimpiade, Act III, set 1: C A G C

L'Olimpiade, Act III, set 2: D E♭ G D

Andromaca, Act 1, set 1:   G D C F G

Vivaldi uses closed sets more rarely than Leo; indeed in the four works I have examined there are only two, and both occur in final sets. Interestingly, Handel, too, seems to use closed sets predominantly in the last acts, as in *Rodelinda*, Act III, perhaps as a way of achieving stability and closure for the opera (see Chart XII).[19] The Vivaldi ex-

---

[19]Donald Jay Grout, *A Short History of Opera* (New York, 1965), 162, states that many of Handel's operas "show a preference for one tonality . . . [that] is strongly confirmed in the finale," and he gives a list of such operas in note 24. Although the argument that Handel's operas generally revolve around a single key cannot be maintained and is anachronistic, there is little doubt that Handel strove to achieve harmonic stability in a variety of ways at the ends of his operas. (See also note 12 above).

amples (Chart XIII) additionally illustrate the reduced number of keys and predominance of the major mode already discussed in Leo. In *Orlando*, using just the da capo arias and the final chorus, the plan looks as it appears in (a), but this act is full of important ariosos, accompagnatos, and alternate song forms, all of which clearly have single tonics. If these are added, as in (b), the plan of C major alternating with related keys is not disrupted, only expanded. *La fida ninfa* offers an example of a closed final set that does not cover the entire act.

Chart XII. Handel's *Rodelinda*, Act III

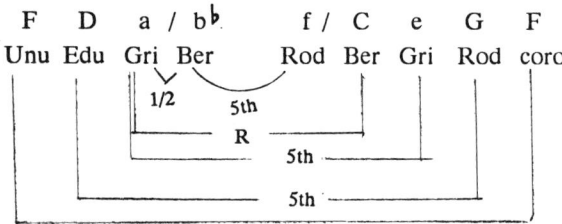

Chart XIII. Closed sets and acts in Vivaldi's operas

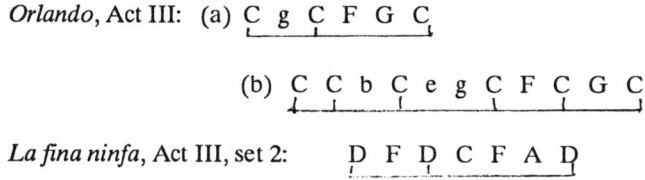

The sets of Vivaldi and Leo given in Charts XIII and XI additionally illustrate that neither composer uses the kind of harmonic conflict at this level that is so typical of Handel. Only one example of a half-step shift appears (in *L'Olimpiade*). There are no consecutive arias a tritone apart.

Handel's use of conflicted sharp and flat key areas follows the same basic principles used by Bach and described by contemporary German composers and theorists. It differs from Bach's method by its immediacy; Baroque opera demands faster changes than the set-by-set speed of the German passion. When Hugo Leichtentritt discussed "Handel's Harmonic Art," he touched on the problem of comparisons to Bach.

> With Bach, however, an inquiry would encounter special difficulties . . . . In his vocal works he was mainly a church composer, and he is therefore hardly comparable with the opera composer, Handel, in the variety of his character delineation and the range (though, of course, not the depth) of his emotional expression.[20]

And he continues by pondering Handel's originality.

> Whether Handel's system of tonal architecture, with its emotional, expressive and color connotations was entirely or partly his own property, is a question open to investigation. And if it was only partly his, the further question arises: what portion, if any, did he inherit from Italian opera of about 1700?[21]

This, of course, is a crucial question. I have found no Italian opera composer from the first half of the eighteenth century who uses similar key-area conflict. In this regard, therefore, Handel's music seems to have a Germanic basis. However, Handel does not, like Bach, use stable sets or extended circle-of-fifths motion as discussed by Chafe. Rather, Handel appears to have adapted and intensified a Scarlattian pattern of harmonic continuity through the recitative link that is better adapted to operatic drama. That is, in his harmonic patterns as in other aspects of his style, Handel seems to have adapted and combined in a unique fashion elements of Germanic and somewhat old-fashioned Italian musical practice.

Harmonic patterns in Handel's operas are an important aspect of his personal compositional style, and they are perfectly adapted to the patterns found in opera seria librettos. It must be emphasized, however, that they are simply patterns. One cannot turn to the operas expecting them to operate 100% of the time; some, such as the normal A/B pattern occur in an overwhelming majority of cases, others, like the recitative link, simply represent the most pervasive pattern. However, their importance for Handel, and perhaps even additional evidence for his awareness of them, can be inferred from the cases where he abandoned them. Thus, it is necessary to discuss the harmonic patterns, at least briefly, in relation to Handel's borrowing practices, his revisions, his instrumentation, and his use of *Affektenlehre*.

---

[20]Leichtentritt, "Handel's Harmonic Art," 213.
[21]Leichtentritt, "Handel's Harmonic Art," 214.

Handel's borrowing practice, for example, tends to confirm his concern for aria keys and key conflict. Thus, in *Agrippina*, Act II, set 2 (Chart XIV), the central conflict of the tritone, which occurs when Poppea learns that Agrippina has tricked her, separates a flat area from a sharp area (each bounded by a fifth relation) and creates a tritone between the outer movements of the set as well.[22] Poppea's arias in B-flat and A were both borrowed; the B-flat aria was originally in A; the A aria was originally in B-flat. These transpositions of a half-step make no difference to the range of Poppea's role, but they create the symmetrical harmonic plan and allow the harmonic conflict to occur in the right place dramatically.[23]

Chart XIV. Handel's *Agrippina*, Act II, set 2

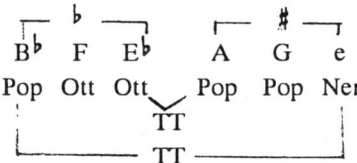

Rodelinda, II, 1 offers a second example. In this set, as discussed above, the tonal conflict occurs between Rodelinda and Grimoaldo (see Chart VI). Their arias are a half-step apart, in B-flat major and A major. Both these arias are based on earlier arias by Handel, and both original arias are in the key of G major. Handel only uses the ritornello material from his source for Rodelinda's aria, completely rewriting the vocal line. His source for Grimoaldo's aria is a duet for two sopranos that obviously demanded adaptation to make it suitable for solo tenor voice. Both arias from *Rodelinda* could have been adapted in any key. However, it is

---

[22] I would like to thank David Hurley, a former graduate student at the University of Chicago, whose work on *Agrippina* for a 1984 seminar I directed on Handel's harmonic plans largely underlies this discussion. His dissertation on "Handel's Compositional Process in Selected Oratorios" was completed in 1991, and is forthcoming from Oxford University Press.

[23] In *Agrippina* II, 2, the A section of Poppea's first aria, "Bella pur nel mio diletto" in B-flat major, is nearly a contrafactum of "Una schiera di piaceri" in A major from *Il trionfo del tempo*. The A section of her second aria, "Ingannata una volta" in A major, is a contrafactum of "Dolce Amor" in B-flat major from *Rodrigo*, which is itself closely modelled on "Se Licori" from the cantata "Tu fedel?," also in B-flat major.

important to an understanding of in Handel's tonal methods that in both cases he used material originally presented in the key of G major, discarded that key, and chose instead to place these consecutive arias in keys a half-step apart. The final aria of the set, which derives from a piece in B-flat major (the key used finally for Rodelinda's aria) was then placed into G major.[24]

Rodelinda offers contradictory evidence of Handel's harmonic awareness during revisions. Its first performance took place during the 1724–25 season, and it was revived the following season with two changes of cast. Winton Dean and Merrill Knapp suggest that two of Grimoaldo's arias were transposed at this time.[25] One of these is a transposition of Grimoaldo's aria in Act II, 1 ("Prigoniera") from A major to B-flat major, which puts this aria apparently into the same key as Rodelinda's preceding aria. Looking at this, the would-be analyst despairs. Bukofzer states the case bluntly.

> ... Both Bach and Handel betray in their revisions, many of which introduce new keys, what would have to be considered as a deplorable lack of appreciation for their own key architecture, had it really existed.[26]

But this argument lacks force. That is, it is unneccesary to conclude that key relations exist only in the mind of the interpreter if the composer weakens or destroys those relations upon revision. For example, we willingly accept the exigencies that called for Gluck to revise his operas for the French stage, even when these changes affect the fabric of the original. We do not say that because Gluck damaged the tonal architecture of *Orfeo* with revisions and additions for the French performance that he never intended such tonal architecture.[27] All opera composers

---

[24]In *Rodelinda* II, 1, "Spietati" is based on "No! non basta" from *Il pastor fido*, "Prigioniera ho l'alma" on "Senza occhi" from the cantata "Tu fedel," and "Fra tempeste" on the minuet of the Overture from *Rodrigo*. See Dean/Knapp, *Handel's Operas*, 664.

[25]Dean and Knapp, *Handel's Operas*, 590.

[26]Bukofzer, *Music in the Baroque Era*, 367.

[27]Patricia Howard, in *C. W. Gluck: "Orfeo"* (Cambridge, 1981), writes (p. 74), "There is evidence that Gluck planned the key sequences of the original *Orfeo* very carefully indeed," but (p. 75) that "key sequences constituted the first aspect of *Orfeo* that Gluck was prepared to jettison—as early as 1769, in the transposition of the role for Millico, and again in 1774 for Le Gros." The frequently damaging effect of revisions on key schemes is not, of course, limited to the eighteenth century. One can find examples throughout the history of opera.

must face changing demands, but this does not discredit their original ideas. Sometimes alterations even prove beneficial.

John Hill has addressed this problem in the operas of Vivaldi.[28] He demonstrates how revisions, even those using parodied arias from other operas, often lead intentionally to a dramatic strengthening of the whole. He writes that often the revision process itself "encourages us to take seriously the dramatic integrity of opera seria."[29] This is true also of the tonal integrity of Handel's operas.

Returning, then, to *Rodelinda*, we find that Handel revived this opera a second time in 1731. Three arias, including Grimoaldo's aria "Prigoniera," were replaced with pieces from other operas. The substitution for "Prigoniera," transferred from *Lotario* (1729) is in the same key, A major, as the original aria and, like that piece, modulates in the B section to C-sharp minor. Similarly, the duet at the end of Act II in F-sharp minor (see Chart VI) is replaced by a duet from *Tolomeo*, also in F-sharp minor. The third substitution, less felicitious, replaces Grimoaldo's final E minor aria with one in C minor. Speculation on the reasons for these changes does not lead far. Dean and Knapp suggest that the changes were hurriedly made to give singers new to their roles songs they had previously sung.[30] No doubt this is true. But the important fact remains that in the two cases where the arias were part of a set's central tonal conflict, Handel made the effort to retain the original key structure. In no instance do practical necessities eliminate the possibility of aesthetic solutions, any more than poor revisions prove the lack of an original harmonic conceit.

The question may also be raised, however, whether Handel's choice of key was not determined either by choice of instrument or affect, rather than by dramatic tonal design. In the case of instrumentation, the answer can be sought by a determination of priorities. That is, did Handel choose his instrumentation or his key structure first? The initial choice of either one limits the range of the other. Looking at

---

[28]John Hill, "Vivaldi's *Griselda*," *Journal of the American Musicological Society*, XXXI (1978): 53–82.
[29]Hill, "*Griselda*," 78.
[30]Dean and Knapp, *Handel's Operas*, 592.

Poppea's B-flat major and A major arias from Act II, 2 of *Agrippina*, discussed above, one finds that their instrumentation and that of their sources presented no tonal limitations. In every case, only strings and oboes are used. The same is true of the borrowings and their transpositions in *Rodelinda*, also discussed above. Indeed, in the vast majority of cases, Handel uses only strings and oboes in his arias, and his choice of key is unrestricted by these instruments.

The instruments that tend to limit the choice of keys are flutes, recorders, trumpets, and horns. Transverse flutes are most comfortable in sharp keys, whereas recorders favor flat keys. Horns are used most often in F major, and trumpets are found predominantly in D major or C major. Furthermore, these instruments and their keys tend to be related to specific affects. Flutes and recorders complement either the pastoral or poignant mood, trumpets color military or rage arias, and horns relate to hunting or formal celebration. These generalizations cannot, however, be codified into rules. Handel wrote military marches without trumpets, even when they were present in the orchestra; he wrote nature pieces without flutes or recorders, and hunting pieces without horns. That is, the subject of the aria might have limited his choice of instrument, in that pastoral texts were not set with trumpets, but it did not limit the choice of key, as specific instruments were never required.

There is a particularly nice example of this in *Rinaldo*, where Handel, as is typical, associates the aggressors (here, the pagans) with flat keys and the righteous victims (the Christians) with sharps. Therefore, in Act III when the libretto states that the "Christian trumpets sound," Handel writes a march in D major with parts for four trumpets and timpani in addition to string orchestra and oboes. A few scenes earlier, the libretto has a similar direction: "The Pagan Trumpets sound." But here Handel writes a march in B-flat major, effectively eliminating the possibility of trumpets, and the march is scored for strings only. That is, Handel prefers to keep the flat-sharp tonal conflict (paralleling the dramatic conflict) rather than use the keys or the instruments usually associated with military marches. In doing so, he even overlooks a specific direction in the libretto. Similarly, a pastoral can be set in F major (with recorders), as in "Un Zeffiro spiró" from *Rodelinda* or in G major (with transverse flutes), as in "Par che mi nasca in seno" from *Tamerlano*, offering Handel the obvious opportunity to set this affect in a sharp or flat key; but pastorals can also be found in keys other than F or G major, and without either recorder or flute.

These examples point to the primacy of key selection over affect as well as instrumentation. Indeed, the idea that Baroque composers followed a rigid scheme of key affect has been largely discredited.[31] But not only was an affect not limited to a single key, the aria text was also not limited to a single affect. This is clearly demonstrated by Johann David Heinichen in his *Der Generalbass in der Composition* (1728) where he offers multiple settings in different keys of four different texts. With a set of sixteen partial settings, Heinichen shows us the freedom with which a contemporary composer could choose both the affect of the aria and the key.[32]

In conclusion, Handel's keys reflect tonal patterns that both parallel the structure of the opera seria libretto and express its content. The patterns discussed stretch from the aria itself, to the scene, to the set, and sometimes groups of sets. By recognizing these patterns, we can begin to understand the musical integrity of Handel's operas as a linear and interlocking series of juxtapositions. The concepts of organicism, thematic transformation, and harmonic resolution were for the future, but this does not mean that Baroque opera lacks a constructive principle.

Handel's particular solution to the harmonic form of the opera seria seems to be unique, and it represents a specific example of his eclectic and para-national style. Three harmonic patterns exist. The A/B pattern is typical of da capos in the works of most of Handel's contemporaries and predecessors. On the other hand, the recitative link appears to be a pattern that is used most frequently before Handel by Alessandro Scarlatti. Even in his first opera of 1704, however, Handel uses this link more than Scarlatti does in his last operas of 1719 and 1720,

---

[31]See especially George Buelow, "Johann Mattheson and the Invention of the 'Affecktenlehre'," in *New Mattheson Studies*, ed. George J. Buelow and Hans Joachim Marx (New York, 1983), 393–408.

[32]See George Buelow, *Thorough-Bass Accompaniment according to Johann David Heinichen*, rev. ed. (Ann Arbor, 1986). Also, Roger Lustig, in a paper presented to the American Musicological Society Meetings in 1986, "*Affeckt* and *Ausweichung*—A Reading Between Heinichen's Lines," discussed the apparent importance to Heinichen of the relation between the primary and secondary keys as opposed to the choice of a specific primary key to the expression of affect.

and he uses it differently, not just as a typical pattern, but as a dramatic tool. Finally, the organization of sets around a tonal conflict seems to be a German trait, used primarily by German musicians and discussed by German theorists. Handel takes these three patterns, integrates them with one another, and uses the first two as normative procedures that can be disrupted to create tension and surprise. The harmonic patterns play a large role in his depiction of the content of the libretto, and, to the same extent, they underscore the structure of the libretto.

Handel's use of these patterns also helps to place him chronologically as the culminator of a tonal tradition. His devotion to the somewhat modal relations of I to iii and i to v identify him with late seventeenth-century practices more than with the modern composers of his own lifetime who favored dominant/tonic and relative relations. There is already little in common between Handel and Vivaldi or Leo. However, the possible comparisons have obviously not been exhausted, and investigations of Steffani's or Gasparini's harmonic practices, in particular, could well prove that Handel had closer colleagues in this regard than Keiser, Scarlatti, Bach, Vivaldi or Leo have proven to be.

Handel's use of harmonic patterns helps to guide the modern editor or conductor of his works. Recitative should not be cut or altered without considering the recitative cadence. B sections should not be cut without considering dramatic uses of both the recitative link, and the da capo convention. And arias should not be cut without considering their tonal position within the set. That is not to say that Handel's operas cannot be cut or that Handel himself did not at times do damage to his own creations. However, the recognition of tonal patterns in Handel's operas offers an important tool to modern editors when cutting is deemed necessary. The operas may be linear, but they are not merely a collection of unrelated events that can be added to, subtracted from, and jumbled without ill effect. Handel's harmonic patterns illustrate his concern at various levels of composition for musical and dramatic conflict and continuity, and that deserves our respect.*

---

*Preliminary versions of this paper were read in Hofgeismar, West Germany (1984), at the Accademia di Santa Cecilia, Rome (1985), at the Gesellschaft für Musikforschung, Stuttgart (1985), and The University of North Carolina at Chapel Hill (1986). I am grateful to those who offered criticism and suggestions. An abstract of this paper appears in *Kongressbericht Stuttgart 1985*. A version of this paper was also scheduled for presentation at the Fondazione Cini in Venice (1985), but a mechanical failure on my flight prevented my arrival; I would like to thank the Fondazione in writing for their forbearance. I would also like to take this opportunity to thank all of the students in my 1984 seminar at The University of Chicago on Handel's harmonic patterns, and to thank C. Steven LaRue, whose work on *Ottone*, *Tamerlano*, and *Tolomeo*, and David Achenbach, whose work on *Alcina*, offered new insights into those operas and kept me working when administrative work might have overwhelmed me. Last but not least, I would like to thank my former research assistant Joseph Auner, who advised and assisted in innumerable ways. Since this paper was completed, much time has elapsed, and it has not been possible to update all the bibliographical references. However, the reader is encouraged to seek out the more recent publications from various authors cited. In particular, please note: Robin F. C. Fenton, "Mattheson's *Cleopatra* and Handel's *Agrippina*: the Transmission of a Tradition or a Case of Indebtedness?" *Göttinger Händel Beiträge* III (1987): 50–70, and "*Almira* (1705): the Birth of G. F. Handel's Genius for Characterization," *Händel-Jahrbuch* XXXIII (1987): 109–30; and Eric Chafe, *Tonal Allegory in the Vocal Music of J. S. Bach* (Berkeley: University of California Press, 1991).

Hellmut Federhofer

JOHANN JOSEPH FUX AND EQUAL TEMPERAMENT*

Translation by John Rothgeb

Controversy continues to surround the question of the tuning practice of Johann Sebastian Bach, especially for stringed keyboard instruments. James Murray Barbour was the first to cast doubt on the opinion, common at least since the nineteenth century, that by the term *wohltemperiert* Bach referred to equal temperament: "The title of Bach's famous '48' meant simply that the clavier was playable in all keys."[1] Other modern authors (Herbert Kelletat, Herbert Anton Kellner, John Barnes, Otto Bernhard Billeter, Owen Henry Jorgensen, Claudio Di Véroli) shared this opinion, and advocated for performance of Bach's works an unequal temperament.[2]

---

*This article first appeared in German in *Die Musikforschung* XLI (1988): 9–15. The editor wishes to thank Bärenreiter for permission to publish this translation.

[1] J. M. Barbour, *Tuning and Temperament, a Historical Survey* (East Lansing, Mich., 2nd ed. 1953), 12.
[2] R. Rasch, "Does 'Well-Tempered' Mean 'Equal-Tempered'?," in *Bach, Handel, Scarlatti, Tercentenary Essays*, ed. P. Williams (Cambridge, 1985), 293ff.

Hellmut Federhofer is University Professor emeritus in musicology at Johannes Gutenberg-Universität (Mainz).

John Rothgeb teaches at the State University of New York at Binghamton and writes on music theory.

For Martin Vogel, "the thousand-times parroted opinion that Bach's well-tempering was identical with equal-stepped tuning . . . is false, and should not be repeated. . . . *The Welltempered Clavier* had a tuning by fifths, and also a portion of pure intonation."[3] Vogel does not doubt that "Bach's Well-Tempered Clavier was tuned according to Kirnberger's system."[4] But Rudolf Rasch, on the contrary, citing testimony of contemporaneous theorists (Andreas Werckmeister, Johann Georg Neidhardt, Johann Mattheson, and Georg Andreas Sorge, among others), has most recently represented the view that "the arguments put forward in favor of an unequal temperament for Bach's WTC are at best undocumented modern views. The conclusion must be that the traditional view, that Bach's WTC expects an equal-tempered keyboard, is correct."[5] Rasch qualifies this statement, however, as follows: "Nothing is being said explicitly about the tuning(s) practiced."[6]

In agreement with this statement is the fact that the extraordinary care devoted by the master to the tuning of his instruments, as witnessed by the obituary of Johann Sebastian Bach and by both Carl Philipp Emanuel Bach and Johann Nikolaus Forkel, was merely a matter of everyday practice. Writings by him on this matter do not exist. Composers, to be sure, hardly felt obliged— unless they were also deeply interested in theoretical problems—to issue treatises about problems of tuning. Their task, rather, was to cultivate purity of intonation. The resulting mathematical-acoustical problems they left to the province of the theorists. The statements of the latter, however, valuable though they may have been, cannot completely answer the question of how the composers of the eighteenth and nineteenth centuries—especially those centuries' most important representatives—dealt with the problem of tuning their instruments.

---

[3]M. Vogel, *Anleitung zur harmonische Analyse und zu reiner Intonation* (Bonn, 1984) (= *Orpheus- Schriftenreihe zu Grundfragen der Musik* 34), 15: die tausendfach nachgebetete Behauptung, dass Bachs Wohltemperierung mit der gleichstufigen identisch war, ist falsch und sollte nicht wiederholt werden. . . . Das 'Wohltemperierte Klavier' hatte eine Quintstimmung, mithin einen Ausschnitt der reinen Stimmung.

[4]Vogel, *Anleitung*, 14f.

[5]Rasch, "Well-Tempered," 308.

[6]Rasch, "Well-Tempered," 303.

It must therefore be viewed as a stroke of good fortune that unequivocal statements exist on this question by two masters—Jean Philippe Rameau and Johann Joseph Fux—who not only earned great recognition as composers in their own lifetimes but who also exerted through their theoretical works an important influence on the evolution of the new music theory. Rameau's comments have been discussed by Wilhelm Dupont, James Murray Barbour, Wolfgang Auhagen, Rita Steblin, and Mark Lindley.[7]

While Rameau in his *Nouveau système de musique théorique* (Paris, 1726) still advocated unequal temperament,[8] he made a commitment to equal temperament in his *Génération harmonique* (Paris, 1737). His original opinion that the distinctive characteristic of scales were to be credited to unequal temperament—an opinion shared by theorists of the subsequent period, and especially by Johann Philipp Kirnberger—he emphatically disavowed in later years:

> Celui qui croit que les différentes impressions qu'il reçoit des différences qu'occasionne le Témpéramment en usage dans chaque Mode transposé, lui élevent le génie, & le portent plus de variété, me permettra de lui dire qu'il se trompe; le goût de variété se prend dans l'entrelacement des Modes, & nullement dans l'altération des intervales, qui ne peut que déplaire à l'Oreille, à la distraire par conséquent de ses fonctions.[9]

It remained almost unnoticed, however, that Fux, in spite of his involvement with the a capella style, unconditionally endorsed equal temperament.[10] Possibly the latter system was common in the Viennese

---

[7]W. Dupont, *Geschichte der musikalischen Temperatur* (Nördlingen, 1935), 39 and 92; J. M. Barbour, *Tuning*, 224; W. Auhagen, *Studien zur Tonartencharakteristik in theoretischen Schriften und Kompositionen vom späten 17. bis zum Beginn des 20. Jahrhunderts* (Frankfurt a.M./Bern/New York, 1983) (= *Europäische Hochschulschriften*, series 26,6), 41f; R. Steblin, *A History of Key Characteristics in the Eighteenth and Early Nineteenth Centuries* (Ann Arbor, Michigan, 1983) (= *Studies in Musicology* 67), 59; M. Lindley, "Temperaments," in *The New Grove* (London, 1980) Vol. 18, 668f.

[8]J. P. Rameau, *Nouveau système de musique théorique* (Paris, 1726), 120. Compare also Dupont, *Geschichte*, 39; Barbour, *Tuning*, 135; Lindley, "Temperaments," 668.

[9]Rameau, *Génération harmonique* (Paris, 1737), 104. Compare also Dupont, *Geschichte*, 92; Auhagen, *Studien*, 42f; Steblin, *History*, 59f; Lindley, "Temperaments," 669.

[10]H. Federhofer, "Johann Joseph Fux als Musiktheoretiker," in *Hans Albrecht in memoriam*, ed. by W. Brennecke and H. Haase (Kassel, 1962), 112.

musical circles of Fux's time, since it had already been used by the court organist Johann Jakob Froberger, who was admired by J. S. Bach.[11] More probable, however, is that Fux got acquainted with it through Marin Mersenne, to whom he refers in his *Gradus ad parnassum* (Vienna, 1725).[12] Fux concerns himself in detail with establishing the mathematical foundation of the tonal system—almost the whole first book of the *Gradus* is devoted to this task—but with the qualification that "Some musical intervals are, with regard to their quality of being proportioned, judged by the ear rather than by reason."[13] Ventures of a practical nature already led Mersenne to the demand for equality of whole-steps and of half-steps, and thus to twelve-step equal temperament. Since "all the tones and all the half-tones are equal,"[14] Mersenne designated the intervals according to half-steps, which Fux modified only to the extent that he presented the intervals as sums of whole- and half-steps. Thus the minor third, for example, consists of a whole- and a half-step; the augmented fifth of three whole- and two half-steps; the octave of five whole- and two half-steps.[15] Fux was of course aware of the difference between large and small whole-steps as well as of that between large and small half-steps—for the latter he supplies the ratios 16:15 and 25:24 respectively. He ponders even their actualization in practice, but rejects it for practical reasons because of the resultant proliferation of keys.

> If indeed separate appropropriate keys were provided in order to distinguish both major and minor tones and semitones as well as some smaller intervals—as many ancient and more recent specialists actually have done in their keyboard constructions—thus, in fact, all intervals used today, and even those derived from Ptolemy's division, could be accorded their proper proportional nature. Perceiving,

---

[11] Lindley, "Temperaments," 665.

[12] Federhofer, "Johann Joseph Fux," 111f. Fux refers not to Mersenne's *Harmonie universelle* (Paris, 1636-37), which he may well have known, but to his *Harmonicorum libri XII* (Paris, 1648), in particular to *liber I, propositio II*: "Mersennus lib. I harmon. propo. 2 ex mente Arist. sonum ait esse motum aëris"; Fux, *Gradus ad parnassum* (Vienna, 1725), 1.

[13] Fux, *Gradus*, 34: "pleraque Musicae intervalla proportionibus suis rationalibus consistentia, aurium judicio potiùs, quam ratione nitantur."

[14] H. H. Dräger, "Marin Mersenne," in *MGG* (Kassel, 1961) vol. 9, col. 133: ". . . tous les tons & et les demy-tons sont esgaux."

[15] Fux, *Gradus*, 37f.

however, a full use of such keyboards with difficulty, yet putting their minds to considering the inadequacy of intervals with a view toward their improvement and an acceptance of imperfect intervals, they attempted to divide the tone and semitone into equal parts. In their realization that this could not be done by mathematical operations, they relied upon the judgement of the ear, taking away from one interval an almost imperceptible part and adding it to another; and they accomplished by this provision that the complexity of the keyboard was enriched, so that today music—released from the problem of differentiated intervals as if from confinement—can move freely in a vast expanse of melodic and harmonic motions. . . . How much benefit and splendor it added to the cause of music, and how much praise is therefore due to its first proponent (which honor is rightfully accorded to the ancient philosopher Aristoxenus), no one even moderately versed in music will fail to see.[16]

Since Aristoxenus divides the octave into six equal parts and the whole-step into equal half-steps, he was considered guardian of equal temperament.[17] Precisely because of the principle of division mentioned, Fux refers to Aristoxenus respectfully in the above passage, but continues by speaking explicitly of the elimination of inequality of whole- and half-steps, which was to be replaced by the "established equality of tones and semitones."[18]

---

[16]Fux, *Gradus*, 34f: Etenim si utriusque tonis majori, & minori, semitoniis majori, minorique, & aliquibus adhuc minoribus intervallis cuilibet singillatim sua peculiaris etiam statuatur clavis, id quod multi Musices periti, & veteres, & recentiores suis Claviaturis rebus ipsis monstravêre, utique omnia hodie usitata intervalla, maximè secundùm Ptolomaei divisionem, suis proportionibus rationalibus probè consistentia haberi possent. Cùm autem Claviaturae usum difficultate plenum perspexissent, & nihilominùs penuriae intervallorum consulturi ad amplificationem eorum, & acquisitionem consonantiarum imperfectarum animum adjecissent, tonum & semitonium in duas partes aequales dividere tentaverunt. Postquam autem numeris id effici non posse, compererunt, aurium judicium in subsidium vocavêre, auferendo ab uno intervallo quandam quasi insensibilem quantitatem, eamque alteri adjiciendo, per quam industriam, sublatâ Claviaturae difficultate effecêre, ut Musica nostra ex intervallorum egestate, tanquam carcere eluctata, in vastissimum modulationis campum hodie latissimè excurrere valeat [. . .]. Quantum inde rei Musicae beneficii, splendorisque accesserit, quantisque propterea primum Autorem (quae gloria Aristoxeno antiquo Philosopho, optimo jure attribuitur) laudivus efferamus, neminem Musicâ vel leviter tinctum latere existimo.

[17]R. P. Winnington-Ingram, "Aristoxenus," in *The New Grove* (London, 1980) vol. 1, 592.

[18]Fux, *Gradus* 35f: "supposita tonorum, & semitoniorum aequalitate."

Thanks to the influence of Fux as composer, theorist, and teacher of, among others, Gottlieb Theophil Muffat, Georg Christoph Wagenseil, and Jan Dismas Zelenka, the extent of the dissemination of equal temperament is scarcely to be underestimated. When Johann Georg Neidhardt in his text *Sectio Canonis Harmonici* (Königsberg, 1724) characterizes three unequal temperaments and, as a fourth, equal temperament with the words, "in my view, the first is often best suited for a village; the second for a small city; the third for a large city; and the fourth for the court,"[19] the fourth temperament exactly corresponds to the requirements that must have evolved at the Viennese imperial court for the performance of music, including that of Fux. J. S. Bach owned a copy of the *Gradus*, and it is noteworthy that his student Lorenz Christoph Mizler, who elsewhere added various critical comments as footnotes to his translation of the work, refrained from adding any to the above passage concerned with temperament, because "this work is written primarily for musical practitioners, who are not always well served by long-winded discussions of such things; this author has dealt only with this point as well."[20] From this it can be inferred that Mizler considered equal temperament suitable in practice—in particular, for "musical practitioners." Had J. S. Bach rejected it, Mizler's silence on the matter in this passage would be very difficult to understand.

That J. S. Bach intended to designate Kirnberger's tuning with the word *wohltemperiert* is assumed by M. Vogel.[21] This assumption, however, is based on a dubious interpretation of the well-known communication from Kirnberger to Friedrich Wilhelm Marpurg, which the latter repeats as follows: "Herr Kirnberger himself has often told me and others how the renowned Johann Sebastian Bach taught him to

---

[19]Quoted after Rasch, "Well-Tempered," 300: "Meines Erachtens schickt sich die Erste, mehrenteils, am besten vor ein Dorff, die Andre vor eine kleine Stadt, die Dritte vor eine Grosse, und die Vierdte vor den Hof."

[20]Fux, *Gradus ad Parnassum [. . .] Aus dem Lateinischen ins Teutsche übersetzt, mit nöthigen und nützlichen Anmerkungen versehen und herausgegeben von Lorenz Mizlern* (Leipzig, 1742), 53: "dieses Werck hauptsächlich vor die practischen Musikverständigen geschrieben ist, denen nicht allzeit mit weitläuftigen Beweisen von dergleichen Dingen gedienet, der Verfasser auch hierin gantz kurtz gegangen." Regarding Mizler, compare F. Wölke, *Lorenz Christoph Mizler* (Würzburg/Aumühle, 1940) and G. F. Buelow, "Mizler," in *The New Grove*, vol. 12, 372f.

[21]Vogel, *Anleitung*, 14f.

tune his keyboard during the time he enjoyed instruction from the latter, and how this master expressly required of him that he make all major thirds sharp."[22] Vogel identifies "sharp major third" with the Pythagorean third 64:81, of which Kirnberger's tuning, however, shows only eight; as Vogel himself acknowledges, "the remaining four thirds must then be taken as they are found."[23] But Kirnberger speaks of Bach's requirement that *all* major thirds be made sharp, "thus ruling out any unsubtle irregular temperament (such as used by Kirnberger himself)."[24]

Kirnberger's unequal temperament was advocated by his pupil Johann Abraham Peter Schulz in the article "Temperament" in Johann Georg Sulzer's *Allgemeine Theorie der schönen Künste* (Leipzig, 1794),[25] which drew criticism from Daniel Gottlob Türk:

> As much as I value the services of a Sulzer and a Kirnberger.... I would nevertheless prefer, for various reasons, not to confuse the unequal temperament recommended by them with equal or almost equal temperament, even though it characterizes the keys more exactly; for if one were obliged to hear only certain triads in completely pure form and others all the more impurely, I do not know whether more would be gained than lost.... I think the Kirnbergerian temperament should not so soon become the common one; for it might be difficult to apply it to all instruments, and such would then nevertheless be necessary. It is a pity, however, that this article in Sulzer's *Allgemeine Theorie* has had so much influence on various others.[26]

---

[22]F. W. Marpurg, *Versuch über die musikalische Temperatur* (Breslau, 1776), 213: "Der Hr. Kirnberger selbst hat mir und andern mehrmahl erzählet, wie der berühmte Joh. Se. Bach ihm, währender Zeit seines von demselben genoßnen musikalischen Unterrichts, die Stimmung seines Claviers übertragen, und wie dieser Meister ausdrücklich von ihm verlanget, alle grosse Terzen scharf zu machen."

[23]Vogel, *Anleitung*, 14: "die restlichen vier Terzen muß man hinnehmen, wie sie sich dann ergeben."

[24]Lindley, "Temperaments," 670.

[25]2nd ed. (Leipzig, 1794), vol. 4, 516ff.

[26]D. G. Türk, *Von den wichtigsten Pflichten eines Organisten* (Halle, 1787), 200f: "So sehr ich auch die Vedienste eines Sulzer und Kirnberger schätze [...]. so möchte ich doch, aus verschiedenen Gründen, ihre vorgeschlagene ungleichschwebende Temperatur, ohnerachtet sie die Töne, genauer, charakterisirt, nicht mit der gleich- oder fast gleichschwebenden vertauschen; denn wenn man z. B. blos Einige Dreyklänge ganz rein, und Andere dagegen desto unreiner hören solte: so weiß ich nicht, ob dadurch mehr gewonnen, als verlohren würde; denn es möchte schwer seyn, sie auf alle Instrumente überzutragen; und das wär' alsdenn doch wohl nöthig.—Schade ists aber, daß dieser Artikel in Sulzers allgem. Theorie so vielen Einfluß auf verschiedene Andere gehabt hat."

That influence appears not to have been overly great, however, for Schulz himself writes in the above article: "A good many composers recommended the so-called equal temperament."[27]

Speaking unequivocally in favor of the latter were Marpurg (Kirnberger's opponent) and Georg Friedrich Wolf, who was connected to C. P. E. Bach and Georg Simon Löhlein. Although Löhlein, in the prefatory remarks for his musical lexicon, expressly invoked Sulzer, whom "the best and greatest musical authorities diligently assisted and provided with musical articles for the preparation of the book in question," Wolf writes as follows in the article "Tuning": "How a keyboard is to be tuned properly is showed by Barth. Fritze [!] in his instructions on how one should tune keyboards and the like (Vienna, 1799).[28] The reference is to Barthold Fritz, who cites C. P. E. Bach in the second printing of his *Anweisung, wie man Claviere, Clavecins, und Orgeln, nach einer mechanischen Art, in allen zwölf Tönen gleich rein stimmen könne* (Leipzig, 1756; second ed. 1757), and comes down decisively in favor of equal temperament.[29] His book appeared in five printings up to 1829. Although there is no direct evidence of unequivocal advocacy of equal temperament by C. P. E. Bach, "if the music of any leading 18th-century German composer ought to be performed in equal temperament, C. P. E. Bach is the best candidate."[30]

The keyboard treatise of the aforementioned Löhlein went through eight printings from 1765 to 1848, and therefore stood in practical use for about a century. Löhlein too opted for equal temperament, as may be inferred from the sixth and final paragraph of the first part:

> § 6. For purposes of tuning, in addition to a good ear a rather large amount of experience is necessary if it is to be done well. In tuning according to equal temperament, it is crucial to observe that all

---

[27] J. G. Sulzer, op. cit., 517: "Gar viel Tonsetzer erklärten sich für die sogenannte gleichschwebende Temperatur."

[28] G. F. Wolf, *Allgemeines Musikalisches Lexikon* (Vienna, 1800), 103: "Wie ein Clavier richtig zu stimmen sey, lehrt Barth. Fritze [!] in seiner Anweisung, wie man Klaviere etc. stimmen soll. Wien 1799." "Fritze" is a somewhat derogatory form of the very popular German first-name usage, which makes Wolf's slip doubly amusing.

[29] Lindley, "Temperaments," 669.

[30] Lindley, "Temperaments," 670.

octaves are perfectly pure and all fifths slightly low. The procedure to be followed is this: one begins with c1 (to tune the clavier to the appropriate pitch, one must adjust this tone according to a tuning pipe or tuning fork) and fits to it the octave c2; next the fifth, g1, and to it the octave g, and thus on and on through fifths and octaves, as shown in the following:

Example 1.

The remaining tones are then tuned according to the already correct octaves. There are still various temperaments according to which several keys are purer, but others on the contrary all the more faulty. The equal temperament presented here, in which one plays with equal purity in all keys, therefore has many advantages.[31]

In the eighth printing of this work, supervised by Carl Czerny, the choice is left open as to which of two different methods is of greatest practical ease and reliability for achieving equal temperament. The latter is taken as self-evident, while Kirnberger's tuning, mentioned only in a footnote, meets with rejection:

---

[31]G. S. Löhlein, *Clavier-Schule* (Leipzig and Züllichau, 1765). Cited after the fifth printing, revised and expanded by J. G. Witthauer (Leipzig and Züllichau, 1791), 82: "Zum Stimmen wird außer einem guten Gehör, ziemlich viel Uebung darinn erfordert, wenn es gut werden soll. Beym Stimmen nach der gleichschwebenden Temperatur, ist vorzüglich zu merken, daß alle Octaven ganz rein und alle Quinten etwas abwärts schweben müssen. Die Verfahrungsart davey ist folgende: Man fängt bey dem c an (diesen Ton muß man, um das Clavier in der gehörigen Höhe zu stimmen, nach einer Stimmpfeife oder Stimmgabel, abpassen) stimmt hierzu die Octave c̄, dahn die Quinte, g, hierzu die Octave klein g, und so immer durch Quinten und Octaven weiter, wie aus folgenden zu sehen, die übrigen Töne werden dann nach den schon reinen Octaven gestimmt. Man hat noch verschiedene Temperaturen, nach welchen etliche Tonarten reiner, andere dafür aber desto mangelhafter sind. Die hier angegebene gleichschwebende, wo man in allen Tonarten gleich rein spielt, hat daher viele Vorzüge."

an unequal temperament has been suggested, recommended, and—with more sophistry than thoroughness—defended by Kirnberger. According to this process nine fifths are tuned perfectly pure (= naturally), but the others are tempered, and thus necessarily become all the more noticeably impure. Any unspoiled ear immediately judges this temperament to be unusable.[32]

In view of the lifelong close relationship of Czerny to Beethoven, it might thus be erroneous to posit a connection between Beethoven's interest in key characteristics (reported by Anton Schindler) and unequal temperament.[33]

Without doubt, however, Kirnberger's suggestions (known as Kirnberger I, II, and III) represented among the unequal temperaments a strong competition to equal temperament—but only in the eighteenth century; no longer in the nineteenth. When Martin Vogel writes that "the Kirnbergerian tuning was the principal tuning of its time. The *Leipziger Allgemeine Musikalische Zeitung* calls it still in 1848 the most famous and in practice most widely disseminated of all temperaments,"[34] he falls victim to a misinterpretation. He refers to a four-part article signed "Hdt." cited earlier by Dupont, "Ketzerische Rhapsodieen eines musikalischen Skeptikers, Rhapsodia I–IV." Only Sections III and IV relate to problems of temperament, and the subtitle of both instalments, "That it has nothing to do with the characteristic of keys," reveals what the author would like to prove—namely, that "none of our keys possesses, apart from the aspect of higher or lower pitch level, a character that is special to it and differentiated from that of others of the same mode."[35] Here he is in agreement with Marpurg, who likewise makes pitch-level and not type of temperament responsible for the characterization of the keys.[36] Dupont, to be sure, already misunderstands the "Hdt." author

---

[32]Published as A. E. Müller, *Grosse Fortepiano-Schule*, eighth edition by C. Czerny (Leipzig, 1825), 241f.

[33]See in this connection Lindley, "Temperaments," 669.

[34]Vogel, *Anleitung* 14.

[35]*Allgemeine Musikalische Zeitung* L (1848), No. 33 (16 August), col. 529ff., and No. 26 (6 September), col. 577ff. Erroneously in Dupont, *Geschichte*, 102, as 6 August and 16 September 1848. The problem of the anonymity of the author "Hdt.", whose article is cited also by Auhagen, *Studien*, 143ff., and Steblin, *History*, 101ff, remains unresolved.

[36]Marpurg, *Versuch* 217; Dupont, *Geschichte*, 106.

when he ascribes to him the opinion that "the characteristicness of keys is disputed only for equal temperament; it is granted as a fact for the Kirnbergerian system."[37] Rather, a connection between tuning and key-character is denied altogether, both in respect to church modes, whose special character is attributed to both the different positions of the half- and whole-steps and the melodic and harmonic successions specific to each, and also in relation to the major-minor system. Pointing to Andreas Werckmeister, who is viewed in the article—in agreement with an opinion also widely shared later—as the founder of equal temperament, it avers that he had proposed

> to segment the old Wolf into twelve equally large pieces, and to distribute them, as just that many small wolves of little danger or none at all, over the whole half-tone system of the octave. But, the practitioners of the time were and remained of the opinion that this would indeed be quite good in theory, but unfeasible in practice; and thus here, as so often happens with good devices that aim for a radical remedy, human intellectual sloth, prejudice, and clinging to old ways at first formed an obstacle to the realization of an idea that nevertheless came to be honored, but only after a long struggle and five quarter-centuries later.

> Since the twelve major and minor scales were all available—at least for the eye—, however, it was all the more necessary to give consideration to adapting them one and all for the ear as well, for it was desirable to secure completely both the convenience of transposition and the possibility of harmonic excursions in every direction; and thus arose the unequal temperaments, which left only a certain number of fifths completely pure, and distributed the diatonic surplus over the remaining ones as best as possible without causing excessive inconvenience. There were, incidentally, a large number of these unequal temperaments, which differed only in respect to the number, size, and position of the new unharmonious howlers sprouted from the substance of the fortunately slain great Wolf; these descendants, incidentally, if not possessed of so much power as their forebear, nevertheless always made their presence felt.

> The most famous of these temperaments and the one most widely, although by no means generally, disseminated in practice, was the one introduced about the middle of the preceding century by *Kirnberger*, which to some extent remained in use well into the first

[37]Dupont, *Geschichte*, 102.

decade of this century, but then had to yield completely to its colleague that was gaining ever greater acceptance, the one that completely evened out the entire scale —equal temperament.[38]

Kirnberger's temperament, accordingly, only the most famous among the unequal temperaments, found merely residual partial application in the first decade of the nineteenth century, and then receded completely—by comparison with equal temperament—in importance. This circumstance is confirmed twice more in the above article: "Moreover, the Kirnbergerian temperament, as already mentioned, was never generally adopted, and for that very reason the system of characteristics derived from it could never claim general validity." In a similar vein, shortly thereafter it is remarked that "equal temperament has superseded all others for about forty years."[39] Kirnberger's temperament therefore was in 1848 considered long obsolete.

Unfortunately nothing is known about the one-time practice of professional tuners of keyboard instruments, who were doubtless generally of low social standing. Regional particularities must naturally be taken into consideration just as much as different tunings of organs. But the facts that Johann Joseph Fux as early as 1725 spoke out unequivocally in favor of equal temperament, and that some printings of the mentioned treatises by Fritz and Wolf were published also in Vienna, justify the conclusion that this tuning was in use without interruption since the eighteenth century, at least in the Viennese cultural circle. It can further be inferred from the sources cited that Kirnberger's tuning was preeminent only among unequal temperaments, but was by no means used generally in the second half of the eighteenth century, and only seldom in the nineteenth.

---

[38]"Ketzerische Rhapsodieen" III, col. 531f
[39]"Ketzerische Rhapsodieen" IV, col. 534.

Eva Badura-Skoda

ON THE HISTORY OF MUSICAL INSTRUCTION IN THE AUSTRIAN BAROQUE

The upheavals caused in the sixteenth century by the Reformation led to some of the most significant changes which musical instruction has undergone in the German-speaking countries. The pronouncedly democratic element in Luther's teachings resulted in the concept of a wide-ranging education for the common man, and the general improvement of schooling must be counted among the most important achievements of Protestantism. It is a known fact that Luther devoted his particular attention to the education of the young. Again and again he concerned himself with the cultivation of existing schools and with the establishment of new educational institutions. In his statement *To All City Councillors in German Lands Regarding Establishment and Maintaining of Christian Schools* and in his *Sermon on Adhering to Children's Schooling*, he designed an educational program that bore rich fruit wherever his doctrines found a following.[1] The aristocracy and civic authorities took part in the founding and expansion of schools, and new

---

[1] See G. Schünemann, *Geschichte der deutschen Schulmusik* (Leipzig, 1928), 78ff.

Eva Badura-Skoda's many publications focus especially on performance practice problems and on Vienna in the Classic period, and she has prepared editions of music by Mozart, Haydn and Schubert. In 1986 she was decorated by the Austrian government with the Ehrenkreuz für Kunst und Wissenschaft.

school regulations were adopted by order of sovereigns. It was Luther again who demanded not only catechism but singing instruction for children, day by day, or at least every Sunday, for "Musica is a gracious discipline and taskmaster, which renders us kindlier, more compassionate, docile and lenient."[2] In music Luther saw a divine power of enduring value, a guidance for life. Thus he postulated that it be regarded a major subject of schooling. He stated: "A schoolmaster must be able to sing, otherwise he is not worth his salt."[3]

The Protestant church had spread not only within Germany (as understood in the modern sense), but soon also enveloped Austrian territory. A Roman complaint of 1620, coming from the Jesuit priest Conzenius, to the effect that Luther's songs had corrupted more souls than his writings and sermons,[4] shows how truly Luther had recognized the educational effect of music. While the Habsburg dynasty strictly held to Roman Catholicism, the numerous wars against the Magyars and Turks had compelled the Emperor to seek help from all denominations and had prevented a determined stand against the expanding Protestantism.

The Reformation found its main support in the aristocracy and the well-to-do citizenry. It was owing to their initiative that new schools were established throughout Austria, with the exception of Vienna. By the middle of the sixteenth century it was not only Protestant ministers who were appointed, but also Protestant school teachers from Württemberg, Swabia, and northern Germany. Schools for writing and arithmetic, so-called German Schools, were instituted in smaller places; community and regional schools grew in larger cities such as Linz, Klagenfurt and Graz. While the number of students in Protestant schools increased through the growing interest of Protestant citizenry, the Catholic convent schools declined. As early as 1570 there were almost no schools attached to the monasteries of Upper and Lower Austria. The few independent Catholic schools passed into Protestant hands or closed because of dwindling enrolment.

---

[2]*Luthers Tischreden*, in *Martin Luthers Werke: Kritische Gesamtausgabe* (Weimar,1883) I, Nr. 968. "Musika ist eine holde Disziplin und Zuchtmeisterin, so die Leute gelinder und sanftmütiger, sittsamer und vernünftiger machet."

[3]Preface to the *Geistliche Gesangbüchlein* (Wittenberg, 1524). "Ein Schulmeister muss singen können, sonst sehe ich ihn nicht an."

[4]"Hymni Lutheri animas plures quam scripta et declamationes occiderunt," quoted in K. Anton, *Luther und die Musik* (Zwickau, 1928), 3.

With the Imperial reform of 1567, an attempt was made to check the disintegration of cloister schools. And there were requests from bishops to the Emperor or Archduke for support in their routine inspections of parishes and schools—requests which were honored with good results. Thus the effects of the Counter Reformation began to be strongly felt. Not only the parishes but also the schools became a battleground for the warring denominations. The Protestant aristocracy began to fear for the existence of its churches and schools and asked the Emperor at the Diet for official tolerance of Lutheran ministers and teachers. In 1564, under the reign of Maximilian II, an agreement was actually reached by which authorities in Lower Austria were assured of religious freedom in exchange for considerable payments of Imperial debts.[5] A similar agreement was reached for Upper Austria in 1568. Archduke Karl saw himself obliged to follow suit with a settlement concluded in 1578 for the regions of Styria, Kärnten and Krain at a meeting in Bruck an der Mur.[6] Yet only slightly later, immediately after the ascension of the Emperor Rudolf II, Habsburg's persecution of non-Catholic clergy and teachers began in earnest, for Rudolf—like his brother, the Archduke Ernst, who was given administrative power over Lower Austria—had been raised in Catholic Spain. Statistics compiled by Cardinal Melchior Khlesl, *spiritus rector* of the Counter Reformation in Lower Austria, show that as early as 1578 the number of Catholic parishes had risen again to more than 940, whereas that of Protestant parishes had sunk to 165. Jesuit priests from Spain, hastily summoned, were enabled, with help from the Emperor and Archduke, to organize their convents throughout the Imperial lands, and they soon began to open Catholic schools.

By the beginning of the seventeenth century, the Counter Reformation had succeeded almost everywhere, which caused a stifling of the musical life and general culture of the Reformation. On occasion this success was impeded by peasant revolts and the vicissitudes of war. Some proudly resisting village schools managed to retain their Protestant schoolmasters until the middle of the seventeenth century. Local

---

[5]G. Strakosch-Grassmann, *Geschichte des österreichischen Unterrichtswesens"* (Vienna, 1905), 17.

[6]See R. Peinlich, "Geschichte des Gymnasiums in Graz: II. Periode, Collegium, Gymnasium und Universität der Jesuiten," in *Programme des Gymnasiums in Graz 1869–1874* (Graz, n.d.).

authorities often refused financial support to schools unless they were granted freedom in choosing their teachers. But by the second half of the seventeenth century, they could only choose from among Catholic personnel if they did not want to lose their jurisdiction.

Initially the Jesuits working in Austria followed the ascetic principles of their order in not granting a place to the arts in their curriculum. Soon, however, they proved prudent enough in their battle for the recognition of Catholic tenets to provide a place for church music within their schools and to assign music, in fact, a preeminent function. This was not in keeping with the ideas of their order, but it assured them of considerable popularity in Austria.

Whereas in village churches the Catholic cantor (in Austria, *regens chori*) taught the children Psalms and sacred songs and began to form church choirs, the Catholic Latin Schools for the upper grades organized major urban centers of music. Now music became part of the daily instruction, as in the Protestant north. When, about 1600, almost all civic Protestant schools were closed, in keeping with Imperial mandates, musical instruction returned generally to the hands of Catholic orders. Only a few cities could afford to keep their independent writing and arithmetic schools or even *gymnasia*, but an increasing number of cloister schools now opened their doors. Though it was effectively suppressed, the Reformation thus exerted a lasting influence upon civic and local schools in Austria: by 1600 the awareness of the importance of general schooling had grown immensely in comparison with pre-Reformation times, and the need for maintaining schools was more readily recognized by the population.

Regional governments were on the whole interested only in keeping the instruction under Catholic control; they were interested to a lesser extent in maintaining "German" (that is, lower) schools. It was usually left to the communities to further or neglect their schools. They received no financial support. This reveals the negative side of the Counter Reformation. The impoverishment of the population caused by political unrest, by diseases and epidemics as well as by the peasant revolts and turmoil of the Thirty Years' War, resulted in the closing of many German schools. The Thirty Years' War inflicted immense damage on countries north of the Danube. Yet the southern regions of Austria,

Styria, Kärnten, Krain, and the eastern parts of Lower Austria suffered no less through Hungarian and Turkish invasions.

Our sources for the instruction given in the lower and middle schools of the seventeenth and early eighteenth centuries are the visitation reports preserved in the deaneries and diocese offices. At the beginning of the seventeenth century, the inspections were mainly concerned with the religious aspects of instruction; but later they extended to general pedagogical matters. The re-entry of Catholic rule meant at first a lowering of educational aims. The ambitious progress of the sixteenth-century humanistic educators disappeared, primarily with the result that Latin was deemed less and less important as part of general schooling. Increasingly, teachers not trained at a university but at a *gymnasium* received appointments. Nevertheless, it was expected that they should be good singers and generally experienced in music. By 1700 we encounter a sizeable number of aristocratic and civic endowments established for the cultivation of church music instruction. It was through these endowments that the costs for an enlarged school music program or the salary of an organist were defrayed. Often it was assumed that a teaching position was joined to an organist's post.[7]

Whereas the Catholic orders generally showed little concern for the middle and lower schools, toward the end of the seventeenth century numerous *gymnasia* emerged from monasteries, and not only under Jesuit rule. In addition to the Jesuits, it was primarily the order of the Benedictines, who held numerous possessions and monasteries in Austria, and that of the Piarists that guided the rise of Catholic cloister schools. Yet the Jesuits not only directed *gymnasia*, but they soon presided over universities and founded seminaries. The University of Salzburg, established by the Benedictines, formed an exception.

The need for choirboys and instrumentalists in church orchestras and orchestras of the aristocracy was served in the eighteenth century largely through students at community and cloister schools, and the schoolmaster gained favor in his community whenever he was able to add to the execution of his organist's duties the performance of a Sunday mass with voices and instruments, rendering the service more festive.

---

[7]G. Strakosch–Grassmann, *Geschichte*, 79.

We may take it for granted that in those cloister schools which offered elementary instruction, music held a special place in the curriculum, so that at least a small number of their boys could serve in the church choir. Especially in Bohemia and Moravia, the musical training in the elementary grades must have been exceptionally good.

When Burney travelled through Upper and Lower Austria in 1772, he observed, to his surprise, two-part and three-part singing among the country population. Until the abolition of serfdom in 1780, liveried servants in Bohemia and Moravia were as a rule expected to be knowledgeable in music and to be capable of vocal or instrumental performance in order to qualify for their duties. Only this fact can explain why so many members of the aristocracy were able to maintain their own musical establishments. In order to assure advancement in service for their children, members of the population, again primarily in Bohemia and Moravia, were more interested in their musical school training than in the instruction of basic subjects such as reading, writing and arithmetic. "Musical ability served as a criterion for acceptance into a convent, it guaranteed sustenance in the cities and leisure for studies, and opened prospects of a secure future."[8] Thus the schoolmaster had to be first and foremost a musician. "Their value and esteem was determined by their musical talent; therefore general school training became a neglected matter, of little consequence, but music instruction, in the morning and afternoon, was all the more industriously pursued."[9]

The clerical orders entrusted with school instruction during the High Baroque were primarily Jesuits, Piarists and the Ursuline nuns. Not infrequently schools or seminaries were also attached to the monasteries of Benedictines, Augustinian, Dominicans, Franciscans, Premonstratensians and Cistercians. But among all of these, the Jesuit order was the most active and powerful in seventeenth- and eighteenth-century Austria. It was not only the largest with regard to membership and institutions, but also the strongest financially, and the one most

---

[8] *Allgemeine Musikalische Zeitung Leipzig* II (1800): 491. "Die Musik war die Empfehlung für die Aufnahme ins Kloster, Musik verschaffte in den Städten gute Versorgung und Muße zu den Studien, sie eröffnete ihnen Aussichten in eine glückliche Zukunft."
[9] Ibid. "Der Wert und der Grad der Achtung dieser Leute wurde bloss nach ihren musikalischen Talenten bestimmt, daher wurde der Kinder-Unterricht als Nebensache nachlässig, aber desto fleissiger, und zwar früh und nachmittags, der Unterricht in der Musik betrieben."

clearly favored by the house of Habsburg. Around 1600, numerous establishments of other orders were secularized by Imperial decree, their possessions being placed at the disposition of the Jesuits. In 1621, Jesuits in Judenburg took over an Augustinian monastery and immediately opened a grammar school. In St. Veith an der Glan, a Franciscan possession was handed over by Imperial order to the Klagenfurt Jesuits.[10]

As has been mentioned, the Austrian Jesuits had soon reversed their precepts against music and accorded it a stature similar to that assigned by the Protestants. But other orders had likewise shown interest in music and had readily followed the trend of cultivating not only sacred but also secular music. This spurred the Jesuits to giving greater attention to dramatic music, and it drew them into the general intense cultural activity of the High Baroque. By stressing the cultivation of the school drama—invariably with elaborate music, at times resulting in veritable operas—the Jesuit *gymnasia*, with their choral and instrumental instruction, became foremost musical institutions at the beginning of the eighteenth century. This is borne out by the preserved curricula of Jesuit seminaries and boarding schools, and by the well-known fact that foremost Austrian musical figures such as Johann Joseph Fux, Christoph Willibald Gluck, Florian Gassmann and Leopold Mozart attended Jesuit seminaries. Nevertheless, it had required characteristic Jesuit cunning to circumvent the regulations of the order. Intense musical activity stood in clear contrast to the rules laid down by St. Ignatius of Loyola, who had refused music a place in the school. They found a way out by the establishment of seminaries, which meant that music was introduced *outside* the actual school curriculum.[11]

Musical splendor is inseparable from the Baroque. Every event was given rich musical elaboration. Since especially in the larger cities the Jesuits rarely passed up an opportunity for festive display, their musically qualified seminarians had to perform many additional services. Johann Joseph Fux, in his early period with the Jesuits in Graz, must have seen many strenuous days, which may have been a reason for

---

[10]See B. Hassler, "Geschichte des kärntnerischen Schulwesens" (Dissertation, Vienna, 1929), 33ff.

[11]See M. Wittwer, "Die Musikpflege im Jesuit–Orden, unter besonderer Berücksichtigung der Länder deutscher Zunge" (Dissertation, Greifswald, 1934) 53.

his secret escape noted in the seminary files. At universities, not only the formal observance of graduation, but even intermediate exams were occasions for festivities. In particular, the admittance of new students, the so-called deposition, was musically celebrated.[12] Often the deposition proceedings covered as much as a two-day period, with several processions involving music. Above all, the reception and welcoming celebrations of members of the Imperial family gave rise to great jubilation in Jesuit seminaries and other institutions. Unfortunately we know little about the school dramas and operas performed at these events. There are only brief references to be gleaned from the sparsely preserved records and diaries of Jesuit seminarians.[13] Many accounts were lost due to the expulsion of the Jesuits under the Empress Maria Theresia in the third quarter of the eighteenth century.

To give a picture of the manifold musical duties to which Jesuit seminarians had to attend, we might quote the court worship service in Graz. Its unvaryingly elaborate musical frame was provided almost exclusively by the "Ferdinandists" (students of the Ferdinandeum, the Jesuit-directed boarding school and seminary in Graz):

1. High Mass and Vespers for 52 Sundays

2. High Mass and Vespers for all the holy days of the year

3. High Mass, Vespers and preceding services for all festive church gatherings, school and other special events, the Litany to be performed for the congregation at these times *in mausoleo*.

4. The Litany also to be performed at all Sundays and feast days of the year.

5. Instrumental accompaniment to be provided for all the services held at daybreak throughout the Advent season.

6. Solemn Litany, High Mass, Vespers and preceding services throughout the nine feast days of St. Ignatius.

7. The same for the nine feast days of St. Franciscus Xaverius.

8. Solemn Litany for the six Sundays of St. Aloysius; High Mass, Vespers and preceding services on the name day of the Saint.

---

[12]Peinlich, *Programm* 1870, 137.
[13]Wittwer, "Musikpflege," 77ff.

9. Litany for the ten other Sundays of St. Ignatius.

10. On high holidays of Our Lord, such as Christmas, p.p. Litany.[14]

11. Miserere for all Fridays in Lent.

12. Requiem services, and forty-hour fasting service observance p.p. at other solemn holidays such as year's end, Resurrection and Ascension, processions, all court holidays celebrated in the court chapel, as well as university holidays, Holy Week, Christmas midnight service, and memorial services.[15]

Needless to say, the demand for choristers and instrumentalists was especially great at the Imperial court and at courts of princes and bishops. The services of choirboys are listed for the Viennese court chapel as early as the fourteenth century. We have an early seventeenth-century record of regulations for the masters of the chapel, which relates the circumstances of the choirboys' life.[16]

This *Instruction and Order as to the Maintenance of our Chapel Choirboys* indicates that the boys were to be instructed in music every morning and afternoon, by the director of the chapel in person, unless court choristers could be specially assigned to this task. Gifted and industrious students were further to be guided in studies of score reading by the master of the chapel, and to be given organ or other instrumental instruction at the expense of the court. Likewise we gather from documents at the Salzburg archiepiscopal court that "choirboy Coloman Widmann submits to the Princely Ruler a plea for lessons on the bassoon and other instruments."[17] The Bishop of Passau maintained a small court chapel that included four discantists. Normally these were taught by the cantor, who also supplied rather meager room and board.

---

[14]P.p. means *praemissis praemittendis* ("after attending to the necessary preliminaries").

[15]Grazer Diözesan-Archiv III. A XLIII/o, quoted in P.R. Allinger, *Studien zur steirischen Musikgeschichte* (Vienna, 1937).

[16]Haus– Hof– und Staatsarchiv Wien, Hofstaatsfaszikel, Hofkammer–Archiv Ms. 189, folio 139v–153; see A Smijers,"Die kaiserliche Hofmusikkapelle," *Studien zur Musikwissenschaft* VI (1919): 157.

[17]H. Spies, "Die Tonkunst in Salzburg in der Regierungszeit des Fürsten und Erzbischofs Wolf–Dietrich von Raitenau (1587-1612)" I, *Mitteilungen der Gesellschaft für Salzburger Landeskunde* LXXI (1931): 25. "Kapelljung Coloman Widmann bittet, hochfürstliche Gnaden wollen ihn auf dem Vagott oder anderen Instrumenten lernen lassen."

The Innsbruck Court Chapel choirboys and other members received similar sustenance. When in 1724 the Innsbruck court music was disbanded by order of Karl VI, all court musicians found themselves at loose ends. Upon demand of the Viennese court, however, the five chapel choirboys were admitted to the Jesuit "Nicolaihaus" in Innsbruck.

While the private lodging of court chapel boys offered the advantage of close proximity for teacher and student, there were obvious disadvantages when the master of the chapel began to tire of the constant supervision or when his was not a well-regulated household. Thus the choirboys were at times placed in clerical institutions or in the seminaries for the priests, or else arrangements were made for a special chapel house such as the Rupertinum in Salzburg, founded by the Archbishop Max Gandolf von Kuenburg (1661–1688), in which a total of twelve choir boys could receive their tutelage at a given time.

The choirboys were trained not only in music, but also in general subjects. This is evident from old expense accounts that show entries for books needed by the boys "ad humaniora" as well as from salary items for "chapel boy schoolmasters." Yet there was little time for the youngsters' academic studies, since they needed to perform both at court and church, and since musical instruction, especially the study of new works, required their primary attention. With the developments of the later eighteenth century, the preponderance of a homophonic style and the ease afforded by modern notation, the demands placed upon them decreased, so that they found greater opportunity for instrumental studies, and also for studies in Latin.

Through the years of *gratis* instruction in music, of which the choirboys of the Imperial and princely chapels could avail themselves, the course of their lives was often determined in that they became professional musicians. Some of them received court appointments in their turn, among them Joseph Haydn. In an autobiographical sketch, Haydn gave a brief description of his choirboy days:

> In my seventh year, the late Capellmeister Reutter, on a journey that took him through Hainburg, happened to hear my weak but pleasant voice. He took me immediately to the chapel house where I, aside

from studies in the art of singing, was taught on the clavier and the violin by very good masters. I then sang soprano at St. Stephen's as well as at the court with much success until my eighteenth year.[18]

It does not need to be stressed that music was often taught privately during the Baroque era. Private tutoring can be traced as an indispensable means of instruction through all centuries. Girls, above all, had to rely upon private lessons, for only very rarely was it possible for them to attend a school. On the other hand, music was a mandatory part of a girl's good education. Boys, as well, for reasons of high birth or poverty, often learned the rudiments of music through private guidance. It is obviously not easy to find documentation of private music study in past centuries, except that autobiographical statements of musicians often make mention of pedagogical chores. In this connection we therefore need to refer to these documents.

At the waning of the Baroque period, in the 1750s, the Empress Maria Theresia appointed a body of commissioners to deal with school reform in the Austrian lands. When this group had completed its mission in 1774, having assured that aside from mandatory school attendance, a mandatory basic curriculum was instituted, illiteracy had all but disappeared. Yet musical instruction had lost the primary place it had held in the schools of the Austrian Baroque. In subsequent decades, it deteriorated and sank in most of the public schools to the low level it still holds in our century. Private music instruction, however, greatly gained in importance, and to it, above all, music in the Imperial Vienna of the nineteenth century owed its flourishing life.

That in all segments of the population there were always devotees to be found in the eighteenth century is evident from contemporary accounts of the nobility's predilection for music, as well as from Burney's Austrian travel diary of 1774:

---

[18]Cited in W. Kahl, *Selbstbiographien deutscher Musiker des 18. Jahrhunderst*, Facsimiles of Early Biographies V (Amsterdam, 1972): 84. "In den 7ten Jahr meines alters hörte der Seel: Herr Capell Meister v: Reutter in einer durchreise durch Haimburg von ungefähr meine schwache doch angenehme stime, Er nahm mich alsogleich zu sich in das Capell Hauss, allwo ich nebst dem Studiren die singkunst das Clavier, und die Violin von sehr guten Meistern erlernte. ich sang allda sowohl bey St: Stephan als bey Hof mit grossen Beyfall bis in das 18te Jahr meines alters den Sopran. . ."

At this place the soldiers, and almost all the young people that were walking by the water side, were frequently singing, and never in less than two parts.... It is not easy to account for this facility of singing in different parts, in the people of one country, more than in those of another: whether it arises in Roman Catholic countries from the frequency of hearing music sung in parts, in their churches, I cannot say; but of this I am certain, that in England it costs infinite trouble, both to the master and scholar, before a young practitioner in singing is able to perform, with firmness, an under part to the most simple melody imaginable; and I never remember hearing the ballad singers, in the streets of London, or in our country towns, attempt singing in two different parts.[19]

---

[19] Charles Burney, *The Present State of Music in Germany...* I, Monuments of Music and Music Literature in Facsimile, series 2, CXVII (facs. of 1775 ed., New York, 1969): 203–4.

Peter Williams

TOWARDS A CLOSE READING OF CARL PHILIPP EMANUEL BACH

The problem for most of us in trying to understand what a composer or theorist knew and assumed—in trying to *contextualize* him, as literary studies would call it today—is that we are unlikely to know enough about him. To discover "where somebody is coming from" requires us to know a very great deal, not only of music theory or cultural history or biographical documentation but a great deal of *music*. A lifetime would not introduce us to all the music known to Carl Philipp Emanuel Bach, and even if it did, we would not have the real narrowness of understanding that alone seems to give us close intimacy to music. Clearly, he was brought up from an earliest age in a phenomenally active musical family environment, and it is no idly romantic notion on our part to imagine that that family lived, breathed and ate music as no one today ever did or could. The environment in which J. S. Bach lavished so much effort on his beloved son Wilhelm Friedemann and gave due encouragement to Philipp Emanuel and the other sons, is not easily grasped by us, nor has it been for nearly two centuries now.

Previous admirers of the Bach family have often been speculative and even rather sentimental (attributing weight to feelings they are not

---

Peter Williams is Arts and Sciences Distinguished Professor of Music at Duke University and Director of the Center for Studies in Performance Practice in the Graduate School there. Among his many writings on the study and performance of keyboard music are The Organ Music of J. S. Bach, *3 vols. (Cambridge University Press, 1980–84) and* The Organ in Western Culture, 750–1250 *(Cambridge University Press, 1993).*

close enough to define accurately), while more recent scholarship has tended to avoid the personal impact and stick to musicological documentation. But behind the bits of documentation lay that famous hectic household, a veritable beehive of activity (Philipp Emanuel's word was *dovecot*), difficult for us to imagine because we are *college people* in a sense totally unknown to the Bachs. Our college notions of education, of literacy, of a polite regard for the arts, and of a more or less passive and (by Bachian standards) part-time involvement with music, mean we cannot know from personal experience what such involvement with music amounted to. No doubt a useful approach would be to see the family not as college-educated, middle class musicians but as guildsmen: the family business was not making shoes or goldsmithing but playing the organ or being a *Stadtpfeifer*. This was the business sons were expected to take up, though perhaps social betterment was an increasingly important aim and the reason why young Sebastian's elder brother confiscated (if he did) that little keyboard codex. (Because if you discouraged a child from exclusive interest in keyboard music, which could only lead to a cantorship at best, he might develop violin and other studies, enter the opera world and become a city's music director, as Telemann did?) Times were always changing, of course, so that Wilhelm Friedemann and Philipp Emanuel did become college students and unwittingly contributed to that historical development whereby guild apprenticeship gradually gave way to liberal education, with what ultimate benefit to us all is hard to say. But they had the best of both worlds: liberal education and constant musical activity in a household full of music—contact with other musicians, students and senior choirboys coming in and out, many visitors, publishers, clergy, something of a retail trade in selling music and instruments (not enormous, but telling), fixed schedules of rehearsal and auditions (singers, instrumentalists), and no doubt discussions about up-to-date music especially in the 1730s when the three eldest sons were looking for employment and their father was evidently eager to learn about German-Italian opera. It is this sheer, massive amount of musical activity that one should bear in mind as one traces the development taking place in Philipp Emanuel's understanding. As a young professional, away from the dovecot and on his own, he must have had less, not more stimulus.

In turning to some samples from Philipp Emanuel's writing, we could also usefully ponder the word *influence*, a word everyone (from earliest written assignments as young students onwards) uses and takes for granted. What exactly does it mean for a composer to be "influenced," how does it come about, what form does it take, why does it take that form and not another, is it (as historians need to ask about any document) witting or unwitting? Experience may suggest that influence is often specific rather than general; we should speak not so much of Corelli's influence on Handel as the influence of Corelli's Op. V or Op. VI on Handel, even of specific movements or contrapuntal types within Corelli's Op. V or Op. VI. On the other hand, it is possible to overdo this, and some scholars even use the word *database* for what they see as specific influences; for example, a Vivaldi Concerto op III is a database for J. S. Bach's Organ Sonata in G major BVW 530. This is indeed specific and therefore useful, but the problem is that here too, in the case of the Source *A* that is supposed to have influenced Piece *B* , there have also been huge backlogs of previous influence. Vivaldi's Op. III did not exist out of the blue. It too is the bearer of countless allusions, witting and unwitting, countless details of harmony or structure that could be found in music which he can be safely assumed to have known. The lines of knowledge have to be traced far enough back for one to be able to say anything trustworthy about "influence," and even recognizing everyday common knowledge—the kind of detail everyone would be familiar with—is curiously difficult, more than one would think.

Let us begin with one of Philipp Emanuel's most famous contributions to music studies, his remarks on keyboard fingering as it affects the thumb. Clearly, in any account of the changing nature of keyboard music and keyboard playing between, say, the virginalists and the classical pianists—between the twin peaks of John Bull and Carl Czerny—Philipp Emmanuel's position would be amongst the most significant. This is so because of what he knew about older music (because of whose son he was!) and because of what he suggests about new trends and the musical priorities of the later eighteenth century.

> My late father told me how in his youth he heard great men who used the thumb only when it was necessary for big spans. But as he lived during a time when gradually a striking alteration in musical

taste was coming about, so he was compelled to think out for himself a much more complete use of the fingers, particularly the thumb which, in addition to other good uses, is indispensable primarily in the difficult keys. He thought out how to use the thumbs as Nature intended them to be used. By this means they were promoted from their previous inactivity to being the principal finger.

As this new king of fingering is so made that with it one can easily bring about at the right time everything that is possible, I am taking it here as the foundation.[1]

Now at face value, everything that he says here is very reasonable and, as we know, something of a foundation for the detail he goes into in his book. Not only his further remarks on fingering but also what he says about ornaments and figured-bass playing later in the book, assume this foundation of what we might call the "versatile thumb." But there are several important implications that raise questions. Firstly, the historical point, namely that his father's seniors used the thumb only for stretches. But stretches of what? I assume he means chords rather than widely spaced contrapuntal lines, since at least in the overwhelming amount of music that has come down to us, counterpoint (organ fugues and the like) rarely did pass beyond narrow confines of compass and stretch. Part of the skill in composing a fugue was to keep it within a certain compass; this was still true for the *Art of Fugue*. It seems to me a point of some interest that in, say, a Praeludium of Dietrich Buxtehude, the thumb could well be less necessary in the fugal sections than in the toccata sections, for this may imply that articulation as between prelude and fugue was customarily somewhat different and in fact consciously varied. What Philipp Emmanuel is after is uniform flexibility, and this is a new development—not the flexibility but the uniformity, the levell-

---

[1]C. P. E. Bach, *Versuch über die wahre Art das Clavier zu Spielen* I (Berlin, 1753): 17: "Mein seeliger Vater hat mir erzählt, in seiner Jugend grosse Männer gehört zu haben, welche den Daumen nicht eher gebraucht, als wenn es bey grossen Spannungen nöthig war. Da er nun einen Zeitpunckt erlebt hatte, in welchem nach und nach eine gantz besondere Veränderung mit dem musicalischen Geschmack vorging: so wurde er dadurch genöthiget, einen weit vollkommnern Gebrauch der Finger sich auszudencken, besonders den Daumen, welcher ausser guten Diensten hauptsächlich in den schweren Tonarten gantz unentbehrlich ist, so zu gebrauchen, wie ihn die Natur gleichsam gebraucht wissen will. Hierdurch ist er auf einmahl von seiner bisherigen Unthätigkeit zu der Stelle des Haupt-Fingers erhoben worden.

Da diese neue Finger-Setzung so beschaffen ist, das man damit alles möglich zur bestimmten Zeit leicht herausbringen kan; so lege ich solche hier zum Grunde."

ing-out for the sake of other Enlightenment details such as tempo contrast. One sees levelling-out too in the area of tuning and temperament.

Note that Philipp Emanuel says his father told him. Now of course we do not know that this is untrue, and again on the face of it, it is very likely. But it is surely true too that Philipp Emanuel knew about another major book that had raised these issues: Johann Joachim Quantz's book on the flute, published in the same city a year before Emanuel's *Versuch* and published incidentally with much the same title.[2] Presumably both books were in preparation in or around the court at Potsdam at much the same time. Now Quantz, when discussing German keyboard playing in general, refers in particular to the old Netherlanders, and while this has mostly been taken to denote the Dutch legacy of Sweelinck, it is very likely that for a resident Berliner, *Netherlands* could include all the low-lying lands of northwest Germany (like *Frisia* for the Romans). It is as a successor to these that Sebastian "brought to perfection" the art of playing keyboard instruments. Now Quantz was Emanuel's senior at Potsdam, the director of music, the only one allowed to praise the king's playing. It is not far-fetched to imagine that Philipp Emanuel was making the same point in his book as Quantz was in his, but now in a more personal form—the player recently admired in print by Emanuel's chief was of course Emanuel's father. Quantz's assistant, his continuo-player, could speak with more authority on the late composer whom Quantz himself had gone to some trouble to praise. Establishing such authority would have been important to Philipp Emanuel, as one can easily imagine, though one might also wonder what Quantz's evidence was—those performances of Sebastian at Potsdam in 1747 at which he was presumably present? Or something Emanuel himself had told him? In any case, what would they tell us about Sebastian's style of playing while he was writing most of his keyboard music thirty years before?

One might also wonder what "great men" of the past Philipp Emanuel's hearsay (for this is what it was) was understood to include. Did he mean northern masters like Buxtehude and Reincken or the more homely, local talents like Johann Kuhnau and Friedrich Wilhelm Zachau? Perhaps these local players of the Province of Thuringia, to one lineage of which J. S. and C. P. E. Bach belonged, were less strict,

---

[2] J. J. Quantz, *Versuch einer Anweisung, die Flöte traversiere zu spielen* (Berlin, 1752).

less classical, more pragmatic, more inclined to use their fingers howsoever they could? Despite Sebastian's well-known studies in north Germany and the high incidence of north German music found in the sources associated with him, it could well be that the Kuhnaus and Zachaus of his native province had at least as strong an influence, even though they may not be so admired today. (It could be a mistake to assume "great" composers had stronger influence on a young composer than "lesser.") The very diverse cultures of which "Germany" was made up could well mean that the central German pragmatism that produced J. S. Bach had the strength of native influence comparable to the strength of, say, English tradition for Purcell.

Then there is the question of the use of the thumb itself. Now it can not be true that Sebastian and hence his second son were alone in advocating the versatile use of thumbs. I know that Emanuel does not say that they were, but there is an "implication of patent" about his remarks and one that is not justified. Surely he was not unaware of what Rameau had written over a quarter of a century before:

> [in fast scale passages] one need only get used to passing the thumb under whichever finger one wishes, and to passing one of the other fingers above the thumb. This method is excellent, particularly when one comes across sharps and flats.[3]

Note that Rameau too makes the point about thumbs being particularly excellent when one is playing in the "difficult tonalities," though he uses different words from Philipp Emanuel. Yet is it the case that remoter keys require more frequent use of the thumb? All things being equal, does F sharp major require the thumb more than F major in the idioms of Rameau and the Bachs? In conventional piano-fingering, white-note keys like C have their own needs, if anything calling on strong fourth fingers less often than remoter keys like E flat minor: it is this that makes the latter difficult for children, even in the form of scales. Of course, Carl Czerny's parnassus of twenty-four equal keys was not quite what Philipp Emanuel was talking about.

---

[3]J.-P. Rameau, Preface to *Pièces de Clavecin* (Paris, 1724): "il n'y a qu'à s'accoutumer à passer le 1. par-dessous tel autre doigt que l'on veut, et à passer l'un de ces autres doigts par-dessus le 1. Cette maniere est excellente, sur-tout quand il s'y rencontre des *Dièzes* ou des *Bemols*."

At much the same time that Emanuel's *Versuch* was in the press, his late father's obituary was being composed, partly from information supplied by Emanuel. Now the obituary had also tried to summarize what new fingering methods were owed to Sebastian:

> With him all fingers were used equally... He had worked out for himself so comfortable a fingering that he did not find it hard to surmount the greatest difficulties with the most fluent ease. Before him, the most renowned keyboard-players in Germany and other countries had made little use of the thumb.[4]

Naturally, an obituary celebrates its regretted subject as warmly as it can, and there can be no doubt that Philipp Emanuel (more than the other sons?) took his father as something of a reference point and contributed to the hero worship as much as any other pupil. Although the *Versuch* had a very different tone from the *Obituary*, it is as if it takes the *Obituary* commendation a little farther, for is there not a hint that the mantle of authority is falling on his, Emanuel's, shoulders? His father, the late master but new hero of German art, did so-and-so and he, Philipp Emanuel, is continuing the line by basing much of a treatise on it, now adapted to a newly stylish kind of music. One can often find in Philipp Emanuel Bach an implication that the Apostolic Succession has passed to him.

In order not to overstress this point, consider the next example:

> One plays with arched fingers and relaxed muscles... He who plays with extended fingers and stiff muscles experiences, as well as an ungainliness that results naturally from this, also a serious problem, namely that he is distancing the other fingers (because of their [stretched out] length) far from the thumb...[5]

---

[4]Obituary of J. S. Bach, in *Dokumente zum Nachwirken Johann Sebastian Bachs 1750–1800* (= *Bach-Dokumente* III) ed. H.-J. Schulze (Leipzig, 1972), 80–93: "Alle Finger waren bey ihm gleich geübt... Er hatte sich so eine bequeme Fingersetzung ausgesonnen, dass es ihm nicht schwer fiel, die grössten Schwierigkeiten mit der fliessendesten Leichtigkeit vorzutragen. Vor ihm hatten die berühmtesten Clavieristen in Deutschland und andern Ländern, dem Daumen wenig zu schaffen gemacht."

[5]C. P. E. Bach, *Versuch*, p. 18: "Man spielt mit gebogenen Fingern und schlaffen Nerven... Wer mit ausgestreckten Fingern und steifen Nerven spielt, erfährt ausser der natürlich erfolgenden Ungeschicklichkeit, noch einen Haupt-Schaden, nehmlich er entfernt die übrigen Finger wegen ihrer Länge zu weit von dem Daumen..."

This too is a fair point—Philipp Emanuel goes on to say that those who do not use the thumb are generally inclined to play stiffly, while those who do cannot play stiffly even if they wanted to (a remark many teachers would find it hard to agree with). Now had he been constantly on the lookout to take credit from his father—even keen to establish the Apostolic Succession—he could have invoked him again here, but does not. J.N. Forkel, indebted to Philipp Emanuel for his Bach biography, accredited the curved finger, the drawing-in of the fingertips towards the player as the finger leaves the key, to Johann Sebastian Bach.[6] But he did so probably because Quantz had before him.[7] Quantz attributes curved, effortless fingers to Johann Sebastian, while Emanuel does not; there may be a general implication that his father approved such technique, but Emanuel does not emphasize it in his own book. Nevertheless, a general moral emerges very clearly from such point-by-point comparison between what Quantz, Philipp Emanuel and Forkel have written, namely that the interconnection between them renders very doubtful any evidence about Johann Sebastian Bach they appear to offer.

Philipp Emanuel may not have referred to his father in connection with curved fingers, but neither does he note that, again, Rameau had anticipated him in his harpsichord book of 1724:

> The first and fifth fingers, finding themselves at the [front] edge of the keys, make the other fingers curve, so that they can likewise find themselves at the edge of the keys... one should not then straighten nor curve them any further.[8]

I think that in the *Versuch*, Philipp Emanuel never actually refers once to Rameau, and François Couperin's *L'Art de toucher* is mentioned only to be criticized for not using the thumb more for finger-substitution on a held note. But Rameau's curved fingers could not be clearer, and his French buyers would have seen any such remarks (1724) as glosses on

---

[6] J. N. Forkel, *Über Johann Sebastian Bachs Leben, Kunst and Kunstwerk* (Leipzig, 1802).
[7] Quantz, *Versuch*, 232.
[8] Rameau, Preface to *Pièces de Clavecin*: "Le 1 & le 5. se trouvant sur le bord des touches, engagent à courber les autres doigts, pour qu'ils puissent se trouver également sur le bord des touches... on ne doit plus ni les alonger, ni les arondir d'avantage."

what Couperin had written only recently (1716). We should remember, however, that Rameau's remarks occur only in the form of a preface to a volume of harpsichord music, while Philipp Emanuel's thoroughness of exposition (though less than perfectly organized from our post-Enlightenment point of view) puts his *Versuch* on a different footing. Such thoroughness is an aspect of German consciousness in the Age of Enlightenment, one with good pedigree in all the thorough and comprehensive treatises written since Praetorius in 1620, and also one very much *au fait* with the desire to categorize, the systematic marshalling of information, inspiring the French encyclopedia-authors of Philipp Emanuel's generation. It is in the first chapter of the *Versuch* that we find one of the first, if not the first, fully systematic listings of the scales of all major and minor keys. With such a list, players were on the way to the systematic practising of all scales and arpeggios, something still so far from being fixed as a norm by the time of Beethoven's *Emperor Concerto* that he could work novelty from introducing the piano soloist with various arpeggios and chromatic scales.

Certainly as one looked at the German music-writers and theorists of the Enlightenment—C. P. E. Bach, J. P. Kirnberger, Quantz and Forkel in particular—one could frequently recognize French or other sources for many of their more technical, less theoretical points. In J. G. Sulzer's now familiar *General Theory of Fine Arts* (edited in the 1770s), somebody, probably Kirnberger, remarked on Sebastian's physical composure as a player, a player barely moving his body and playing in such a way that you barely saw his fingers move.[9] Forkel took up that idea, saying that his motion came only from the first finger-joint, while the hand itself remained still. Now all this may be quite correct, and Kirnberger certainly saw Johann Sebastian Bach play during his later Leipzig years, and wished later to contrast his composure with the more publicly-minded virtuosi of later decades (though Kirnberger does not put it in these terms). But again, Rameau had also said the following in his preface of 1724:

---

[9] J. G. Sulzer, *Allgemeine Theorie der schönen Künste in einzeln* II (Leipzig, 1774) 1256. Extract in *Bach-Dokumente* III, 215.

> The movement of the fingers takes place at their root [= first joint] ... and never anywhere else... without any other finger or the hand [as a whole] at that moment making the slightest movement.[10]

Now these German writers should not be seen as exceptionally derivative or secretive in their hidden use of earlier material: writing always means using older books. Our problem is that so often this fact of literate life is forgotten and we fail to define influences or contextualize sufficiently. Sometimes, one can do this only to the extent of asking unanswerable questions. For instance, if it is true that the newer virtuosi of Kirnberger's period made a point of obtrusively, graphically moving as they played, are we to take the report that Beethoven too barely seemed to move his hands as his fingers glided over the keys (in a description given to Thayer by the painter W. J. Mähler, who saw him in 1803) as being either (a) a typical view of the genius as someone unlike other people, (b) an atypical view suggesting that Beethoven was a good deal more controlled and classical than the mass-entertaining improvisers of his day, or neither, merely a matter-of-fact remark?

The various German writers from 1750 onwards certainly shared views and ideals; this is what one means when using such a phrase as "The early German Enlightenment." In the Horatian claim that *art is to hide art* lies a distinct philosophical or aesthetic stance, but there is also a strictly technical side: your fingers hide their art by barely moving and therefore being all the more miraculous and mysterious. Philipp Emanuel describes his father's effortless playing at least partly because it was an ideal of the later period. Other indications of Enlightenment attitudes abound in these writings, and we are so used to the prophetic element in Emanuel's music (as acknowledged by some later composers in Germany and Austria, though seldom elsewhere) that we can easily miss the peculiar blend of the traditional and modern in his outlook. That is true of most authors as they amalgamate what they learn from their own experience with what they learn from other authors. In the passages quoted above, there have already appeared some instances of terms and ideas fashionable in the German Enlightenment. In the first

---

[10]Rameau, Preface to *Pièces de Clavecin*: "Le mouvement des doigts se prend à leur racine... & jamais ailleurs... sans qu'aucun autre doigt, ni sans que la main fassent pour lors le moindre mouvement."

quotation, C. P. E. Bach uses the word *nature*, that veritable buzzword of this period in Germany, as in other countries ("... to use the thumbs as *Nature* intended them to be used"), and later, he speaks of "... the ungainliness that results *naturally* from the stretched-out fingers."

These words are specific flags alerting us to the battle-lines being drawn. If we think nothing of them, it is because we are products, beneficiaries, of Philipp Emanuel's bequest, or at least that of his period. One cannot even take what he says here as being true: nature is invoked no more justifiably than it would be by a landscape gardener of the 1750s deliberately planting trees and digging lakes in order to imitate what he claimed to be nature. After all, no kind of cultivated or man-made garden is, in any real sense, more natural than any other, whether it is formal ("artificial") or carefully made not to be ("natural"). Similarly, no kind of keyboard-fingering is of itself more natural than any other; the nature of fingers is not exclusively to be effortless-seeming. Nature cannot herself have intended the thumb to be used on keyboards since keyboards are very sophisticated artefacts of western man, and earlier players even within that culture did not use it, as indeed Philipp Emanuel had himself just pointed out. A word like *Nature*—the use of which has become quite *natural* to us—becomes a stick by which one fashion beats an earlier fashion, as can be seen in any anthology of music-writings.[11] As an experienced keyboard-player knows, one can become so used to the earlier repertories—such as the English virginalists—that indeed it becomes unnatural to use the thumb in them, especially on the very differently designed keyboards of the sixteenth century. Did Philipp Emanuel not know or not care about earlier keyboards?

It is also in remarks about his father that one learns of some of the layers of significance authors of Philipp Emanuel's period would have had in their writings. For example, he says this about his father's practical skills:

> ... he also knew the construction of organs thoroughly... Never has anyone undertaken organ-testing so severely and yet at the same time so fairly. Organ-building as a whole he understood in the highest degree...

---

[11]See, for example, P. Le Huray and J. Day, *Music and Aesthetics in the Eighteenth and Early Nineteenth Centuries* (Cambridge, 1981), 95, 121, 136, 148.

...he also learnt the placement of the orchestra. He knew how to profit well from this experience, together with a naturally [as distinct from "artificially" acquired] good knowledge of architecture as far as it is relevant to sound.

The pure tuning of his keyboard instruments had his greatest attention. He would thank no-one for tuning or quilling his harpsichords.

Any peculiarity of a room he grasped immediately [followed by an anecdote concerning the opera house in Berlin].

The late departed educated his taste through his own efforts. Purely through his own contemplation he was already in his youth the writer of genuine, strong fugues...

In general, however, he did not have the most brilliant good fortune, because he did not do that which was required, namely rove through the world.[12]

Now through these and similar comments move some important motifs. J. S. Bach is said to have understood technical things—organ-construction, tuning, harpsichord-voicing, organ-testing, practical acoustics, orchestral placement—some of which must have been rare skills as the century progressed, although orchestral placement was very much an interest of the symphony composer of the 1770s. At the same time, Emanuel's father understood such basic musical-artistic skills as how to compose fugal counterpoint; and what is more, he had largely taught himself. Now it is not difficult to imagine that composers of his son's generation were less able to boast in either of these areas. They were unlikely to know so much about technicalities because it would

---

[12]C. P. E. Bach (first from *Obituary*, others from *Letters to Forkel*, in *Bach-Dokumente* III [see note 4], 284–89): "...er kannte auch den Bau der Orgeln aus dem Grunde...

... hat er das *arrangement* des Orchesters kennen gelernt. Diese Erfahrung, nebst einer natürlichen guten Kenntnis der Bauart, in wie ferne sie dem Klange nützlich ist... hat er gut zu nutzen gewusst.

Das reine Stimmen seiner Instrumente... war sein vornehmstes Augenmerck. Niemand konnte ihm seine Instrumente zu Dancke stimmen und bekielen...

Jede Ausnahme, was den Ort anlangte, wuste er beym ersten Anblick.

Der seelige hat durch eigene Zusätze seiner Geschmack gebildet. Blos eigenes Nachsinnen hat ihn schon in seinen Jugend zum reinen und starcken Fugisten gemacht...

Ueberhaupt aber hatte er nicht das brillanteste Glück, weil er nicht dasjenige that, welches dazu nöthig ist, nehmlich die Welt durchzustreifen."

have been below their dignity as liberally educated musicians to have been so expert, and they were less likely to have taught themselves than to have roamed from one teacher to another, much as we do today. Thus we do not know exactly how true are any of Philipp Emanuel's remarks because he is writing from the point of view of his generation, and he was out to make a statement that reflected not absolute truth (whatever that could mean), but certain ideals of his own period, often rather *romanticized*, as we now say of his period's poetry and novels. How far his father-hero conformed to these ideals is another question. I am not sure his father *was* such an expert on organs or that a cantor really would have felt it to be a source of pride if he were. Organ-making was a craft, being a cantor was a profession, and as we all know, crafts and professions are by no means blood-brothers. They certainly are not in our post-Enlightenment culture of today.

I am aware that whatever we may now say about Philipp Emanuel is in turn subject to the same principle of period-conditioning: we now contextualize, often as a substitute for real involvement in what someone has said in the past. Particularly interesting as a literary genre, one clearly indicative of its particular period, is the biography, the telling of someone's life and the various desires and motives that went with it. Here, perhaps, contextualizing is at its most useful, acting as a brake on our reception of its enthusiastic message. For example, in praising his father, Emanuel says that he was uniquely gifted in his understanding of organ registration:

> He understood the art of handling organs, of uniting the stops...
> No one understood so well as he the registering of organs... these sciences died out with him.[13]

Notice, by the way, the use of the words *art* and *science* here, themselves very typical words of the period. Now half a century later, C. F. D. Schubart, one of today's most studied writers of the German aesthetic movement of that period, said this in his book on music:

---

[13]*Obituary* and *Letter to Forkel*: "Er verstund... die Art die Orgeln zu handhaben, die Stimmen... mit einander zu vereinigen.

Das Registriren bey den Orgeln wuste niemand so gut, wie er... Diese Wissenschaften sind mit ihm abgestorben."

> He made himself master of the organ's nature; no one has yet imitated him in his understanding of the stops. He mixes them... and thereby produces a wonderful whole.[14]

Only—he did not say it about Johann Sebastian Bach but about Wilhelm Friedemann Bach! In other words, for these German biographers, it was important to be able to show their subjects as having both technical and creative expertise. Of course, they very likely did, though the idea of mixing disparate elements to produce the unified whole (as in Schubart's remarks) is such an Enlightenment motif that one has to flag it as precisely that. As with other, very early biographies in western literature, such as the Lives or *vitae* of early medieval saints, one has to see that the subject's recorded attributes necessarily conformed to the conventions of the biographical mode in question. It was important, for example, to show a saint as curing blindness or even fatally terminated disease. The biography must also conform to literary models such as Suetonius's *Lives of the Caesars* or even the *Gospels*; and *they* conformed to their models. And so on. The form of your information does not necessary consume its content, but it certainly governs it.

There is an additional motif in the last quotation, significant in many of these German books, biographies, histories and encyclopedias: what one might today call the element of national pride, the pushing of German interests in a manner that was really rather new and certainly characteristic of the period. Philipp Emanuel and his friends, when writing the *Obituary* for J. S. Bach, must have been perfectly aware that another German composer, quite as spectacularly gifted as their subject (thus as fine an *exemplum* for the definitions of genius that Kant and others were working on), had already achieved worldly fame and riches in other lands, the riches bringing a higher social level than was ever within the sights of a Lutheran cantor. How could they reconcile the obviously special musical position of Bach with his obviously provincial situation, moreover a milieu to which they too belonged? One answer was: he achieved so much because he taught himself by assiduous observation and emulation, and did not need to write successful operas

---

[14]C. F. D. Schubart, *Ideen zu einer Aesthetik der Tonkunst* (Vienna, 1806), 90: "Der Natur der Orgel hat er sich ganz bemächtiget; sein Registerverständnis hat ihm noch niemand nachgemacht. Er mischt die Register... und bringt dadurch ein bewundernswürdiges Ganzes hervor."

in Hamburg or play with Corelli in Rome, as Handel's biographer described *his* hero as having done at an early age. Another answer lies in the strength of Germany itself, in particular Thuringia, which had produced those generations of Bachs:

> It might be wondered why such excellent men were so little known outside their native land, if one did not consider that these honorable Thuringers were so satisfied with their homeland and with their station that they did not even wish to venture far outside it to seek their fortune. They preferred the favour of the princes in whose areas they were born and of a mass of their loyal countrymen (whom they had close by) to the uncertain signs of approval they would seek from a few, even perhaps jealous, foreigners.[15]

Of course, the *Obituary* authors were not to know that within a few years of their remarks, the first monograph biography of a composer was to be published (John Mainwaring's *Memoirs of Handel*)[16] in which Handel is actually quoted as saying that "he never could endure the thought of staying long at home" in Germany. An irony is that he meant Halle, which, as a major trade-city linked with both Thuringia and Saxony (though not strictly within Saxony), was a good deal more cosmopolitan than the Bach family's Eisenach. Sebastian's bid to succeed Handel's teacher Zachau, and Wilhelm Friedemann's position in that church thirty years later, must have underlined Handel's rise to greater heights in distant lands.

National or provincial pride is not the same as nationalism in the modern sense, but I think we would not quite understand what happened in later eighteenth-century music if we could not somehow interrelate these various motifs in writings—the various definitions of genius and what it was that geniuses had to be shown to be capable of,

---

[15]*Obituary*: "Es würde zu verwundern seyn, dass so brafe Männer, ausser ihrem Vaterlande so wenig bekannt worden; wenn man nicht bedächte, das diese ehrlichen Thüringer mit ihrem Vaterlande, und ihrem Stande so zufrieden waren, dass sie sich nicht einmal wagen wolten, weit ausser demselben ihrem Glücke nachzugehen. Sie zogen den Beyfall der Herren, in deren Gebiete sie gebohren waren, und einer Menge treuherziger Landsleute, die sie gegenwärtig hatten, andern noch ungewissen, mit Mühe und Kosten zu suchenden Lobeserhebungen, weniger, und noch dazu vielleicht neidischer Ausländer, mit Vergnügen, vor."

[16]*Memoirs of the Life of the late George Frederic Handel* (London, 1760).

the nature of natural talent, of industrious self-instruction or self-application, and of the German *Geist*. In proposing that such writers as Philipp Emanuel come with their own baggage of allusions and illusions, their own philosophical agenda and aesthetic stance, one would not reduce their value to us or render it uninteresting and unenlightening. On the contrary, for as one can see with the last example and its hidden allusions (to Handel, to traditional German regard for Italy, to the lessening indebtedness to France, and so on), a better appreciation of the context for remarks made during the period opens up very fruitful lines of enquiry. There is so much that must be learned about these people if we are to grasp the interior meanings, the real meanings, of what they say.

David Beach

THE INFLUENCE OF HARMONIC THINKING ON THE TEACHING OF SIMPLE COUNTERPOINT IN THE LATTER HALF OF THE EIGHTEENTH CENTURY*

When considering the topic of counterpoint instruction in the eighteenth century, the first name to come to my mind—and I suspect to the minds of most knowledgeable musicians—is Johann Joseph Fux. Though one might cite various reasons for the continued influence of his *Gradus ad Parnassum* (1725), my own awareness of and interest in his approach to the teaching of counterpoint is due in large part to the work of two very different individuals. The first is Heinrich Schenker, whose two-part study of strict counterpoint[1] is based on the five-species approach set down by Fux. But, where Fux sought to codify the Palestrina style, Schenker was concerned with presenting in a systematic way the principles of voice leading that transcend the confines of any particular style. This adaptation of Fux's work is the basis for many

---

*An abbreviated version of this paper was read at the joint meeting of the American Musicological Society and the Society for Music Theory, Austin, Texas, 29 October 1989.
[1]Heinrich Schenker, *Counterpoint*, trans. John Rothgeb and Jürgen Thym, ed. John Rothgeb, 2 vols. (New York, 1987).

David Beach *is Professor of Music Theory at the Eastman School of Music and University Dean of Graduate Studies at the University of Rochester. He has published widely on Schenkerian theory and analysis, and eighteenth-century theory.*

courses in simple counterpoint taught at the collegiate level today in North America. The second individual is my esteemed colleague at the Eastman School of Music, Alfred Mann, whose interest in Fux and counterpoint instruction dates back some fifty years. It is Mann who has provided us with English translations of that portion of the *Gradus ad Parnassum* dealing with simple counterpoint—that is, the section presenting the five species in two, three and four parts[2]—and, in a separate volume, the chapters on imitation, fugue and double counterpoint, along with portions of treatises by Marpurg, Albrechtsberger and Martini.[3] He is also responsible for providing us with a translation and commentary of Haydn's abstract of the opening chapters of the Fux treatise in the hand of his student, F. C. Magnus,[4] and, along with others, what I think is a truly remarkable document, the transcription of Thomas Attwood's studies with Mozart in harmony, counterpoint and composition.[5] Finally, Professor Mann has published several studies during the past two decades detailing the connection between Fux and the following composers: J. S. Bach, Martini, Haydn, Mozart, Beethoven and Schubert.[6]

---

[2]Johann Joseph Fux, *The Study of Counterpoint*, translated and ed. Alfred Mann (New York, 1971).

[3]Alfred Mann, *The Study of Fugue* (New York, 1965).

[4]Alfred Mann, "Haydn's Elementarbuch: A Document of Classic Counterpoint Instruction," *The Music Forum* III (1973): 197-237.

[5]*Thomas Attwoods Theorie- und Kompositionsstudien bei Mozart, Neue Mozart-Ausgabe* X (suppl.) 30, 1, ed. Erich Hertzmann, Cecil B. Oldman, Daniel Heartz and Alfred Mann (Kassel, 1965).

[6]*Theory and Practice: The Great Composers as Students and Teachers* (New York, 1987). See also *"Bach und die Fuxsche Lehre: Theorie und Kompositionspraxis,"* in *Johann Sebastian Bach und Johann Joseph Fux*, ed. Johann Trummer and Rudolf Flotzinger (Kassel, 1985), 82-86; "Padre Martini and Fux," in *Festschrift für Ernst Hermann Meyer zum 60. Geburtstag*, ed. Georg Knepler (Leipzig, 1973), 253-55; "Eine Textrevision von der Hand Joseph Haydns," in *Musik und Verlag: Karl Vötterle zum 65. Geburtstag*, ed. Richard Baum and Wolfgang Rehm (Kassel, 1968), 433-37; "Haydn as a Student and Critic of Fux," in *Studies in Eighteenth-Century Music: a Tribute to Karl Geiringer*, ed. H. C. Robbins Landon (New York, 1970), 323-32; "Haydn's Relationship to the *stile antico*," in *Haydn Studies: Proceedings of the International Haydn Conference* (1975), ed. Jens Peter Larsen, Howard Serwer and James Webster (New York, 1981), 374-76; "Zur Kontrapunktlehre Haydns und Mozarts," *Mozart-Jahrbuch* (1978-79), 195-99; "Zum Salzburger Studienbuch," *Mozart-Jahrbuch* (1984/85), 71-74; "Leopold Mozart als Lehrer seines Sohnes," *Mozart-Jahrbuch* (1989), 31-35; "Beethoven's Contrapuntal Studies with Haydn," *The Musical Quarterly* LVI (1970): 711-26—also in *The Creative*

Having acknowledged the value of Fux's work and paid tribute to those, like Mann and Schenker, who have contributed to our understanding of its historical and theoretical significance, I would now like to voice my concern at the lack of attention paid in the recent literature to alternative approaches to counterpoint instruction from the eighteenth century. While I cannot remedy this situation in total, it is my intention in the following study to fill at least a small part of the lacuna. My reason for choosing the present topic is that the study of harmony was a central concern—actually a preoccupation—of that time. But the topic is far too inclusive to cover adequately here, and thus I have decided to focus on those approaches to the teaching of simple counterpoint from the latter half of the century that take harmony as their point of departure and thus break with the established tradition of species counterpoint. These limitations exclude many fascinating topics, for example, Rameau's approach to adding a part to a given melody or bass,[7] or Albrechtsberger's adaptation of Fux.[8] These and other related topics will be explored sometime in the future.[9]

This paper will present the approaches to counterpoint expressed in the writings of the following three theorists: Johann Philipp Kirnberger (1721–1783), Johann Friedrich Daube (1730–1797) and Henrich Christoph Koch (1749–1816). While there are many differences among these three individuals, particularly in their orientations and in their intended audiences, there is a common thread—the study of harmony as a prerequisite to the study of counterpoint. Though their ideas on the subject had little influence, possibly because the relationship of studies in counterpoint to the art of composition was soon to

---

World of Beethoven, ed. Paul Henry Lang (New York, 1971), 209–24; "Haydns Kontrapunktlehre und Beethovens Studien," in *Bericht über den internationalen musikwissenschaftlichen Kongress Bonn 1970*, ed. Carl Dahlhaus, Hans Joachim, Magda Marx-Weber und Günther Massenkeil (Kassel, 1970), 70–74; *Schuberts Studien, Neue Schubert–Ausgabe*, vii (suppl.) 2 (Kassel, 1986).

[7]See, for example, chapters 38 and 41 of his *Traité de l'harmonie* (Paris, 1722).

[8]Johann Georg Albrechtsberger, *Gründliche Anweisung zur Composition* (Leipzig, 1790), chapters 7–22.

[9]Recent research in this area has been done by Joel Lester. See chapter 7, "Harmonic Perspectives on Counterpoint," in his *Compositional Theory in the Eighteenth Century* (Cambridge, MA, 1992).

decline, I find their approaches appropriate to the times, more so than was Fux's, and thus most worthy of our attention.

I. JOHANN PHILIPP KIRNBERGER

Kirnberger's discussion of counterpoint is divided into two main topics: simple counterpoint, which is further divided into plain or equal and embellished or florid; and double counterpoint. The former, which is of concern to us here, is contained in the final two chapters of the initial volume of *Die Kunst des reinen Satzes in der Music* (1771). The latter topic is treated extensively in parts two and three of the second volume of the same work, published in 1776 and 1779 respectively.

While Kirnberger's division of counterpoint is traditional, his approach to it—at least to the teaching of simple counterpoint—clearly is not. Shortly after the opening of the initial chapter on the subject, he makes the following now-famous statement.

> Simple plain counterpoint can be for two, three or more voices. It is best to begin with four voices, because it is not possible to write for two or three voices perfectly until one can do so for four voices. Since complete harmony is in four parts, the harmony in two- and three-part compositions must always be incomplete. Therefore it is impossible to judge with certainty what must be omitted from the harmony in the various situations that arise until one has a thorough knowledge of four-part composition.[10]

Though there is a negative side to this statement, namely, that composition in less than four parts can be viewed in terms of what has been omitted rather than what is there, this should not detract from the significance of the underlying concept. For this is the first and, as far as I know, the only time in the eighteenth century we find a theorist advocating beginning the study of strict counterpoint with four-part harmony.[11] This is not at all a surprising development when one considers how central to music theory the study of harmony had become by this time. What is perhaps surprising is that Kirnberger's idea seems to have fallen pretty much on deaf ears.[12]

---

[10] Johann Philipp Kirnberger, *The Art of Strict Musical Composition*, trans. David Beach and Jurgen Thym (New Haven, 1982), 159.

[11] One exception is Augustus Frederic Christopher Kollmann, whose theoretical writings were based directly on those of Kirnberger. See his *Essay on Musical Harmony* (London, 1796), chapter 13.

[12] In addition to Kollmann (see note 10), see Ernst Friedrich Richter, *Lehrbuch des einfachen und doppelten Kontrapunkts* (Leipzig, 1872).

It is not until a later publication, *Gedanken über die verschiedenen Lehrarten in der Komposition als Vorbereitung zur Fugenkentniss* (1782), which is both a tribute to his teacher, J. S. Bach, and, at the same time, an attack on Fux's method,[13] that we get some clue as to what has led to Kirnberger's approach.

> Johann Sebastian Bach follows a thoroughly pure style in all of his compositions; every piece by him has a definite character which leads to unity. Rhythm, melody, and harmony, in short all that makes a composition really beautiful, he has completely in his power, as evidenced in his practical works. His method is the best because he progresses thoroughly from the easiest step to the most difficult, through which even the step to fugue itself is no more difficult than any other. For this reason, I maintain that Johann Sebastian Bach's method is the only one and the best one. It is regrettable that this great musician has written nothing theoretical about music, and that his teachings have been made available to posterity only through his pupils.
>
> I have sought to reduce the method of the late J. S. Bach to basic principles and to present his instruction to the very best of my ability in my *Kunst des reinen Satzes*.[14]

Though Kirnberger does not specify just what Bach's method is, only that it leads systematically from the easiest to the most difficult step, it would seem from the context that he is referring at least indirectly to Bach's approach to teaching counterpoint. And though there is no direct evidence that Kirnberger's work in its entirety represents Bach's method of teaching, I think we can surmise from the indirect evidence—for example, from the following statement by C. P. E. Bach—that there is some basis for this claim, at least in regard to the reliance on four-part writing as the basis for further study.

---

[13] In some respects this is a most curious work. Why, after not even mentioning Fux in his earlier work, does Kirnberger decide it is time to air his objections, except possibly in answer to some criticism of his own work? Furthermore, despite his objections, it is clear that what follows is derived from Fux. This is reminiscent of his not–so–gentle gibes at Rameau's ideas: the more he objects, the more it becomes apparent to what extent he was influenced by them.

[14] "Thoughts on the Different Methods of Teaching Composition as Preparation for Understanding Fugue," translated with an introduction by Richard B. Nelson and Donald R. Boomgaarden, *Journal of Music Theory* XXX (1986): 75–76.

> ... In composition he started his pupils right in with what was practical, and omitted all the *dry species* of counterpoint that are given by Fux and others. His pupils had to begin their studies by learning pure four-part thorough bass. From this he went to chorales; first he added the basses to them himself, and they had to invent the alto and tenor. Then he taught them to devise the basses themselves. He particularly insisted on the writing out of the thorough bass in [four real] parts.
>
> The realization of a thorough bass and the introduction to chorales are without doubt the best method of studying, as far as harmony is concerned.[15]

Let us return now to Kirnberger's consideration of simple plain counterpoint in four parts. Following a brief review of two matters affecting purity of writing, the avoidance of forbidden octave- and fifth-progressions and the proper treatment of close or open harmony, he elaborates on the following three points: 1) that the harmony must have appropriate variety and diversity along with good continuity; 2) that the progression in all voices, together as well as separate, be strict; and 3) that each voice have a simple and flowing line. This section is followed by a rather brief consideration of writing in three and then in two parts, and finally for five, six and more voices. Though there are many valuable insights in this chapter, particularly in the portion dealing with four-part writing, taken by itself it is not a systematic treatment of the subject suitable for instruction. Rather it must be understood in relation to the preceding chapters.

Kirnberger opens his discussion of embellished or florid simple counterpoint with the following descriptive analogy.

> Simple plain melody, which is called chorale, resembles the common walk, which progresses by equal steps; embellished melody, on the other hand, is analogous to the decorative motions that occur in dances, where each step is embellished.[16]

After developing this idea, he then defines and discusses two main types of embellished counterpoint. The first arises from melodic embellishment, which can be of two kinds: either it results from the harmony

---

[15]From a letter to Johann Nicolaus Forkel (dated January 13, 1775), *The Bach Reader*, ed. Hans T. David and Arthur Mendel (New York, 1966), 279.
[16]Kirnberger, *Art of Strict Musical Composition*, 205.

HARMONIC THINKING AND 18TH-CENTURY COUNTERPOINT 165

(arpeggiation) or from passing motions. Here Kirnberger points out the necessity of understanding harmony in order to distinguish properly between the decorative note (for example, the accented or unaccented passing tone) and the note representing the step in the walk. The second type arises from anticipation or retardation of one of the parts, which results in staggered or syncopated counterpoint, which the French call *contretems*.

Kirnberger does provide several examples in the body and at the end of the chapter. Most interesting, perhaps, are the excerpts from two Graun arias, since they summarize very nicely the relationship between plain and embellished writing. They are given here as Examples 1 and 2.

Example 1.

Example 2.

In the first, the top part is the original melody, below which Kirnberger has provided only the main notes, which form note-against-note counterpoint with the supporting bass. In the second example, Kirnberger provides two stages of reduction, the second of which once again is in a note-to-note relationship with the bass. In this way one can clearly see decorated melody as an embellishment of a much simpler and underlying framework.

In the four chapters that comprise the first installment of volume two of *Die Kunst des reinen Satzes*, published in 1774, Kirnberger turns his attention to those features of song or melody that give it its particular character and expression (for example, the choice of key and meter, the harmony and types of modulation employed, etc.). The initial chapter, titled "Different Types of Harmonic Accompaniment to a Given Melody," is a practical application of all that has come before, including

HARMONIC THINKING AND 18TH-CENTURY COUNTERPOINT 167

the chapters on counterpoint. Here Kirnberger is systematic in his presentation, the result being the most lucid and, in my opinion, the most valuable chapter in the entire treatise.

To demonstrate the expressive power of harmony, Kirnberger identifies four types of accompaniment, progressing from the simplest to the most complex. The first utilizes only those triads built on the tonic, dominant and subdominant in the main key, or, if the piece modulates, also those chords and their inversions in the new key(s). An example of the former type is given in Example 3, second staff.

Example 3.

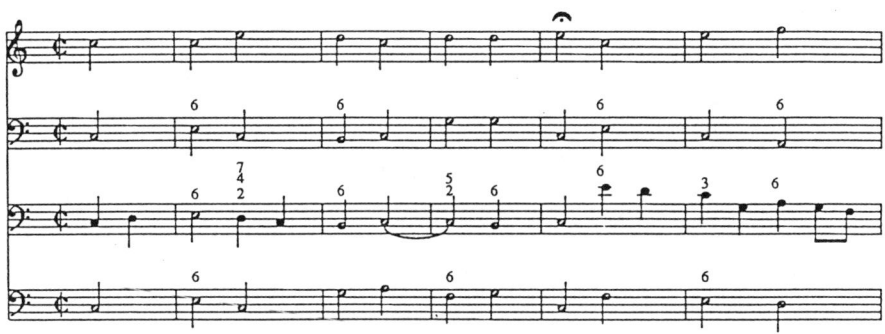

Example 3 (continued)

Such an accompaniment, Kirnberger tells us, is "suitable only for the most common listener, whose ear is incapable of grasping anything more complex."[17] Even elaboration of the bass, as demonstrated in the third staff of the same example, is insufficient to counteract the monotony created by the limited harmonic resources. This leads to the second type of accompaniment, which utilizes not only the tonic, dominant and subdominant harmonies, but the other diatonic harmonies as well, as demonstrated by the bottom staff in Example 3. The third type utilizes what we today call "secondary dominants," or, as Kirnberger worded it, "dominants of triads contained in the scale of the key."[18] This type is demonstrated in Example 4, where the chromatic chords of the bottom

[17]Kirnberger, *Art of Strict Musical Composition*, 286.
[18]Kirnberger, *Art of Strict Musical Composition*, 295.

staff are shown as substitutes for their diatonic counterparts in the type two harmonization given immediately above.

Example 4.

"Finally," Kirnberger tells us, "if required by the expression, sudden digressions to remote keys, enharmonic progressions and transitions, sudden shifts, and similar harmonic devices that can produce great effects can be applied to a *cantus firmus*."[19] Rather than provide an example of this fourth type of accompaniment, I refer you to Kirnberger's twenty-six different harmonizations of the chorale, "Ach Gott und Herr, wie gross und schwer sind mein begangne Sünden."[20]

II. JOHANN FRIEDRICH DAUBE

One can hardly find a greater contrast to Kirnberger's approach than that favored by his contemporary, Johann Friedrich Daube. Kirnberger was a conservative, an advocate of thorough mastery of the strict style, either as an end in itself or as prerequisite to composition in

---

[19]Kirnberger, *Art of Strict Musical Composition*, 298.
[20]Kirnberger, *Art of Strict Musical Composition*, 300–5.

the newer galant style. Though perhaps pedantic at times, he attempted to develop his ideas thoroughly and to present them clearly. Daube, on the other hand, oriented his *Musikalische Dilettant* of 1773 toward the growing number of amateur musicians in Vienna who were eager to learn to write chamber music in the contemporary idiom. While the treatise contains much valuable information, particularly about the various contemporary styles of composition, it has serious shortcomings as an instructional manual, often moving from one idea to the next, not always in logical sequence and without properly developing one or the other. This situation, no doubt, contributed to its rather limited and brief period of acceptance.

Daube expected the readers of his composition manual to be acquainted with his ideas on thoroughbass—on chords, their succession, and on the relationship of keys. These ideas are contained in his initial treatise, *Der Generalbass in drey Accorden* (1756), but stated in abridged and simplified version specifically for his Vienna readership in the periodical immediately preceding the work being considered here and published under the same general title.[21] The basic premise given by Daube is that all chords used in music are derived from three fundamental harmonies: 1) the triad built on scale degree one; 2) the six-five chord on scale degree four; and 3) the seventh chord on scale degree five. These are referred to simply as the first, second and third chords, respectively, and the first is often called the "ruling chord," what we today would call the tonic. When a piece modulates, then there is a change of ruling chord, no matter how transient the modulation may be. The natural progression of chords is from the first to second to third, back to the first, and so on; the only apparent exception is the deceptive cadence. The second chord can be omitted, but when it is used it always progresses to the third chord, never to the first, as it can in Rameau's theory.[22]

---

[21]*Der musikalische Dilettant: eine Wochenschrift* (Vienna, 1770–71).

[22]There is a striking resemblance between Daube's and Rameau's ideas, which led Marpurg, under the pseudonym Dr. Gemmel, to criticize *Der General-Bass in drey Accorden* in installments published in the second, third and fourth volumes of his *Historische-Kritische Beyträge zur Aufnahme der Musik* (1754–78) as an inaccurate plagiarism of Rameau's system. Though Daube denied any connection, Marpurg's characterization has persisted. A dissenting opinion is given by Susan Snook, who thinks Daube may very well have arrived at his ideas independently. See "J. F. Daube's *Der musikalische Dilettant: Eine Abhandlung der Komposition* (1773): A Translation and Commentary," (Ph.D. dissertation, Stanford University, 1978), 450–53.

HARMONIC THINKING AND 18TH-CENTURY COUNTERPOINT

Daube's instruction in two-part composition is given in the third chapter of his treatise. He distinguishes between two types, one formed by a single melodic voice supported by a bass, the discussion of which occupies all but the final few pages of the chapter, and the other involving two equal voices. Daube begins by considering each of the three chords separately: first, which note or notes from each chord would best support any given melodic note under various circumstances, and immediately thereafter various means of connecting different positions of the same chord (for example, by passing tones in either or both parts) and then imitations between the parts. The latter is in reality a brief consideration of diminution technique along with a few comments about imitation (at the octave only), which bridges the gap between the individual chord and the use of several chords in succession to form simple two-part pieces. The first example of such a piece is provided at (a) in Example 5.

Example 5.

Example 5 (continued)

Daube's comments reveal his harmonic orientation.

> In this example the three chords proceed in order until the seventh measure, where the third chord follows directly upon the first chord, and then these two chords alternate until the end. In constructing a bass to the upper voice, one merely examines each melody tone to determine to which chord it belongs and, since some tones are found in two chords, one simply heeds the order of succession of the three chords.[23]

Following a detailed explanation of his choice of harmony and bass note for each note of the melody, Daube considers ways to transform this simple exercise into a little piece. First he provides a variation, where the bass line is embellished, as shown at (b) in Example 5. Then he shows how to improve the melody by the addition of appoggiaturas and accented passing tones (c), and finally he provides a variation of the improved melody at (d). This series of examples is representative of his

[23]Snook, "J. F. Daube's *Der Musikalische Dilettant*," 38.

approach to teaching composition. Though the end product is not without flaws, it is certainly a vast improvement over the original version. And though the transformation is in some respects impressive, one must keep in mind that Daube has progressed from plain to embellished counterpoint in just over three pages of text, hardly adequate instruction for the aspiring amateur.

Elsewhere in the chapter, Daube discusses other matters one should consider when harmonizing a given melody, either with a bass or with a countermelody. (Unfortunately he doesn't tell us at this point what makes a good melody or bass line.) First, one must be aware of modulations in order to adjust the harmony accordingly. Second, one must be able to identify melodic notes that do not receive their own harmonic support, such as appoggiaturas and passing tones, but also anticipations and retardations. And finally, where it is not clear which of two possible harmonies to choose, one should look to the next note and consider which harmony it implies in selecting the one more appropriate to the natural progression of chords.

In his consideration of three-part composition, Daube once again distinguishes between two types:

> It [three-part composition] can conveniently be divided into two classes, natural and artificial construction. In the former class all three voices are merely drawn from the three chords, and the upper voice constantly asserts its authority as the primary voice, while the second voice neither ascends above it nor introduces anything concerting or imitative, but simply proceeds with the bass according to the rules of harmony.... The second class, on the contrary, is a product of the aforementioned artificial construction. Here nature and art must be united to produce true beauty. The second type is characterized by the three motions of the voices, the imitation of a melodic motive in all three voices, concerting in some passages, the alternation of brilliant and singing styles, beautiful symmetry or division of the main melody, along with the varying of the harmony by means of Piano and Forte.[24]

In his discussion of the first type, Daube follows the same procedure as before. He begins with a consideration of each chord separately, then their use in succession. Of the examples he provides, I have chosen two,

[24]Snook, "J. F. Daube's *Der Musikalische Dilettant*," 58.

one in the major mode (Example 6) and the other in the minor mode (Example 7).[25]

Example 6.

The first requires no comment, since it follows Daube's prescription for normative progression. The second, however, is more complex in its use of chords and in its digressions from the main key. Daube's comments about bars 4–8 reveal much about his conception of harmony.

> [In the fourth measure] the ruling chord is heard twice, after which the second and third chords appear in order. Now the bass ascends a tone, causing a deceptive cadence. Instead of the harmony of the first chord, a partially similar harmony follows, namely the inversion of the third chord in D minor. The bass descends a tone to E, in contrary motion to the upper voice. The second voice has G, its third, and A, thereby completing the chord. The natural resolution into the ruling chord of D minor follows. Now even D sharp appears in the upper voice. Which harmony should one furnish here? This foreign D sharp indicates the third chord in E minor, which requires either B, A or F sharp in the bass. But since this tone [the D sharp] ascends a half step to E, and the preceding bass F likewise is situated a half step above the lower octave E, contrary motion permits the harmony of the chromatic chord in E minor here, all the more because F can then remain stationary in the bass with only its third, A, in the second voice.

[25]The original examples were written on three separate staves, but they have been rewritten here on two to save space.

The resolution takes place as with the third chord in this key, namely into the ruling chord in E minor.[26]

Example 7.

Most interesting is Daube's interpretation of the augmented-sixth chord in measure 7 as an alteration of the third chord in E minor (as opposed to an alteration of the second chord in A minor), meaning that the altered pitch is taken as the bass note F rather than the melodic D sharp. Whether this interpretation is dictated by the following E minor chord (as opposed to the expected E major chord) or whether this E minor chord follows because of the supposed quasi-dominant function of the augmented-sixth chord is not at all clear.[27] In either case, this

---

[26]Snook, "J. F. Daube's *Der Musikalische Dilettant*," 76–77.

[27]Daube is not particularly clear in his interpretation of the origin of the augmented sixth chord in his earlier writings. For example, in the sixth chapter, section 7, of *Der Generalbass in drey Accorden*, he implies that the augmented sixth results from alteration of the chord on scale degree four, where the interval of the augmented sixth above the bass results from melodic embellishment borrowed from another key. However, in section 13 of the following chapter, he mentions that the augmented sixth chord above F should resolve to the ruling chord in E minor, implying that it is an alteration of the chord on the fifth degree of that scale.

interpretation allows Daube to describe the succession of chords from this point up to the deceptive cadence in measures 14–15 as a series of dominant-tonic relationships, to put it in modern terms, in a succession of keys. The first use of a chord from the second class beyond the fifth measure occurs on the downbeat of measure 16.

When it comes to giving advice to the amateur composer, Daube recommends the following procedure. First, write the melody, and then below each note write the number one, two, or three to indicate the harmony to which it belongs. Second, write a bass line appropriate to the melody, and finally add the inner part. Daube ends this section with an example demonstrating everything discussed so far, which is reproduced here as Example 8.

Example 8.

The following discussion of the artificial style, in which "art and nature are combined," contains much valuable information about styles and categories of composition. Daube provides examples of "unusual modulations," imitation of a melodic motive in all three voices, concerting passages, alternation of the brilliant and singing styles, and a summary example. These and Daube's descriptions of them are well worth studying, but they will not be discussed here, since they do not add anything to the topic under consideration. Likewise with Daube's treatment of four-part composition. Perhaps the one feature worth repeating in this context is his advice to the amateur composer. In writing for string quartet, he recommends the following procedure. First decide what type of piece you want to write; then write the melody and *analyze it harmonically*. After this is accomplished, write in order the 'cello part, the second violin part, and last, of course, the viola part. Though Daube can hardly be held responsible, his advice does bring to mind all those dull viola parts from the early Classical period!

III. HEINRICH CHRISTOPH KOCH

The final theorist to be considered here, Heinrich Christoph Koch, is perhaps best known today for the thorough discussion of phrase structure and formal organization found in the second and third volumes of his *Versuch einer Anleitung zur Composition*,[28] published in 1787 and 1793, respectively, and for his *Musikalisches Lexikon* of 1802. Yet he wrote extensively about counterpoint in the initial volume of the *Versuch*, published in 1782, and, like Kirnberger and Daube, his approach to the discipline is entirely harmonic. One reason this section has long been overlooked may be the imprecise and often confusing terminology used by Koch, which makes it next to impossible to provide an accurate and faithful translation. Furthermore, much of what he does say, and in particular the terminology he does employ, is dependent upon an understanding of certain ideas presented in the preceding section of the treatise. Thus we must digress momentarily to review

---

[28]Heinrich Christoph Koch, *Introductory Essay on Composition*, translated and with an introduction by Nancy Kovaleff Baker (New Haven, 1983). See especially Part II, "The Mechanical Rules of Melody."

these concepts, thereby establishing a basis for our understanding of his approach to counterpoint.

First, let us consider Koch's three-stage generation of the major scale from the sonorous body. He begins by pointing out that when a note is sounded we hear not only the fundamental but also the next five partials [*mitklingende Töne*].[29] For example, if the sounding body is the open C string of the 'cello, we hear not only the fundamental but also the partials c, g, c^1, e^1, g^1, which together form the major triad on C. Next he considers the simplest divisions of this sounding body: 1/2 the string length produces the octave c; 2/3 the string length produces the fifth g; and 3/4 the string length produces the fourth f. The two new pitches produced in this way, the fourth and fifth above the fundamental, are called principal tones [*Haupttöne*] by Koch to indicate their important relationship to the fundamental. Finally, he considers the sounding partials above the fundamental (c–e–g) and above the two principal tones (f–a–c and g–b–d), which, when put in ascending order above the fundamental within a single octave, produce the C major scale. Later Koch designates these triads—those that produce the major scale—as the essential [*wesentlich*] triads of the key; those built on scale degrees two, three and six are called non-essential [*zufällig*]. This distinction is the basis of our current designations of primary versus secondary triads of a key.

Koch's general approach to counterpoint follows the standard practice of beginning with two parts, then progressing through three to four parts; he does not discuss composition in more than four parts. He also makes the standard distinction between equal and embellished counterpoint, but his treatment of the latter is unusual in that he subdivides it into unequal and mixed. By unequal, Koch means that the note values of the added part are a consistent division of the *tactus*, for example, two eighth notes or four sixteenths for each quarter note of the *cantus firmus*; in short, the counterpoint consists of equal values throughout that are unequal in relation to the given part. Mixed counterpoint, on the other hand, consists of a variety of figures and note values in relation to the tones of the *cantus firmus*. In his examples and

---

[29]Koch credits Marpurg (and indirectly Rameau) as the source of his information. See Marpurg's *Anmerkungen über Sorgens Compendium harmonicum* (Berlin, 1760), chapter 1, paragraph 6.

commentary, he makes a distinction between the bound or fugal style and the free or galant style. As we shall see, these examples are rather primitive, which is perhaps the greatest weakness of the presentation. For the sake of space, we will consider only a limited number of his two- and three-part examples, all but one with the *cantus firmus* (chorale melody) in the uppermost voice.

Koch divides equal counterpoint into five types, progressing from the simplest and most natural to the most complex. The first type of harmonic accompaniment is defined as one where each note of the upper voice is a sounding partial [*mitklingende Ton*] of the note supporting it, or, stated conversely, where each bass note is the fundamental of the tone it supports and thus the root of the chord. Koch goes on to explain that only the essential triads of the key—those built on scale degrees one, four and five—are used here. This type is demonstrated in the top line of Example 9 (chorale melody I); the only exception to the stated guidelines occurs on the downbeat of the fourth measure, where the third of the chord appears in the bass.

Example 9.

Example 9 (continued)

The second type is essentially the same, except it routinely permits use of the third as well as the root in the bass, but Koch cautions against use of the six-four in two-part writing, except under special circumstances. This type is demonstrated by the second line of Example 9, marked 2a. At this point Koch digresses for a brief time to discuss two matters: the use of the diminished triad with its third in the bass; and standard cadence patterns occurring in four-part writing, including what today would be designated by the labels ii^6–V–I. This leads to variants of the type-two accompaniment, the two illustrations of which are labelled 2b in Example 9. The third type, an example of which is given on the second line under chorale melody II, permits the use of the non-essential triads, that is, those built on scale degrees two, three and six. Koch points out that these chords are used much more frequently in the fugal style than in the galant style. The fourth type permits the use of dissonance. The principal rule given here is "that any note on an accented beat can be used as a dissonance when it occurs on the preceding weak beat and [subsequently] resolves down by step."[30] This applies to both the strict and free styles. Situations described by Koch that apply only to the free style are limited to the following:

> When the top voice progresses down from the fourth to the third degree in either mode, the minor seventh can be set against this fourth degree on either an accented or an unaccented beat; and, in the situation where the minor sixth degree in the minor mode leads down by step, the diminished seventh can be set against it.
>
> When, in either the major or minor mode, the top voice has the fifth degree, which either is repeated or progresses upward by fourth to the final, the major second can be set against it.[31]

An instance of scale degree four being treated as a dissonant seventh can be found on the fourth beat of the next setting of our second chorale melody (II). Koch goes on to explain that when scale-degree four supports either scale-degree three or one before a cadence on the dominant, the fourth degree must be raised, as in the next measure of this example. Finally, the fifth type involves various non-essential or optional digressions, so-called because they are not required by the melody.

    This is the core of Koch's approach to equal counterpoint in two parts. One might be tempted to make a comparison with Fux, but in fact the only similarity is the division into five species. The real similarity is with Kirnberger's four types of harmonic accompaniment, which, as we have seen, follows much the same path. Though Koch relies heavily on Marpurg's writings, he was also influenced to some extent by Kirnberger's ideas, and in this instance the parallel could not be clearer.

---

[30]*Versuch*, 287.
[31]*Versuch*, 287.

At the bottom of Example 9 I have provided illustrations of unequal and mixed counterpoint in two parts, both of them settings of the first chorale melody. Regarding the former, note that the added part consists almost exclusively of consonances in relation to the *cantus firmus*; the only exceptions are two unaccented passing tones and two unaccented fourths resulting from arpeggiation of the underlying harmony. Koch does mention in passing that accented dissonances can occur, but for the most part his examples of unequal counterpoint consist of consonant skips and arpeggiations mixed with unaccented passing tones. Regarding mixed counterpoint, Koch's main advice in choosing figures is that they should not counteract the established meter.

Our consideration of three-part counterpoint will be very brief, since little new that is pertinent to the study is added here. Koch begins by distinguishing between two types—1) where a single line (for example, a bass) is to be added to two already composed parts in consideration of their implied harmonic progression; and 2) where a given chorale melody is to be accompanied harmonically with two added voices—but, in reality, he develops only the latter. His treatment of this topic follows the same general outline as his discussion of two-part writing, though greatly abbreviated: first, equal counterpoint, then unequal and finally mixed. In Example 10 I have reproduced his illustrations of the various types of equal counterpoint in three parts. The top system provides an example of the first type, where only the essential triads of the key are used with the root of each chord in the bass, the only exception occurring in the same place as before. An example of the second type—actually the variant of the second type labelled 2b in Example 9—is given in the second system, and directly below is the third type, which permits the use of the non-essential triads. The fourth and fifth types, involving dissonances and optional digressions, are combined in the final setting, which is provided *in toto*. Finally, a brief example of mixed three-part counterpoint in the fugal style with the *cantus firmus* in the inner voice is given in Example 11.

HARMONIC THINKING AND 18TH-CENTURY COUNTERPOINT

Example 10.

Example 11.

In summary I would like to speculate briefly on why the approaches of these three theorists to the topic of simple counterpoint did not enjoy greater success. To a certain extent I have already provided the answers. Koch's approach is derivative (from Kirnberger), his terminology is often confusing or unclear, and he made no apparent attempt to bridge the gap between theory and musical practice. Daube's approach is dependent upon an understanding of a system of harmony that appears to be derived from Rameau, and, furthermore, his presentation is often inadequate from a pedagogical point of view. At the same time, his consideration of current musical styles and some of his more polished examples are far more engaging than what either Kirnberger or Koch had to offer. Of the three, Kirnberger was the most influential, but it was primarily his ideas on harmony rather than counterpoint that had some impact on succeeding generations of musicians. While all of this may be true, it does not explain why Fuxian counterpoint persisted and these harmonically based approaches did not. Part of the answer lies, I think, in the fact that the Fux approach is entirely self-contained, whereas each of these others is dependent upon a particular system of harmony and its accompanying terminology. In addition, I think Fux had the advantage of being in the right place at the right time, so to speak. He provided something that was lacking and apparently much needed, a basic and clearly organized manual in strict counterpoint. Being the first didactic work of any substance on the topic published in Germany, it soon gained a foothold, and by the 1770s—when Kirnberger's and

Daube's works were first published—it was already established as the standard text. Whatever advantages might have been offered by the methods proposed by Kirnberger, Daube and Koch, including their closer connection to contemporary composition, were apparently not equal to the simplicity and pedagogical strengths of the *Gradus ad Parnassum*.

George J. Buelow

A BACH BORROWING BY GLUCK*
Another Frontier

In his article entitled "Bach's Parody Technique and its Frontiers,"[1] Alfred Mann explored with his usual thoughtfulness the question of Bach's reuse of musical ideas in subsequent compositions. He ends the essay with the memorable phrase, "'borrowing' with abiding inspiration," to characterize this type of Bach's compositional procedures. These words might also give tribute to other composers who have taken musical ideas of their own or others and made use of them in new works. When a composer perceives in a given musical concept new musical potentialities, indeed, new frontiers to be explored, then the new work must be said to have been created with the same musical genius that distinguishes any original composition. In addition to Bach, this cogent phrase applies equally as well to numerous works by George Frideric Handel. More than any other composer, he has been condemned in the

---

*This article appeared originally in the Spring/Summer 1991 issue of *BACH: The Journal of the Riemenschneider Bach Institute*, and is included here with the kind permission of its editor.
[1] In *Bach Studies*, ed. Don O. Franklin (Cambridge, 1989), 115.

George J. Buelow is Professor of Musicology at Indiana University. He is the author of Thorough-Bass Accompaniment according to Johann David Heinichen, *as well as numerous articles concerning Baroque music.*

past for his procedures of borrowing when creating new works out of previously existing musical materials. However, Handel's achievements with this form of musical creativity, "borrowing with abiding inspiration," deserve the same serious analysis and reflection as any other kind of successful compositional procedure.

Other composers have also used similar techniques for inventing new works based on borrowed musical ideas. The one who most closely resembles Handel in this regard is Christoph Willibald Gluck. Throughout his career, he used, adapted, and was inspired by musical materials taken almost exclusively (as far as is known today) from his own previously composed scores. These "borrowings" often reveal the composer rethinking the potential of the music at hand and his adaptation of it for new texts and dramatic situations in his operas.[2] Unquestionably, the most unusual example of Gluck's adaptation of a borrowed composition is his use of the gigue from the Partita No. 1 in B-flat major by Johann Sebastian Bach. Although two earlier versions exist, Gluck's borrowing is most familiar from its appearance in his last great French *tragédie opéra*, *Iphigénie en Tauride* (Paris, 1779), Act IV, which opens with Iphigénie's "Je t'implore et je tremble."[3]

This borrowing was already mentioned in the Gluck literature at the beginning of the nineteenth century. Otto Jahn, in his Mozart study, refers to it as the most remarkable use of borrowed materials in music, which he says receives its "impulse" from the gigue. However, typical of the need for nineteenth-century writers to dispel any suggestion of plagiarism in the work of a great composer, Jahn adds: "With these masters no one would imagine that they stole for lack of ideas."[4] Philipp Spitta picked up the reference to Bach's work from Jahn and included it in his great study of J. S. Bach.[5] Beginning with A. B. Marx's *Gluck und die Oper*,[6] almost every Gluck biography mentions the composer's

---

[2]See Klaus Hortschansky, *Parodie und Entlehnung im Schaffen Christoph Willibald Gluck*, Analecta musicologica 13 (Cologne, 1973).

[3]C. W. Gluck, *Iphigénie en Tauride*, Sämtliche Werke I/9, ed. Gerhard Croll (Kassel, 1973), 240.

[4]Otto Jahn, *W. A. Mozart*, IV (Leipzig, 1859): 715. "Bei diesen Meistern wird Niemand an Diebstahl aus Erfindsnoth denken."

[5]Philipp Spitta, *Johann Sebastian Bach* (Leipzig, 1873–80; Eng. trans., London, 1884–85, repr. New York, 1951) 3, p. 161 fn.

[6]Adolf Bernhard Marx, *Gluck und die Oper*, I (Berlin, 1863): 201.

use of Bach's gigue, including Alfred Einstein,[7] Roland Tenschert,[8] Anna Amalie Abert,[9] and Jacques-Gabriel Prod'homme.[10] Most of these references also acknowledge that the aria is in fact a revised version of the same one appearing in *Telemaco* (Vienna, January 24, 1765), where it is used for Circe's aria in Act II, "S'a estinguer non bastate."[11] An even earlier version can be traced back to Gluck's *Antigono* (Rome, February 9, 1756), in Act III, for Berenice's "Perchè, se tanti siete."[12]

A. B. Marx describes the borrowing as a "wonder," and comments, incorrectly, on its extensive agreement with the original gigue. Only Anna Amalie Abert examined the aria sufficiently to see that its connection to the gigue only "liegt in den ersten Takten den Anfang." None of these authors, however, gives any details to clarify how Gluck used the Bach gigue in the aria, while most of them express surprise at the achievement. Except for Abert, the discussions incorrectly imply that Gluck based his composition on the entire gigue, even though only the first measures are reflected throughout much of the aria. The aria itself stands as an entirely new composition, the result of the same abiding inspiration that both Bach and Handel could draw from an existing musical idea.

Bach's Partita in B-flat major, his first published work, appeared in the *Clavierübung* I, a set of six partitas published between 1726 and 1731. The title page describes the set as the composer's Opus I. The gigue itself is unique among Bach's keyboard works. A brilliant technical exercise involving the continuous crossing of hands, it was perhaps influenced by Domenico Scarlatti's keyboard sonatas, which often employ this same technical feature. In the original published version Bach labelled the movement as a *giga*. However, the piece is neither a French nor an Italian dance, lacking the characteristic style features: it has no imitation nor dotted rhythms, does not have a particularly melodic substance, and is written in duple not ternary meter, which is

---

[7]Alfred Einstein, *Gluck: Sein Leben—seine Werke* (Zürich/Stuttgart, n.d.,) 237.
[8]Roland Tenschert, *Christoph Willibald Gluck* (Freiburg/Breisgau, 1951), 147.
[9]Anna Amalie Abert, *Christoph Willibald Gluck* (Munich, 1959), 250.
[10]Jacques-Gabriel Prod'homme, *Christoph Willibald Gluck* (Paris, 1985), 41.
[11]C. W. Gluck, *Telemaco*, *Sämtliche Werke* I/2, ed. Karl Geiringer (Kassel, 1972), 303.
[12]Gluck's *Antigono*, MS in Paris, Bibliothèque nationale, has not been published. See Hortschansky, *Parodie und Entlehnung*, 103–5.

usually basic to most gigues of the early eighteenth century including all of Bach's other dances of this type.

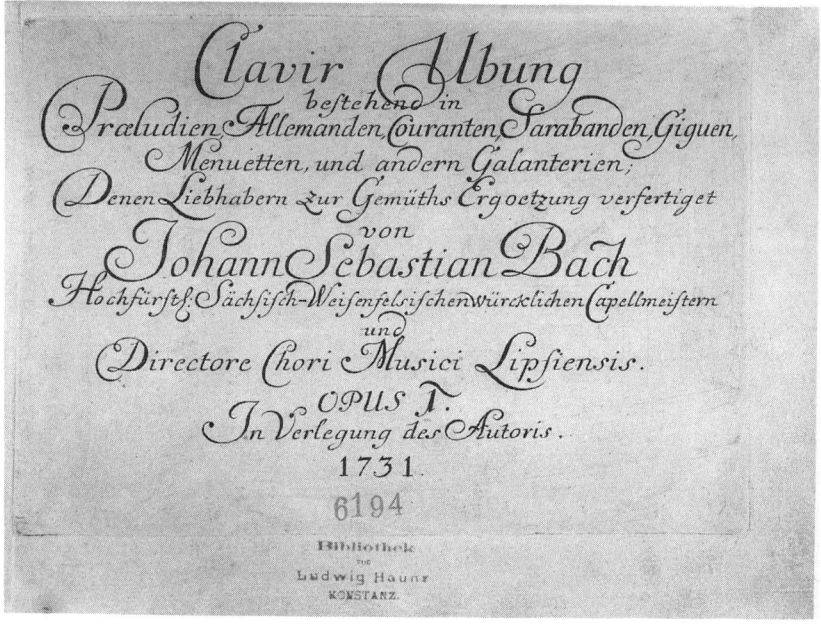

Plate 1. J. S. Bach, Title page of the Clavier-Ubung I. (Reproduced with permission from the exemplar held by the Riemenschneider Bach Institute of Baldwin-Wallace College.

What attracted Gluck to this harpsichord piece, and how did he discover the Partita? The second question can be answered by a passage found in Forkel's biography of Bach, when he commented in regard to the Partitas:

> In its time, this work caused a great sensation in the musical world; no one had ever seen or heard such splendid clavier compositions. Whoever learned to perform pieces from it really well could make his fortune in the world.[13]

---

[13]J. N. Forkel, *Ueber Johann Sebastian Bachs Leben, Kunst und Kunstwerke* (Leipzig, 1802), 50. "Diese Werk machte zu seiner Zeit in der musikalischen Welt grosses Aufsehen; man hat noch nie so vortreffliche Claviercompositionen gesehen und gehört. Wer einige Stücke daraus recht gut vortragen lernte, konnte sein Glück in der Welt damit machen."

Gluck traveled extensively, living at times in Italy, England, Austria and Germany. His attention could have been drawn to Bach's first published works while visiting Handel in London, or possibly during the period when he lived in Dresden or Vienna. The more important question concerns why this keyboard piece attracted Gluck to use it as a touchstone of inspiration for a totally transformed composition, a dramatic aria of large dimensions serving three of his operas.

Example 1 gives the opening section of Bach's gigue as it appears in the original publication (Gluck borrows nothing from the second half of the gigue):

Example 1.

Reproduced by permission from the copy of the *Clavierübung I* (Leipzig, 1731) in the Riemenschneider Bach Institute library, Baldwin-Wallace College, Berea, Ohio.

Gluck takes musical substance from only the initial eleven of the sixteen measures making up the first section of the piece. No doubt he was attracted by the agitated nature of the accompaniment which he imitates by constant 16th–note articulations in violins II and violas (see the aria from *Iphigénie en Tauride* at the end of this article). More important to Gluck's aria are the unusual melodic motives, the leaping melodic line of the left hand as it moves above, below, and into the midst of the accompanying right-hand figure. Even more crucial to the entire affective character of Gluck's aria are the reiterated dissonant appoggiaturas. These dissonant seconds permeate much of the aria and inevitably cement the association between aria and gigue (see especially measures 9–11). Although the gigue, as a brilliant demonstration of a particular aspect of keyboard virtuosity, does not seem especially expressive of an affection of agitation, distress, or emotional crisis, Gluck finds these musical elements perfectly suited to expressing these very feelings found in all three aria texts. In each case, the singer tells of suffering inner torments and an emotional crisis. The texts for all three settings of the aria have a similar emotional basis of despair:

ANTIGONO, III/7

Perché, se tanti siete	Why, if so many of you
Che delirar mi fate,	make me rave,
Perché non m'uccidete,	why do you not slay me,
Affani del mio cor?	pangs of my heart?
Crescete, oh Dio! crescete,	Rise up, O God, rise up
Fin che mi porga aita,	until you offer me aid
Con togliermi di vita,	by taking away from life
L'eccesso del dolor.	the excess of grief.

TELEMACO, II/8

Se a estinguer non bastate	If it is not enough for you
Il mio funesto ardore,	to quench my distressing ardor,
Perchè mi lacerate,	why will you rend my heart,
Vani rimorsi, il cor?	futile remorses?
Cessate, Oh Dei! cessate	Cease, o gods, cease
Di tormentarmi il core,	to torment my heart,
O a uccidermi il dolore	or act so that it suffices at least
Fate, che basti almen.	to kill my grief.

IPHIGÉNIE EN TAURIDE, IV/1

Je t'implore et je tremble	I implore thee and I tremble,
Ô Déesse implacable!	O implacable goddess!
Dans le fond de mon coeur	In the depths of my heart
mets la férocité.	place ferocity,

Etouffe de l'humanité	Stifle from [my] humanity
La voix plaintive et lamentable!	the woeful and pitiable voice!
Hélas! ah! quelle est donc	Alas! how then is
la rigueur de mon sort:	the harshness of my lot,
D'un sanglant ministère,	Of a bloody office
Victime involontaire!	to be the unwilling victim!
J'obéis!	I obey!
Et mon coeur est en proie au remords.	And my heart is a prey to remorse.

Gluck's aria sets the complete text twice, casting the music into a large binary form as follows:

    Key: A major
    INSTRUMENTAL INTRODUCTION (mm 1–10), cadence on   V of A major

    PART ONE
        A (mm 11–24) A major to V of E major
            Text: *Je t'implore et je tremble, Ô Déesse implacable!*
                Dans le fond de mon coeur mets la férocité. Etouffe de l'humanité
                La voix plaintive et lamentable!
        B (mm 25–36, ending with fermata), V of E pedal to I_6
            Text: *Hélas! ah! quelle est donc la rigueur de mon sort:*
                D'un sanglant ministère, victime involontaire!
                J'obéis!
        C (mm 37–42), cadence in E major
            Text: *Et mon coeur est en proie au remords.*
    INSTRUMENTAL INTERLUDE (mm 50–56 = 37–42), with V–I cadence in E

    PART II
        A (mm 57–68 = development of 15–21), transition to A major
        B (mm 80–90, ending with fermata), A pedal to I^6 of A
        C (mm 91–103)
    POSTLUDE (mm 104–112 = 50–56 in A major)

Of these 106 measures, a little more than half (or fifty-eight) consist of musical material based on Bach's gigue, as follows:

Gluck's aria		*Bach's gigue*
Measures 1–10	=	Measures 1–4 plus 9–11
Measures 11–21	=	Measures 1–11
Measures 31–36	=	Based on string motive (a) and appoggiatura motive)
Measures 37–39	=	Measures 9–11
Measures 50–52	=	Measures 9–11
Measures 57–69	=	Measures 1–11
Measures 85–93	=	Measures 1–11
Measures 104–06	=	Measures 9–11

Example 2. Opening measures of Gluck's aria[14]

[14]This example, as well as the entire aria reproduced at the end of the article are taken, for practical reasons of spacing, from the edition of the opera by Alfred Dörffel (Leipzig, 1884), 130–35.

The "borrowed" material has undergone immediate reinterpretation: Bach's gigue begins on the downbeat, Gluck's, however, with an upbeat. And to this initial upbeat and every subsequent fourth beat Gluck adds an ornamented turn which energizes the motive in a way not found in Bach's piece. There are also other slight though important changes in the overall melodic line departing from Bach's top part.

Gluck's insistent, ostinato-like stress on the ornamented upbeat motive alters completely the musical impact of Bach's original concept. The music now has an intensity and a forward drive making Gluck's aria a perfect reflection of the text, in which Iphigénie's emotions seethe with fear and uncertainty as she faces her duty as priestess to sacrifice the stranger Orestes—whom she does not as yet recognize as her brother. This creative impulse applied to the borrowed idea is not found in Gluck's earlier setting of the same aria in *Telemaco*, where the same upbeat is decorated with a less intense rhythmic figure of an eighth and two sixteenths.

Example 3: Opening of the aria, "S'a estinguer non bastate" from *Telemaco* (*Sämtliche Werke*, I/2, 303).

Example 3 (continued)

The six-note phrase in measures 5–8 of the gigue, where it functions melodically, Gluck uses as the bass line supporting the vocal melody (see measures 15–18). It remains to be observed that of all the aspects of Bach's gigue that Gluck found suggestive of new expressive potential, it was the descending accented appoggiaturas that were the most compelling. From these piquant dissonances arising from the harpsichord figure, Gluck creates a motive of striking dramatic effect in both violins as well as cellos and basses. They are the key aspect capturing the affection of intensity, stressfulness, and even terror.

As is true of Handel and other composers when they adapted borrowed musical ideas, Gluck does not reveal in his score the origins of the musical impetus leading to the aria. Few in his audience attending any of the three operas containing this aria would have known Bach's gigue (in fact even today I have found that graduate students—many of them professional pianists—remain oblivious to the keyboard origins of Gluck's aria). Yet the Bach gigue is immediately recognizable by anyone who has performed the piece. Was Gluck committing an act of plagiarism in keeping his source unstated, dare we say secret?

The answer obviously is no, for Gluck, as was true of many other composers, was employing an age-old tradition connected to language as well as to the visual and musical arts that stressed imitation rather than the more modern concept of "originality." Indeed, it was often considered an act of admiration, even homage to base a new work on one by a writer, an artist, or a composer who was revered for the greatness of his achievement. Classical sources on oratory stress imitation as a means to creation. For example, Quintillian declared that "it is from these [a list of great writers of his and previous Greek culture] and other authors worthy of our study that we must draw our stock of words, the variety of our figures and our methods of composition.... It is a universal rule that we should wish to copy what we approve in others."[15] Was Gluck perhaps paying homage to Bach in this way?

This apparently unique borrowing of music from another composer by Gluck is probably the only evidence we shall have that he found Sebastian Bach's music worthy of tribute. Hortschansky, in his study of parody and borrowings in Gluck, believes that Gluck's borrowing from Bach cannot be classified as a borrowing (*Entlehnung*), but rather what he terms a "paraphrase."[16] This too seems an inadequate if not an incorrect usage of a term with different connotations in earlier as well as in nineteenth-century music. Rather, it would be better to describe these instances of borrowing for what they are, new compositions based on previous musical ideas in which the composer crosses a new frontier to discover new musical and expressive potentialities. Gluck, in his adaptation of a part of Bach's gigue, crosses over such a frontier. He moved from the musical milieu of a Baroque harpsichord dance form, to the musical milieu of a Classical opera aria of tragic expressiveness. It is another example, surely, of a composer "borrowing with abiding inspiration."

---

[15]Marcus Fabius Quintillianus, *Institutio oratorio* trans. H. E. Butler (London, 1921), 4 (= Book X), 75. Further concerning the relationships between imitation and originality, see the author's "Originality, Genius, Plagiarism in English Criticism of the Eighteenth Century," in *Florilegium musicologicum, Festschrift H. Federhofer* (Tutzing, 1988), 57.

[16]Hortschansky, *Parodie und Entlehnung*, 12.

APPENDIX

A BACH BORROWING BY GLUCK

A BACH BORROWING BY GLUCK

A BACH BORROWING BY GLUCK

Mario R. Mercado

MOZART THROUGH HIS PIANO STUDENTS

Mozart's role as a teacher of composition is variously documented, most notably in the landmark study undertaken by Erich Hertzmann and completed by Daniel Heartz and Alfred Mann of Thomas Attwood's lessons with the composer. This volume and its critical report, the work of Heartz and Mann, in the *Neue Mozart-Ausgabe* have recently been joined by a companion volume examining Mozart's tutelage of Barbara Ployer and Franz Jacob Freystädtler; Hellmut Federhofer has evaluated the Ployer studies and Alfred Mann those of Freystädtler.[1] But the question of Mozart's vocation as a teacher of the keyboard has remained necessarily less open to examination, given the lack of comparable documents of pianistic pedagogy.[2] To date, only one étude has been

---

[1]*Neue Mozart-Ausgabe*, Serie X: Supplement; Werkgruppe 30: *Studien, Skizzen, Entwürfe, Fragmente*, Varia: Band 2: *Barbara Ployer und Franz Jacob Freystädtlers Theorie- und Kompositionsstudien bei Mozart* (Leipzig, 1989).

[2]For discussion of Mozart as a teacher of composition, see also Robert Lach, *Mozart als Theoretiker* (Vienna, 1918); Walter Senn, "Barbara Ployer, Mozarts Klavierschülerin," *Österreichische Musikzeitschrift* XXXIII (1978); Walter Senn, "Zur Mozarts angeblichen 'kurgefasste GeneralbassSchule,'" *Mitteilungen der Internationalen Stiftung Mozart* XXIX (1988), 3–4: 28–33; John Hind Chesnut, "Mozart's Teaching of Intonation," *Journal of the American Musicological Society* XXX (1977): 254–71.

Mario R. Mercado is the author of The Evolution of Mozart's Pianistic Style *(Southern Illinois University Press, 1992), and writes on 18th-century instrumental music and 20th-century opera and music theater. He is former Director of Programs of the Kurt Weill Foundation for Music in New York.*

verified as emanating from Mozart's years in Vienna. Yet an impression can be formed of Mozart's role as a teacher through study of correspondence and other documents, as well as consideration of the piano works written or intended for his pupils. Furthermore, the picture that emerges serves to refine aspects of Mozart biography.

As early as 1771, while he was still in Salzburg, there is record of Mozart's giving harpsichord instruction, and, despite his travels and his remarkably intense life as a composer, he remained obliged to teach throughout most of his career. While the extant documentation of his tuition of Attwood, Ployer, and Freystädtler involves the subject of composition, the majority of his students—and during his life they may have numbered over sixty—were clavier or piano pupils. In addition, Mozart gave occasional instruction on the violin, an instrument on which he excelled and for which he had inherited one of the essential didactic treatises of eighteenth-century instrumental performance—his father Leopold's *Violonschule*, published in the year of Mozart's birth.

As with other facets of Mozart's life, it was in Vienna that piano instruction assumed both a prominence and routine; teaching often offered steady income. Mozart's correspondence from the early 1780s reveals that generally he composed in the early morning, then taught from mid-morning to early afternoon, until the time of the midday meal, reserving the evenings for composition, a fact that seems astounding given his artistic achievements during this period. Though the number of pupils he taught varied and can not be determined with certainty, more than a few pianists and students may have influenced his work, including the blind pianist Theresia von Paradis (1759–1824), the dedicatee of the concerto in B-flat major K. 456, and the young Baroness Franziska von Jacquin (1769–1853), for whom the trio in E-flat major K. 458 for piano, clarinet and viola was written. Clearly, his approach varied with the level of each student. In Vienna he instructed a considerable number of genuinely talented pupils (the number and quality of students evidently changed by the end of the decade when Mozart made it known to his fellow Freemason Michael Puchberg that he was anxious, because of serious financial circumstance, to take on additional pupils). Examination of Mozart's relationships with three students, Josepha Barbara von Auernhammer, Barbara Ployer, and Johann

Nepomuk Hummel, brings into focus the picture of Mozart both as a teacher and pianist and enhances understanding of the fundamental body of piano literature that he cultivated.

Josepha von Auernhammer (1758–1820), only two years Mozart's junior, was one of Mozart's most talented pupils and figured significantly throughout the years of his career in Vienna. The daughter of Johann Michael Auernhammer, an Economic Councillor to the Imperial Court, she began studying with Mozart in the spring of 1781, shortly after his dismissal by the Archbishop Colloredo of Salzburg and his permanent settlement in Vienna. Mozart gave von Auernhammer frequent instruction; he taught her three times a week, though early in their association the instruction may have been even more frequent. In a letter to his father, dated Vienna, 27 June 1781, Mozart wrote:

> I go to Herr von Auernhammer almost every afternoon. The young lady is a fright, but plays enchantingly, though in cantabile playing she has not got the real delicate singing style. She clips everything.[3]

In the continuation of the above letter, Mozart relates Josepha von Auernhammer's hope of going to Paris in order to establish a professional career; however, there is a touching, if not pathetic, element to the plan's background.

> She [Auernhammer] said, 'I am no beauty—au contraire, I am ugly. So I prefer to remain as I am and to live by my talent.'[4]

It was in Vienna, however, that she established a career as a performer which she actively maintained until 1813. She also composed, mostly sets of piano variations, as was the custom, on popular arias or songs, and most notable among these is a set of six variations on "Der Vogelfänger bin ich ja," from *Die Zauberflöte*.[5] According to various biographers, von Auernhammer had a romantic interest in Mozart. Her feelings obviously faded after the especially close association of the

---

[3]Emily Anderson, *The Letters of Mozart and His Family*, 3rd edition corrected by Stanley Sadie and Fiona Smart, after the 2nd edition prepared by A. Hyatt King and Monica Carolan (New York, 1989), 748.
[4]Anderson, *Letters*, 748.
[5]Rudolf Angermüller "Josepha von Auernhammer," *The New Grove Dictionary of Music and Musicians*, ed. Stanley Sadie, vol. 1 (London, 1980): 689.

early 1780s. By 1786, she married Johann Bessenig, who later became a civil magistrate.

Mozart honored his pupil with the dedication of his first Viennese publication, *Six sonates pour le clavecin, ou pianoforte avec l'accompagnement d'un Violon, Oeuvre II* (the piano and violin sonatas in C major K. 296, F major K. 376 [374d], F major K. 377 [374e], B-flat major K. 378 [317d], G major K. 379 [373a], and E-flat major K. 380 [374f]), engraved and issued in November 1781 by the firm Artaria. Of these piano and violin sonatas, one in the series, K. 296 in C major, was composed in March 1778 at Mannheim, at which time Mozart had dedicated the work to another keyboard student Thérèse Serrarius. With the possible exception of the sonata in B-flat major K. 378 (317d), the rest of the sonatas in the series were composed at Vienna during the summer of 1781.

In addition to the set of piano and violin sonatas, Mozart composed the sonata for two pianos in D major K. 448 (375a) for Josepha von Auernhammer. This work, Mozart's only ensemble sonata for two keyboards, was written in November 1781 and figured as one of the three works involving two pianos which Mozart performed often with his talented pupil. In letters from the spring of that year, Mozart requested from his father the manuscript score of two "double" concertos—the concerto in E-flat major K. 365 (316a) for two pianos and orchestra which he had composed at Salzburg in 1779, and the concerto in F major K. 242 (originally for 3 pianos) which Mozart recast in a version for 2 pianos, transposed to E-flat major.

Mozart and von Auernhammer first performed the D major sonata in a concert at the Auernhammer residence on 23 November 1781; the concerto in E-flat major K. 365 (316a) was also on the program. Mozart reported to his father that the sonata, written expressly for the occasion, proved very successful. It remained a popular work. Mozart later performed it with Barbara Ployer; and Hummel, who as a young student of Mozart read duet sonatas with his teacher, likely played the D major sonata too. He was familiar with it, in any case; during his concert appearances in London in the 1830s, he performed the sonata on at least two occasions with Ignaz Moscheles.[6]

---

[6]Joel Sachs, *Kapellmeister Hummel in England and France* No. 6 (Detroit, 1977), 49ff.

Indeed, the pairing of the sonata and the concerto must have made an extraordinary effect. The D major sonata exudes a brilliance owing only partly to its key, but also to the antiphonal writing that stresses the *concertante* style in a work for two players at two instruments. For the November 1781 concert, Mozart expanded the orchestration of the E-flat major concerto K. 365 (316a), probably composed in 1779, from 2 oboes, 2 bassoons, 2 horns, and strings, to include 2 clarinets, 2 trumpets and timpani in the first and third movements. The concerto bears the stylistic influences of Mozart's sojourn at Mannheim in 1777–78, and, given the equal footing on which the two keyboard parts are placed throughout, it seems likely that it was written originally for performance by Mozart and his sister. Mozart and von Auernhammer later performed the concerto in 1782 at the pavilion reserved for concerts at the Augarten, one of the two principal pleasure gardens—the other being the Prater—of eighteenth-century Vienna. The performance (Mozart's first at the Augarten) took place in the morning of 26 May 1782. The Archduke Maximilian, brother of Joseph II and Mozart's exact contemporary, was among those in attendance.

In early November 1782, Josepha von Auernhammer organized a concert at the Kärntnertor Theater in which Mozart doubtless took part.[7] In a letter to his father of 26 October 1782, Mozart, explaining the delay in a trip to Salzburg, indicates that "Fräulein von Auernhammer is giving a concert in the theater on that day [3 November]... and I have promised to play with her." Although complete details of the concert program are not known, besides von Auernhammer there were three singers who participated, Desideria von Pauler, a Mlle Berger, and a Mlle Weber (probably one of the Weber sisters, Josepha or, less likely, Sophie, but not Aloisia or Constanze). If Mozart performed with Auernhammer, it would seem likely that the sonata in D major K. 448 figured on the program; a report in a pamphlet, *Über das wiener Dilektante-Konzert*, suggests that Mozart also performed some solo works, but no other details indicate the presence of an orchestra, or, consequently, a concerto on the program.[8] According to Deutsch, von Auernhammer's next performance was in a concert on 24 February 1786

---

[7] Otto Erich Deutsch, *Mozart, A Documentary Biography*, trans. Eric Blom, Peter Branscombe and Jeremy Noble (Stanford, 1965), 207.
[8] Deutsch, *Mozart*, 208.

at the Burgtheater, a significantly more important venue. Mozart probably also took part, though he was intensely involved in his series of Lenten subscription concerts at the Mehlgrube.[9]

Josepha von Auernhammer's talents as a pianist and composer, as well as her familiarity with Mozart's work and manuscript, qualified her to be the editor entrusted with first publications of Mozart's solo sonatas and sets of variations. In the late 1780s, she proofread the first editions of these works for the Viennese firm of Artaria; a report in Karl Friedrich Cramer's *Magazin der Music*, Hamburg, 23 April 1787, gives interesting notice of her efforts: "she it was who supervised and corrected the engraving of many sonatas andariettas with variations by Mozart at Messrs. Artaria's."[10] A similar report comes later, published notably in Ernst Ludwig Gerber's *Historisch–biographisches Lexicon der Tonkünstler*, at Leipzig in 1790. Of the ten sets of variations (including two for piano and violin) published in Vienna during Mozart's life, Artaria engraved six in 1786 and 1791; the firm of Christoph Torricella had issued three variation sets in 1785, including the celebrated variations on "Ah, vous dirai–je maman" K. 256, which Mozart had composed during the period 1781–82. Artaria reprinted these three variation sets (K. 265, K. 398, K. 455) in 1786, probably from Torricella's engraved plates (Torricella became insolvent by the middle of 1786, was forced to close, and sell off all its engraved plates, which were promptly acquired by Artaria).[11] Mlle von Auernhammer likely oversaw the preparation of these six sets and possibly supervised the issue of the additional three assumed by Artaria. The Viennese publisher Johann Traeg issued in 1784 a set of variations in A major K. 460 (454a) on "Come un agnello" from Sarti's opera *Fra i due litiganti*. The authenticity of the publication with eight variations has been called into question by Kurt von Fischer and others; there is little to suggest that Auernhammer was ever involved with this publication.

---

[9]Thomas Attwood in a letter to an unidentified correspondent also comments on Mozart's generosity in participating in such benefit concerts. "...[Mozart] was very kind to all of Talent who came to Vienna & generally played at their Benefit Concerts." Cliff Eisen, *New Mozart Documents, A Supplement to O. E. Deutsch's Documentary Biography* (Stanford, 1991), 39–40.

[10]Deutsch, *Mozart*, 290.

[11]H. C. Robbins Landon, *Mozart, The Golden Years* (New York, 1989), 37–38.

Of the seven sonatas for piano solo published in Vienna, three were issued by Artaria in 1784 as Op. VI, nos. 1–3, in C major K. 330 (300h), A major K. 331 (300i), and F major (300k). Torricella engraved in 1784 Mozart's Op. VII, nos. 1–3, which included two sonatas for piano solo, in B-flat K. 333 and D major K. 284, and one for piano and violin in B-flat K. 454; as in the case of the variations, Artaria later reprinted and reissued these works in 1787. Artaria also published as Mozart's Op. XI the fantasy and sonata in C minor K. 475 and 457, dedicated to another pupil of Mozart, Thérèse von Trattner (1758–1793). The first edition of the movements comprising the sonata in F major K. 533 was published in 1788 by the Viennese firm of Franz Anton Hoffmeister.[12] While the exact number of Artaria publications which Josepha von Auernhammer edited must at present remain open to conjecture, one should recall that, in the later eighteenth century, piano trios and the sonatas for piano and violin were described generically as sonatas for piano, either "with the accompaniment of violin and cello" or "with the accompaniment of violin." Further, the majority of the piano and violin sonatas and piano trios, like the solo sonatas and variation sets, were also engraved by Artaria. Consequently, the citations in Cramer and Gerber may hint at an even larger role for Auernhammer than otherwise first evident.

By the mid 1780s, Auernhammer had established herself as a teacher as well as a pianist and composer, and one is tempted to speculate about the extent to which she had been endowed with Mozart's approach to piano instruction. Was the famous C major sonata K. 545 written in 1788 ("für Anfänger," as Mozart described it in the *Verzeichnüss* of his compositions)—one of the few sonatas not published in Mozart's lifetime—strictly for Mozart's own use as a teacher? It seems likely that Mlle von Auernhammer would have seen a manuscript copy of the work and perhaps used it for instruction herself. A reminiscence in the Abbé Maximilian Stadler's autobiography captures the affinity that Mozart and von Auernhammer shared.

---

[12]See Wolfgang Plath and Wolfgang Rehm, Preface to *NMA*, Serie IX, *Klaviermusik*, Werkgruppe 25: *Klaviersonaten*, Band 2 (Kassel, 1985), xvii.

> When he came to Vienna and had his 6 sonatas for clavier and violin engraved by Artaria and dedicated to Fräulein Auernhammer, he took me to rehearsal, Artaria [either Carlo or Francesco, one of the two brothers running the Viennese firm] brought the first printed copy with him. Fräulein Auernhammer played the fortepiano—and Mozart accompanied on a 2nd fortepiano that stood at hand, instead of on the violin, and I was wholly enchanted by the playing of master and pupil, and I never in my life heard it performed so incomparably again.[13]

Mozart dedicated to Thérèse von Trattner—the second wife of a prominent Viennese printer, Johann Thomas Edler von Trattner (1717–1798)—the fantasy and sonata in C minor K. 475 and 457 (composed in 1785 and 1784 respectively, and published by Artaria in 1785). From January to September 1784, Mozart and his family had lived in rooms rented from the Trattners in a large building known as the Trattnerhof in the Graben, of which a hall was often hired for concerts (Mozart gave his 1784 Lenten subscription concerts there). Mme von Trattner, like Josepha von Auernhammer, counted as one of Mozart's first pupils in Vienna, beginning her piano studies in 1781. If the fantasy and sonata were written expressly for her as well as dedicated to her, she must have possessed a formidable talent and technique. The fantasy, especially, stretches the bounds of contemporary pianistic idioms and exploits to a new degree the expressive powers of the piano. A lamentable loss is that of correspondence which Mozart had with Thérèse von Trattner, described by Constanze as "two interesting letters to Frau von Trattner about music"; according to Gustav Nottebohm, Constanze mentioned these documents in a letter of 27 November 1799 to the publishers Breitkopf and Härtel. Whether Mozart discussed the fantasy and sonata in particular, or general musical matters, is not known. There is no trace of either letter. However, of great interest is the discovery in 1990 of Mozart's autographs of the Fantasy and C minor Sonata, which differed in significant details from the first and subsequent published editions.

Among Mozart's piano students, Barbara Ployer (1765–1811) was the only one known to have undertaken contrapuntal instruction. She

---

[13]Deutsch, *Mozart*, 543.

was the daughter of Franz Kajetan Ployer, a tax collector and timber tradesman (and not the daughter of Gottfried Ignaz von Ployer as is incorrectly stated in Deutsch and repeated in subsequent sources; Gottfried Ignaz was her uncle and the family member with whom she lived in Vienna from 1780 onward). Barbara Ployer began studying with Mozart in 1784. She possessed an impressive talent—one particularly well-developed for a nineteen-year-old—that prompted Mozart to dedicate two concertos to her, the concerto in F major K. 453 (completed on 9 February 1784) and the concerto in G major K. 453 (entered by Mozart into his catalogue on 12 April 1784). The two works form part of a series of four concertos (the other two are those in B-flat major K. 450 and D major K. 451) written within the astonishingly short span of eight weeks, during which Mozart also composed the Quintet in E-flat for piano and woodwinds K. 452.

Excerpts from Mozart's correspondence provide some details of the background for both works. To his father, Mozart wrote on 20 February 1784, some eleven days after the completion of the E-flat major Concerto K. 449:

> The concerto is also in the original score and this too you may have copied; but have it done as quickly as possible and return it to me. Remember, do not show it to a *single soul*, for I composed it for Fräulein Ployer, who paid me handsomely.[14]

In a letter of 10 April, Mozart informs his father that he has that day completed a new concerto, in G major K. 453, for Ployer, although he did not enter it into his catalogue of works until two days later. On 15 May 1784, Mozart again exhorted his father to be careful with the copying:

> ... but I do ask you to have the four concertos copied at home, for the Salzburg copyists are as little to be trusted as the Viennese... and no one but myself possessed these concertos in G-flat and D [K. 450 and 451], and no one but *myself* and Fräulein Ployer (for whom I composed them) those in E-flat and G [K. 449 and K. 453].[15]

---

[14] Anderson, *Letters*, 868.
[15] Anderson, *Letters*, 876.

The link between Barbara Ployer and the concerto in E-flat major K. 449 bears consideration, given the concerto's stylistic significance. K. 449 initiates a series of highly mature concertos, although its orchestration is still written to afford the possibility of performance with strings only (omitting the winds) as with the concertos composed over the period of 1782–83 (in A major K. 414 [385p], F major K. 413 [387a], and C major K. 415 [387b])—the first group of concertos Mozart wrote in Vienna. Nonetheless, the overall texture stresses strong contrasts between soloists and orchestra, and other features, including the tightly constructed first movement with its focused development of an initial thematic motif, place this work on the evolutionary path forged by the concerto in E-flat major K. 271, composed in 1777. Accordingly, this concerto assumes a position of significance, as the first entry in Mozart's personal catalogue, the *Verzeichnüss aller meiner Werke*.

Alan Tyson's paper studies offer compelling evidence suggesting that the concerto in E-flat major K. 449—at least the first movement—was begun as early as 1782, taken up again late in 1783, and completed in February of the next year.[16] Therefore, the question arises about the extent to which Mozart actually conceived the concerto with Barbara Ployer in mind (there is no indication of their association prior to 1784), or whether he intended it for her only once he was close to completing it and in order to satisfy a commission. However, although her name does not appear in Mozart's correspondence and the known documents until 1784, one can not dismiss completely the possibility of an earlier association.

Tyson's essential investigations of the sources and composition history for another work, the Rondo in A major K. 386 for piano and orchestra, reveal that Mozart and Barbara Ployer may have been acquainted earlier.[17] This Rondo, dated 19 October 1782, was conceived as an independent work, rather than serving, as was previously thought, as a possible substitute finale for the concerto in A major K. 414 (385p) of 1782. When the publisher Johann Anton André acquired from Constanze Mozart the collection of her husband's manuscripts in late 1799 the autograph of this work was included, though the manuscript

---

[16] Alan Tyson, *Mozart, Studies of the Autograph Scores* (Cambridge, 1987), 153.
[17] Tyson, *Mozart Studies*, 275ff.

was incomplete. According to Tyson, the missing leaves of the Rondo were at that time in the possession of Barbara Ployer. In letters of 21–27 February and 31 May 1800, Constanze suggested to Johann Anton André that Ployer might be able to assist the Abbé Maximilian Stadler in the completion of the work as well as know the whereabouts of some of the missing leaves: "Perhaps the Abbé Stadler can complete the rondo in the piano concerto No. 26 through his connections with Früulein Ployen [sic]" ". . . this [the Rondo in A major] will be in the hands of the former Früulein Ployen, now Frau Bojanowich, who is living *not far from* Kreuz in Croatia."[18] (At the time, Constanze and André believed erroneously that the rondo formed part of a concerto.)

Various scenarios suggest themselves. First, if Mozart had in fact written the work for Ployer, then he had known her at least since 1782, because the paper of the Rondo manuscript conclusively dates from that year, as does the other known information concerning its composition. Second, whether he originally intended the Rondo for her or not, Mozart gave Barbara Ployer the manuscript of the Rondo at a later date (possibly in 1784, or still later) for her own performance or, less likely, as a gift. The vexing question arises why Ployer would have been given only part of the manuscript from Mozart or, for some reason, retained only part of it. Regardless of when Mozart gave the Rondo to Ployer, Mozart himself likely gave the premiere of the Rondo in 1782. In that same year, Mozart enjoyed remarkable success with performances of the newly composed Rondo in D major K. 382 that he employed as a substitute finale for the third movement of the concerto in D major K. 175, written in 1773. In a letter dated Vienna, 23 March 1782, Mozart wrote to his father:

> I am sending you at the same time *the last rondo* which I composed for my concerto in D major and which is making such a furore in Vienna. But I beg you to guard it like a *jewel*—and not to give it to a

---

[18]Tyson, *Mozart Studies*, 265–66. Tyson's re–evaluation of the Rondo's text and its conception as an independent work derives from his discovery in the British Library of three leaves which formed the missing fragment of the rondo's final forty–five measures. His determination is also based upon comparison of the papers of the concertos K. 413–415—the autograph scores of which were "re-discovered" in 1980 at the Bibliotheka Jagiellonska in Kraków—and the paper types of other contemporaneous Mozart autographs; these leaves were not available when the edition of this work was prepared for the *Neue Mozart-Ausgabe* in 1960 but now complete the definitive "score" of the work.

soul to play—not even to Marchand and his sister. I composed it *specially* for myself—and no one else but my dear sister must play it.[19]

Reports of Barbara Ployer's first performances of her concertos document her impressive pianistic prowess, as well as the success of her performance. The premiere of the G major concerto K. 453 took place on 10 June 1784 at a concert at the summer residence of her uncle, Ignaz von Ployer, in Döbling, outside of Vienna. At the concert, Mozart also played the newly written Quintet for piano and woodwinds in E-flat K. 452 and joined his pupil in the duo sonata in D major K. 448. Refined part-writing for the woodwinds, the essential characteristic of the piano quintet, assumes a new stylistic prominence in this concerto. Mozart's correspondence reveals that he was especially anxious for the influential opera composer Giovanni Paisiello (1740-1816)—then in Vienna to prepare the comic opera *Il re Teodoro in Venezia* and on his return to Naples after his eight-year tenure at the St. Petersburg court—to hear both his pupil and his music at this June concert.

Mozart was clearly fond of his talented student. References in his letters were often to Fräulein Babette, a characteristically affectionate use of the diminutive form. Constanze shared Mozart's esteem for his pupil; around 1795, she gave to Barbara Ployer a miniature watercolor portrait of her husband mounted on a leaf of paper on which was recorded a warm inscription by Constanze. The leaf formed part of Barbara Ployer's personal album which was formerly in the collection of the Mozarteum but, unfortunately, has been lost since 1945.[20]

An amusing document of Mozart's association with Barbara Ployer endures in the Kleiner Trauermarsch in C Minor K. 453a composed in 1784, subtitled "Marche funebre del Sig.r Maestro Contrapunto," and contained in the same album described above (now lost, though a photograph copy exists) that included the aforementioned watercolor. The album is distinct from the instruction book containing the theory and composition studies (K. 453b) Barbara Ployer undertook with Mozart in 1784, and which are themselves preserved in manuscript at

---

[19]Anderson, *Letters*, 798.

[20]Otto Erich Deutsch, *Mozart und seine Welt in zeitgenössichen Bildern*, NMA, Serie X: Supplement; Werkgruppe 32 (Kassel), 25 and 301.

the Austrian National Library, Vienna (cod. 17.589). These studies represent the first extant documents of Mozart's teaching in Vienna. (Thomas Attwood and Jacob Freystädtler were to commence their studies in 1786 and 1787, respectively.)[21]

The provenance of the Ployer studies is complicated. Barbara Ployer died in 1811 and, at least through the 1820s, the study book remained in the possession of the Abbé Maximilian Stadler who may have been her cousin.[22] The Ployer studies demonstrate Mozart's strict instruction, involving fundamental study in voice leading and counterpoint, and in this connection the mock funeral march for Lord Counterpoint in Barbara Ployer's album emerges as especially humorous. Through an alternation of suggested tutti and soli forces—underscored by shifts in register and dynamics stressing an independence of part-writing—the march bears the quality of a piano arrangement of an orchestral piece. Because of its parodistic tone, the pianistic writing remains simple, clearly not intended as a virtuoso tribute to his gifted pupil, but rather as a witty commemoration of the interment of contrapuntal ordinance—and dry comment by the teacher on the arduous tasks his pupil faced.

Johann Nepomuk Hummel (1778–1837) studied with Mozart for two years during the period 1786–1787. Comparatively little is known about Mozart's tutelage of his most famous male keyboard pupil, although the only document surviving from all of Mozart's piano teach-

---

[21]See Hellmut Federhofer, *Neue Mozart-Ausgabe*, Serie X: Supplement; Werkgruppe 30: *Studien, Skizzen, Entwürfe, Fragmente*, Varia; Band 2: *Barbara Ployer und Franz Jacob Freystädtlers Theorie- und Kompositionsstudien bei Mozart* (Leipzig, 1989), ix–x.

[22]Federhofer, *Barbara Ployer*. The Abbé Maximilian Stadler did not actually move to Vienna until 1796; in 1799, he, along with Georg Nikolaus von Nissen—Constanze Mozart's second husband—organized the Mozart manuscript collections held by Constanze. Stadler completed some of Mozart's compositions from fragments and sketches; his contributions to the Requiem are well known and discussed. In 1829, Vincent and Mary Novello mention the Abbé Stadler showing them part of certain contrapuntal exercises. These studies are considered to be those of Ployer; yet, debate continues whether the relative of Stadler involved in piano and composition study was not another student, perhaps Elisabeth Stadler, a niece of the Abbé. See Walter Senn, Abbé Maximilian Stadler: Mozarts Nachlaß und das "Unterrichtsheft" KV 453b," *Mozart-Jahrbuch 1980–83*; for a detailed, though perhaps not authoritative, list of Mozart's pupils, see Baird Hastings, *Wolfgang Amadeus Mozart, A Guide to Research* (New York, 1989), 355.

ing—a brief étude—seems to emanate from these years.[23] During this period, the eight-year-old Hummel lived with the Mozart family; Mozart gave Hummel free instruction, in distinct contrast to the arrangements Mozart had with his other pupils, the majority of whom were lady amateurs of noble birth or circumstances. Mozart discontinued Hummel's instruction in 1788 and one suspects Mozart's worsening financial circumstances in that year to have been a factor—a circumstance that no longer allowed Hummel to remain a member of the household. Interestingly, also in the spring of 1787, the sixteen-year-old Beethoven had come briefly to Vienna, where he likely received a few lessons from Mozart, although the exact nature of the tuition remains unclear.

Details of Mozart's and Hummel's relationship indicates it was warm and cordial. Mozart treated the young prodigy as a son and the parallel to his own childhood—through which he had been carefully guided by his father—could not have been lost on him.[24] A memoir of Hummel's father, Johannes (who in 1786 became the music director of the Theater auf der Wieden in Vienna, the venue for the premiere of *Die Zauberflöte* in 1791), relates the details of his son's initial meeting with Mozart and offers a glimpse into the audition and the resulting consequences.

> Mozart was hard at work when we entered, but in spite of that he received me with the friendly words, "Ah look; it's my dear Hummel; where have you been, and how are you? It's good to see you. Sit down; and you, my young friend, find yourself a chair."—I had to sit down on the sofa next to the little man.—"What brings you here?" he then asked me. With some slight embarrassment I brought out my request.

---

[23]See Wolfgang Plath, preface to *NMA*, Serie IX, *Klaviermusik*, Werkgruppe 27: Klavierstücke, Band 2: Einzelstücke für Klavier (Kassel, 1982), xxix.

[24]At the time Hummel became a member of the Mozart household, the Mozarts had only one child; during the following two years, two other infants were born but both passed away. Mozart's first son Raimund Leopold, born in the summer of 1783, survived only two months; Karl Thomas, the second child, born in September 1784, was approximately two years old when Hummel arrived; a third child, Johann Thomas Leopold, was born in October 1786 but died less than a month later; the fourth and fifth infants, born in December 1787 and November 1789, Theresia and Anna Maria, lived only 6 months and 1 hour respectively. Only Karl Thomas and the sixth child, Franz Xaver Wolfgang, born in July 1791, survived to adulthood.

He listened to me with patience, but when I had finished he looked a bit doubtful and said, "You know, my dear friend, I don't much like taking on pupils; it takes up too much time and disturbs me in my work. But let's see and hear what the boy's like and whether he's worth helping—Sit down at the piano, then, and show us what you can do," he said to Nepomuk. The latter came out with a few small pieces by Bach which he had carefully practiced, and spread them out. Mozart left him alone and he began. Wolfgang had sat down beside me again and listened with his arms crossed. He became ever more still, his expression ever more rapt; his eyes shone more brightly and joyously. During the performance he nudged me gently with his arm a few times and nodded appreciatively towards me. When my boy had finished the Bach, Mozart placed another and not exactly easy composition before him, one of his own this time, to see how good his sight-reading might be. It went very well. Wolfgang's attention grew from minute to minute. Suddenly, with a look that sparkled and twinkled for joy, he put his hand on my knee, pressed it gently, and whispered to me, "You must leave the lad here with me, I shan't let him out of my sight—something can be made of him!"—My Nepomuk had just about finished the movement when Mozart got up, hurried over to him, put his hand on his head, and said, "Bravo; you're a splendid lad. Carry on like that and you'll get on all right!"—He then took him by the hand, led him to the sofa, put him on his lap, and petted him continually. And to me he said, "It's agreed, then, I'll teach the lad, but he must live with me so that I can always have my eye on him. He shall have everything free, lessons, lodging, food. You will not have any of the cares of looking after him. Agreed?".... Shortly after, my son Nepomuk moved to Mozart's house, where he was treated like a son of the family. He was as comfortable and well cared for as possible; Wolfgang looked after him like a father, and Konstanze cared for him like a mother.[25]

However colored the recollections of Hummel's father might have been, the essential facts are accurate as other reminiscences bear out. The pianist and composer Ferdinand Hiller (1811–1825), himself a student of Hummel, revealed certain details of Hummel's life with the Mozarts in a report from a trip he made with Hummel in 1827 to the Mozart apartments at Schulerstrasse.

Hummel took me to another building... it was the self same house in which as an eight year old boy he had lived with Mozart and received

[25]Deutsch, *Mozart, A Documentary Biography*, 569–70.

instruction from him. The master was completely absorbed in his memories. As he led me through the various rooms, which seemed not to have undergone any alteration, he described the former furnishings to me. "Here," he said, "stood Mozart's pianoforte, at which I had lessons—here was the writing desk at which he composed—here in this little room stood my clavier and there in the middle of the room was a billiard table. One day I tried to wield the cue and tore a hole in the cloth. The punishment (he mimed it) was not slow in coming."[26]

In this report, the terminological distinction between pianoforte and clavier is significant: clavier, as a generic term for keyboard instrument, was commonly used well into the nineteenth century, appearing even in the mature solo piano works of Beethoven as well as some scores of Chopin; in this report, it is clearly employed to distinguish between the piano and either the harpsichord or clavichord. While Hummel might have practiced on a harpsichord, more likely the reference is to the latter instrument. During the Vienna years, Mozart maintained a clavichord that he utilized at times when he composed,[27] and that, as the above reminiscence suggests, he might have reserved for Hummel's practice instrument. In correspondence Mozart often stated preferences for the clavichord, and the sensitive technique it engendered. There existed, also, a certain affinity between the responsive touch of the clavichord and the light keyboard action of Viennese pianos.

That Hummel had offered to repay Mozart's generosity if he were some day to acquire means was not forgotten by Constanze, when in 1838 (by then married to and widowed of Georg Nikolaus von Nissen, a Danish diplomat, her second husband and author of one of the first biographies of Mozart), she reproached in surprisingly stern and petty fashion Hummel's heirs for what she interpreted as a willful lack of consideration on the part of their father.

> Should not this great man have thought of me at his death? So often he promised verbally that if he ever were to become prosperous, he would surely repay with generosity all my troubles, love, care and expenses, room and board, and lessons, which he enjoyed from my late husband Mozart.[28]

---

[27]Nathan Broder, "Mozart and the 'Clavier,'" in *The Creative Mind of Mozart*, ed. Paul Henry Lang (New York, 1963), 77–78.

[28]The author is grateful to Erna Schwerin for reference to this correspondence. Wilhelm A. Bauer, Otto Erich Deutsch, Joseph Heinz Eibl, Mozart, *Briefe und Aufzeichnungen*, Band IV (Kassel, 1962–63), 516.

Hummel's first appearance in Vienna may have been in 1787 in a concert organized by Mozart. By 1788, as mentioned, Mozart no longer could continue the instruction and encouraged Hummel and his father to undertake a concert tour—one which was to last four years. Among the works on Hummel's program for his appearance at Dresden in March 1789 were the virtuoso set of variations on "Lison dormait" K. 264 and a piano concerto (probably K. 503 in C major). In May, Hummel repeated the program at Berlin, in a concert at which Mozart was present (Mozart was in Berlin and during the month appeared before the Prussian court). Hummel and his father continued throughout northern Europe, Scotland, and England, returning to Vienna in early 1793, by which time, Mozart had been dead a little over a year.

During the ensuing years, Hummel enjoyed success as a pianist, composer, teacher, and conductor in Vienna, Esterhazy and Weimar. In the 1820s, Hummel focused attention on teaching and composition. During this period, he also made arrangements of the last six Mozart symphonies (K. 385, 425, 504, 543, 550, and 551) and seven of Mozart's piano concertos for London publishers. Hummel probably completed the symphony arrangements by 1823, whereas he prepared many of the piano concerto arrangements for his tours to England in the later 1820s and 1830s.[29] The symphony and concerto arrangements were made for piano with accompaniment of flute, violin and violoncello; they seem to have existed also in a transcription for solo piano.

Hummel's arrangements of the symphonies and the concertos reflect the demand for literature addressed to the ever-growing market of amateur performer. The results further demonstrated a shift in musical taste. The arrangements featured changes in tempo (almost always faster) and, in the concerto arrangements, different and elaborate keyboard figurations that tended towards the excessive. Moreover, Hummel occasionally made harmonic and formal changes, which further removed the concerto arrangements from their original sphere. Contemporaries of Hummel, pianist-composers including Johann Baptist Cramer (1771–1858) and Philipp Carl Hoffmann (1769–ca.1830) also made embellished versions of Mozart piano concerto movements (mostly slow movements). Moreover, there exists a

---

[29]Sachs, *Kapellmeister Hummel*, 102–5.

manuscript with written out ornamentation of the piano part for the second movement of the concerto in A major K. 488, of which the author appears to be none other than Barbara Ployer. Its relevance, however, to Mozart's authentic text is dubious.[30]

It is interesting to consider which concertos figured in Hummel's adaptations. Hummel selected a wide-ranging group of seven works, five of which were from the series of concertos Mozart wrote for his subscription concerts in Vienna in the mid-1780s. Perhaps more unusual were Hummel's decisions to adapt the concerto in E-flat K. 365 (316a) for two pianos, which Mozart composed in 1779, and the Concerto in D major K. 537 (the so-called "Coronation" concerto), Mozart's penultimate work in the genre, written in 1788.[31]

The musical style of the concerto in D major K. 537 prefigures markedly the keyboard style of the subsequent generation of pianist-composers, such as Carl Maria von Weber and Hummel (Charles Rosen has described this idiom as "proto-Romantic"; characteristically, the "Coronation" concerto, along with the concerto in D minor K. 466, numbered during the nineteenth century among Mozart's most popular concertos). Since Mozart had completed the concerto in D major K. 537 in February 1788, it is conceivable that Hummel, though a child, was witness to the concerto's composition. The likelihood is also great that Hummel was present at the first performance of the concerto in C major (completed in December 1786). Of the concertos which Hummel selected for his arrangements, none was published in subscription during Mozart's life.

Around the same time when he was preparing the arrangements of Mozart's symphonies, Hummel was at work on his monumental keyboard manual *Ausführlich theoretisch-practische Anweisung zum*

---

[30]Frederick Neumann, *Ornamentation and Improvisation in Mozart* (Princeton, 1986), 251 ff.

[31]*Sept/Grand concertos/de/W. A. Mozart/arrangées/Pour Piano seul/avec Cadences et Ornaments/par le célèbre/J.N. Hummel, à Londres, chez Schott et Cie* [n.d.]. The other arrangements are of the concertos in D minor K. 466 (1785), C major K. 503 (1786), C minor K. 491 (1786), E-flat major K. 482 (1785), and B-flat major K. 456 (1784). The first publication may have been by Chappell as proprietor for J. R. Schulz; Schott later assumed or possibly pirated the edition.

Piano–Forte Spiel, (written during the period 1822–25 and published in 1828).[32] The piano method, in three parts, represents a summary of Hummel's keyboard technique and broad pedagogical perspective, while demonstrating his essentially classical aesthetic and pianistic origins. It stands at the end of a tradition of eighteenth–century treatises on instrumental practice (J. J. Quantz, *Versuch einter Anweisung die Flöte traversiere zu spielen, 1752;* Leopold Mozart, *Violonschule*, 1756; C. P. E. Bach, *Versuch über die wahre Art das Clavier zu spielen*, 1762; Daniel Gottlob Türk, *Clavierschule*, 1789), and at the beginning of the era of manuals or methods addressed expressly to a piano literature whose ever growing technical demands necessarily required a specialized approach in the way of studies, exercises, and drills. The work of one of the most sought after teachers, Hummel's method supposedly sold thousands within days of its initial printing.[33]

As mentioned above, the sole known keyboard study by Mozart (reproduced on page 224, plate 1) is generally believed to have been written in the late 1780s. Wolfgang Plath has speculated that it may have been intended for Hummel. It is a remarkable document: first, it gives a methodical approach to the study of the quintessential accompanimental pattern of classical era keyboard music—the Alberti bass; second, it provides in equal measure the exercise pattern for both the right as well as the left hand; third and perhaps most striking, Mozart gives explicit fingering for every note throughout the pattern, thus indicating not only the fingering for such passage work but also a sound ideal that necessarily resulted from his fingering choices. The autograph is now in the collections of the Institute of Russian Literature, Pushkin House, St Petersburg, Russia.

It is tempting to consider whether Mozart's keyboard study, if intended for Hummel, is somehow represented in Hummel's *An-*

---

[32]The eminently popular study was published in an English version at London, and later in America, under the title *A Complete Theoretical & Practical Course of Instruction on The Art of Playing the Piano Forte Commencing with the Simplest elementary principles and including every information requisite to the Most finished Style of Performances*. Written and most humbly dedicated to His Majesty George IV by J. N. Hummel. New York, Published by Firth & Hall, Franklin Square [n.d.]; Revised and corrected by David Paine.

[33]Joel Sachs, "Johann Nepomuk Hummel," *The New Grove Dictionary of Music and Musicians*, ed. Stanley Sadie, vol. 8 (London, 1980): 784.

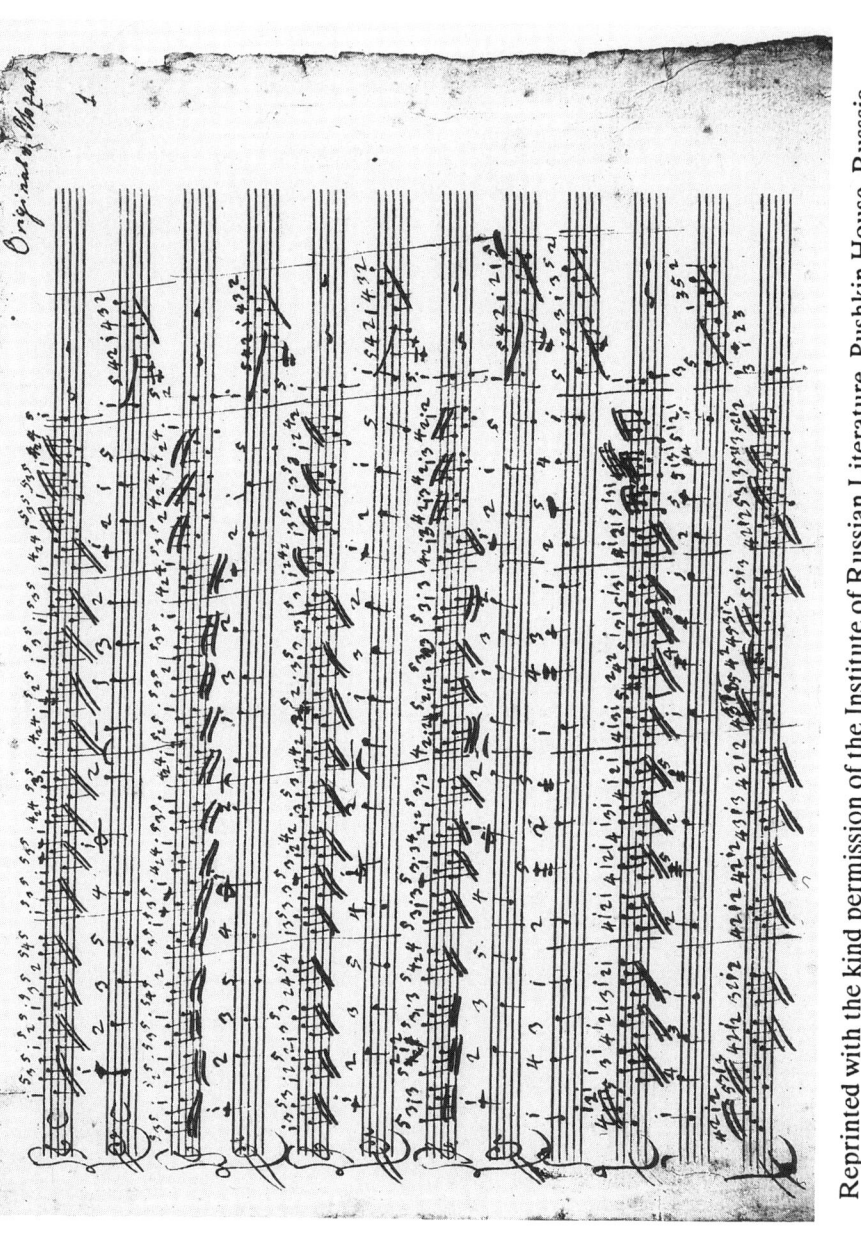

Reprinted with the kind permission of the Institute of Russian Literature, Pushkin House, Russia

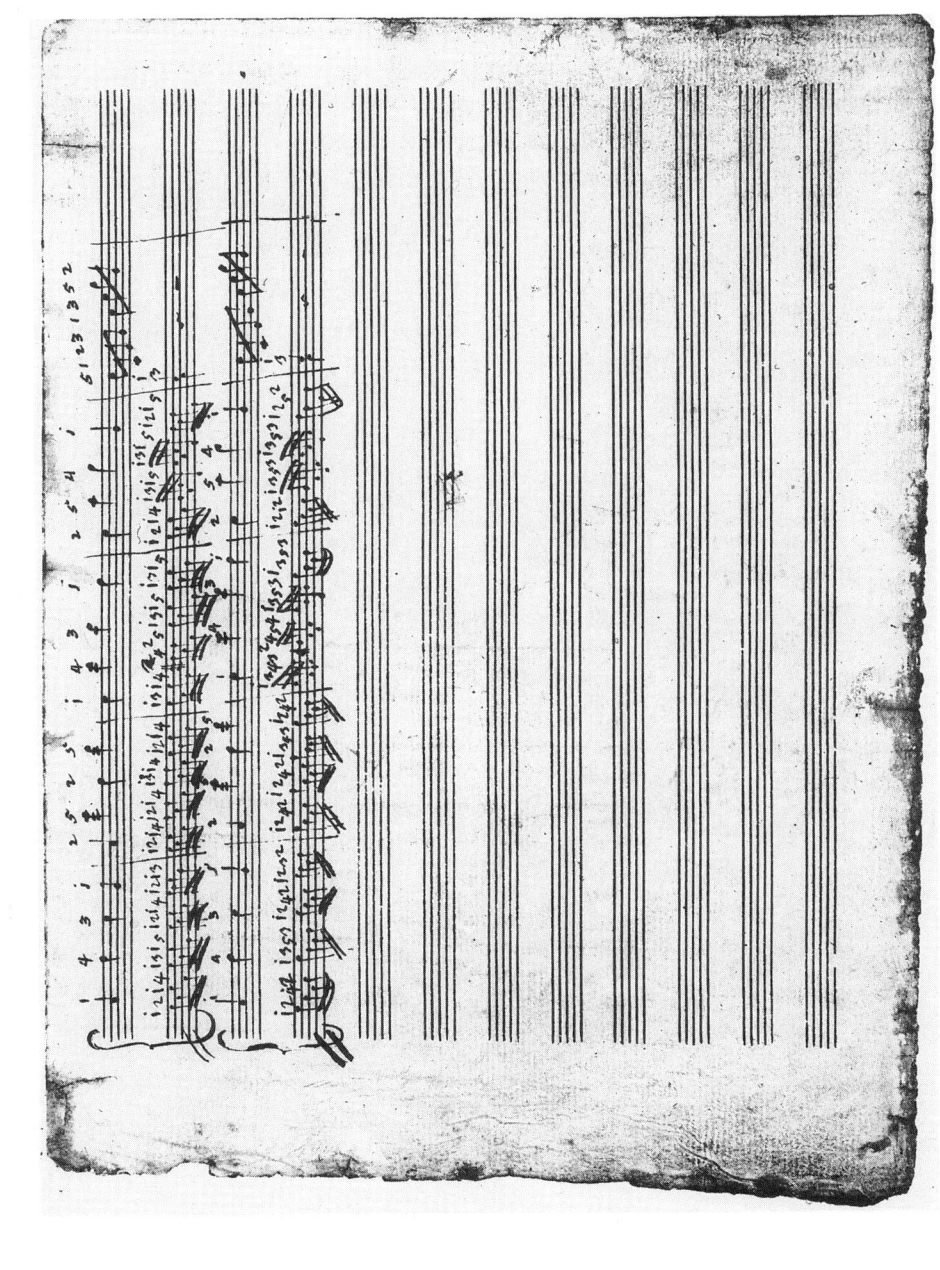

weisung. The study is nowhere literally replicated. Certain exercises in the first section of the third part stress independence of the fingers and their alternation in similar patterns to the Mozart study. None takes up Mozart's specific and meticulous fingering. Similarities could be interpreted as Hummel's assimilation of Mozart, but overall Hummel's exercises typify a wholly different pianistic style born of a new era. Still, Hummel's claims prefacing an exercise on the trill merit quoting: "For this purpose, I recommend the following exercise on the shake with all the fingers alternately, communicated to me practically by Mozart himself."

Throughout the *Anweisung zum Piano-forte Spiel*, Hummel used mostly his own pieces for illustration and instruction. Notably, he specified Mozart's works after the student demonstrated suitable advancement. Given the expressed virtuoso style of a new age and Hummel's "revisions" of Mozart's texts in the concerto arrangements, the recommendation of Mozart's piano works not as the repertoire for the beginner, but as the literature appropriate for the advanced pupil, demonstrates Hummel's keen understanding of the fundamental challenges posed by his master's music.

Walther Dürr

MUSIC AS AN ANALOGUE OF SPEECH
Musical Syntax in the Writings of Heinrich Christoph Koch and in the Works of Schubert

"Next to poetry," says Immanuel Kant in his *Kritik der Urteilskraft*,[1] "I would place music, with its moving effect upon the mind, as the preeminent among the communicative arts. For though music speaks through impressions not guided by intellectual concepts, and thus not calling for direct rational interpretation, it moves the mind more intricately...Its effect, being so direct, seems to be based on the fact that every expression, as if in the context of speech, receives a sound appropriate to its meaning...that the modulation of the sound is, as it were, a language, perceptible to everyone, and that it alone can lay claim to being the language of affections..."

While it is Kant's concern to define music as a language, it remains a language "without concepts"—"impression rather than expression of thought (the play of thought arising, so to speak, merely through an association),"[2] yet closest of all arts to poetry. As the "language of

---
[1] I. Kant, *Kritik der Urteilskraft*, ed.R. Schmidt (Leipzig, 1956), 237.
[2] Kant, *Kritik*, 237.

Walther Dürr is a Professor at the University of Tübingen and a distinguished member of the editorial board of the Neue Schubert-Ausgabe.

affections," it emerges as an analogue of language, reduced—if judged from Kant's point of view—to the very sonority of speech. It communicates through sonorities, through imitation of speech, similar to the art of the mime whose "language" on the stage mimics speech inflection and succeeds in conveying wrath and joy, allurement and rejection, love and hate.

Interpretation through music guides and intensifies the sound of speech, as speech guides the mime; it produces an apt expression. Such parallels are stated as early as the writings of Vincenzo Galilei. He likens the madrigalist, who mauls the continuity of the text with excessive "madrigalisms," to "Zanni" (=Giovanni), the servant figure in the *commedia dell' arte,* who recites comedies not in actual speech but only by imitating the inflections of the portrayed personages. He argues that the composer should not dwell upon the meaning of the individual word but "speak in some manner, with a voice that tends toward the high and the low, with a varying amount of sound, with certain accents and inflections, as one would utter something in rapid or tardy motion."[3]

Vincenzo Galilei was a lutenist—and it was probably not accidental that, being an instrumentalist, he argued so strongly against the commitment to the single word and for a general "language of the affections." And is not the instrumental music of his time predominantly imitation of speech (if not, in fact, intabulated vocal music), declaiming words and sentences in the manner of the orator, yet without fixed concepts, like the "Zanni?" This applies in equal measure to seventeenth-century instrumental music independent of vocal models: the term "canzona" refers in itself to the origin of vocal declamation. Yet the "sonata"—from the outset more instrumentally conceived—is equally linked by its *soggetti* to the model of the motet or madrigal. As an example, chosen at random, we might quote the opening of a *Sonata a due* for violin and continuo from Giovanni Paulo Cima's *Concerti ecclesiastici* of 1610[4] (see Example 1).

[3]V. Galilei, *Dialogo...della musica antica, et della moderna*, (Florence, 1581). Facs. repr. ed. F. Fano (Rome, 1934) 89f. See also W. Dürr, "Sprachliche und musikalische Determinanten in der Monodie: Beobachtungen an Monteverdis *Orfeo*," in *Claudio Monteverdi: Festschrift Reinhold Hammerstein zum 70. Geburtstag*, ed. L. Finscher (Laaber, 1986), 151f.
[4]Modern edition in *12 Sonaten für Violine und Klavier und eine Suite für Violine allein*, ed. G. Beckmann (Berlin/Leipzig, 1921) Heft 1,3.

Example 1.

It is unmistakable: in the first three measures (though not in the subsequent passage) the instrumentalist recites. One is tempted to place syllables under the notes—forming a sentence that leads to the fourth syllable as a climax and ending in an exclamation. The measures trace the sound of a sentence, on its musical rather than its conceptual level. This appears so even though the *soggetto* is doubtless instrumental in character, as the vocally awkward interval of the seventh, filled in by thirds, shows.

Speech, communication, indeed moves on two clearly distinguishable levels.[5] That which a "Zanni" expresses, as he speaks in fantasy sounds (often, incidentally, in imitation of a foreign language—its expression, not its words), and any expression with which the doctrine of musical affections deals, can be transmitted by way of the "musical level" of language. It is, in a way, a "primitive," aboriginal form of speech, anticipating the critical powers of speech; intensified, it grows of itself into music and thus can be directly and totally absorbed in music. With the conceptual, semantic level of speech, however, music has a harder time. It requires an interpretative system—and needs to fall back upon the support of the spoken word.

In the following, we shall deal only with the "musical level" of speech and its analogies. If the instrumentalist follows the example of the "Zanni," he traces not only the inflection and relative intensity of speech; he also divides his discourse into syntactic units, main and subordinate clauses. At first this occurs in direct imitation of the singer; but in the development toward an independent instrumental language, such syntactic units, too, become independent (the model of dance

---

[5]See W. Dürr, *Das deutsche Sololied im 19. Jahrhundert: Untersuchungen zu Sprache und Musik*, Taschenbücher zur Musikwissenschaft 97 (Wilhelmshaven, 1984): 23 ff.

music, *a priori* instrumental, not being the least among the ruling influences). There arise symmetries, correspondences, and periodic structures which, though no longer derived from speech, remain beholden to the analogy with speech. Eighteenth-century theory attests to this abundantly.

There we find music as "speech in musical sound,"[6] analogies to rhetoric (which in Galilei's "Zanni" comparison was first intimated), and reference to "speaking passages" within a work.[7] Quite generally there is the tendency, as expressed in Daniel Gottlieb Türk's *Klavierschule*, "to compare an entire piece of music to an oration; for as in the latter there is a division into larger and smaller sections, so also in music. A major section of a musical work (*Hauptabschnitt*) corresponds to the principal portion of an address. A musical period (*Abschnitt*), which again may be subdivided, is the equivalent of what in a talk is equally called a period, separated from the remainder by the period mark (.). Musical rhythm may encompass smaller sections indicated in speech by a colon (:) or semicolon (;). The smallest musical unit would be that which, in a spoken presentation, is set off by the comma (,)."[8]

Up to this point the analogies do not in fact exceed those of sixteenth-century music theory. In his *Versuch einer Anleitung zur Composition*, Heinrich Christoph Koch moves into new territory; he proceeds from the structure of sound to the syntactical structures on which it is based. In line with musical aesthetics of his time, and indeed with Kant's statements, he expresses the conviction "that music can attain its highest aim, its essential purpose, only with reference to poetry...that its separation from poetry would be to its detriment...

---

[6] J. Mattheson, *Der vollkommene Capellmeister* (Hamburg, 1739), 82. For a selection of theoretical statements, see H. Krones, " 'Meine Sprache versteht man durch die ganze Welt.' Das 'redende Prinzip' in Joseph Haydns Instrumentalmusik," in *Wort und Ton im Europäischen Raum: Gedenkschrift für Robert Schollum* (Vienna/Cologne, 1989), 79ff.

[7] C.P.E. Bach, *Versuch über die wahre Art das Clavier zu spielen* I (Berlin, 1753, repr. Leipzig, 1957): 132.

[8] D.G. Türk, *Klavierschule, oder Anweisung zum Klavierspielen für Lehrer und Lernende* (Leipzig/Halle, 1789, repr. Kassel, 1962), 343.

since the concepts and images of poetry save the composer from the danger of being misunderstood."[9] This implies that it is all the more important for instrumental music to remain close to the model of vocal music and, by structures analogous to speech, reach beyond the natural common basis—the "musical level" of speech.

Koch devotes his attention therefore to this common basis, to those syntactical structures that are at the bottom of the concrete formation of a specific language. Section Three in Chapter Two of the second part of his work deals with the "Nature of Melodic Units." As in Türk's book, what is involved here is a structure expressed through the "resting points in the spirit of the melody" that are comparable to those of speech. The first chapter, however, "Of the Small Units and Their Subdivisions," makes concrete reference to the grammar of language. He writes: "If subject and predicate of a melody could be as clearly distinguished as in speech, one would not have to rely on mere feeling in separating complete from incomplete musical statements."[10] This still leaves the reader with the impression that such strict analogy to the grammer of music might not be practicable. Yet he continues: "I would like to pursue this comparison of melodic with linguistic sentences briefly. If, for instance, we were to consider the following passage (see Example 2) from the point of view of such logic, it would be a complete theme, because the principal motif contained in the first two measures, in its quality of a subject, receives through the subsequent two measures a predicate that lends it a certain direction and intent."

Example 2.

Later, however, Koch does not return to these deliberations, but rather makes reference to his initial skeptical attitude, though an added extensive comment makes it clear that this skeptical attitude is mere pretense:

---

[9]H.C. Koch, *Versuch einer Anleitung zur Composition* II (Leipzig, 1787, repr. Hildesheim, 1969): 33f.
[10]H. C. Koch, *Versuch*, II:350ff.

> In the context of this and the following sections of my discussion, I actually intended. . .to follow up my thoughts regarding the similarities of spoken sentences, with their typical cohesion, and melodic sentences, for I believed that greater definition could thus be given to the periodic structure of melody. But the fact that the sole purpose of my discussion is to be of use to musicians aspiring to the art of composition—with their probable lack of experience in grammatical and logical methods—caused me to give up this plan, since without a thorough command of such methods, a further elaboration might have rendered my discussion obscure to the beginner.[11]

Thus it was primarily for didactic reasons that Koch limited himself to mere suggestions—yet he seems to have had the exploration of "similarities with spoken sentences" at heart, and the topic may have entered his instruction whenever he felt that a student might have been sufficiently receptive.

But what is actually involved? Koch's central concepts—in his Introduction, in the text proper, and again in the added comment—are "precision" and "direction" of the periodic structure and its detailed design. As becomes clear from his specifically musical definitions, he is concerned with "a certain direction and intent" which he links to the function of the grammatical predicate. A complete statement, in music as in verbal expression, requires both parts: the subject which indicates the theme (the opening two measures of a "small unit," that is, a four-measure phrase), and the predicate (the next two measures) which clarifies what the subject is about, elucidates both its very nature and its impact upon the continuation of the spoken or musical statement.

Turning to Koch's own example, we see that the subject leads to the sixth belonging to the subdominant harmony; yet the key remains somewhat ambivalent (the progression from tonic to subdominant could possibly—marginally—be interpreted as one from dominant to tonic). The syncopated formation of the opening measures, though pronounced (and thus particularly suitable for a subject), seems to confuse any attempt to determine the metric design. It is only by the remaining measures that both harmonic and rhythmic structure are clearly defined, and that "direction and intent" are given to the subject.

---

[11]H.C. Koch, *Versuch*, II:356.

It should be observed that there are various critical differences between the two components. One might compare, for instance, the essentially rising tendency of the one with the essentially descending tendency of the other. Such antithesis marks the basic patterns of syntax (the complex of subject-predicate involving that of subject-object).

It seems feasible to test Koch's analytical contentions against compositions of his era. In the following, however, I would like to pursue a different course. Koch's deliberations concerning the analogy of speech and music will be applied to Schubert's instrumental music—for three reasons. First, I owe to the honorand a realization of Schubert's deep indebtedness to eighteenth-century didactic traditions,[12] and my purpose is to view the latter interconnection also with regard to the analogies under discussion. Secondly, Koch analyzes in his text themes that are beholden to the style and taste of his time; and while it is to be expected that the speech patterns to which he refers can be recognized in those, further conclusions may be drawn from works that reflect his teachings, although they are not chronologically concurrent. And thirdly, a declamatory character to be found especially in Schubert's instrumental music has often been noted.

Harry Goldschmidt has sought to relate all of Schubert's instrumental works to prosodic models (which he also understands as semantically expressive of texts). He has used the first movement of the great C Major Symphony as a comprehensive model for his concept and arrived at the following conclusion:

> We can recognize, beyond all principal and subsidiary melodies, one unified, prosodic-semantic image. While preserving all symphonic principles and the entire hierarchy of primary and secondary melodies, the total fabric is determined by it. Through the instrumental foreground, a vocal basis, implied, yet interpretive, invariably shines through.[13]

Goldschmidt's thesis seems to me erroneous. The method of deriving all particles—"principal and subsidiary melodies"—of a major instrumental composition from a few prosodic patterns does not seem

---

[12] A. Mann, *Schuberts Studien, Neue Schubert-Ausgabe* VIII/2 (Kassel, 1986).
[13] H. Goldschmidt, "Der erste Satz der grossen C-Dur-Sinfonie. Eine prosodische Studie," *Beiträge zur Musikwissenschaft* XXI (1979): 281.

plausible. Goldschmidt sees the text "Gross ist Jehova der Herr," which Schubert used in *Die Allmacht*" (D. 852), as well as the same text in the *Alleluja Invocation* (unfinished, D. 875A), as the basis for preliminary compositions of Johann Ladislaus Pyrker's poetry (part of the latter's "Elisa" from *Perlen der heiligen Vorzeit*). This could only be so if at least essential parts of the prosodic models, the rhythmic conformations of the text setting, were to return in the symphony—but this is not the case. From the outset, as early as the horn theme of the slow introduction, any model can be only indirectly applied—it may "shine through" but could easily be supplanted by other models. Perhaps—and this is implied by Koch's insistence on mere analogy—the search for concrete prosodic models is as such illusive, so that Schubert's supposed models constitute a prosody in fact deceptive, in the sense of the Italian "Zanni."

Yet, surprisingly often, Schubert's "statements"—be they "small units," as in Koch's example, or larger—are bi-partite in the manner that a declamatory gesture, as a "subject," is answered by a predicate through which the former is harmonically defined (in reality, as we shall see, only by way of a deceptive cadence), thus giving it a "certain intent." One might quote here the opening phrase of the piano sonata in A Minor (D. 784, February 1823), that of the four-hand piano sonata in C Major (D. 812, June 1824), or that of the later piano sonata in A Minor (D. 845, spring 1825).[14]

Turning to these themes, we find that the A Minor Sonata of 1823 begins with a brief statement quite in keeping with Koch's model (Example 3).

Example 3.

---

[14]Compare with the opening movements of the piano sonatas in C (D. 279, September 1815), in A flat (D. 557, May 1817), in D flat/E flat (D. 568, June 1817), in B (D 575, August 1817), in C (D. 613, April 1818), in f (D. 625, September 1818) and in C (D. 840, April 1825).

The opening gesture of the theme "speaks"; one is tempted to put words to it, or at least articulate syllables, albeit syllables without special semantic connotation. Yet it is not this quality that defines the theme, but rather an aural impression common to music and speech. The declamatory elements—inner structure, melodic high and low points—are outlined by Schubert's phrase markings (elsewhere also by staccato or *portato* signs) as well as by melodic and dynamic accents. It is above all the dynamic symbol—not infrequently giving rise to justified confusion with the decrescendo mark—that suggests the nature of speech. Taken simply as an accent designation, it seems self-evident. The first of these symbols, for instance, occurring on an emphasized beat of the measure, coincides with a tone foreign to the key and is thus emphatic in itself. Schubert uses it in a manner corresponding to that of the raised third in the dominant chord of measure 3, as a tone of similar "utterance." And the phrase marks? In the last measure here quoted, he separates the melodic interval of the third from the preceding. This concluding figure has its own significance; it may be taken as the theme's most essential element. Schubert "articulates" his musical language in a more richly differentiated manner than that found in most works of his time.

But how does he structure this language? The four-measure statement consists of two halves covering two measures each. Adopting Koch's procedure, the first half would constitute the "subject." It supplies the thematic motion characteristic of the movement, the upward skip of the fifth. Granted, taken in itself, the subject lacks "definite" contour: it contains no more than this skip, embellished with a changing note. Only in the second half does it gain definition through the tone c (designating the minor, not the major mode), through the statement's single chord, which marks the dominant of A Minor. Here the theme also receives rhythmic impulse, through the dotted figure, the impulse lending direction to the continuation of the Allegro. In the rising and falling, and in the contrast formed by calm half-note motion and rhythmic impetus, one recognizes the antithetical structure of subject and predicate.

Whereas Schubert's opening themes are rather readily identified with a syntax analogous to speech (in the Sonata D. 784 this applies as well to the "speaking" Andante theme, though not to that of the last movement—dance-like movements reflect a different tradition), the lyrical secondary themes tend toward a more generally obscured structure. Such themes are often rounded in themselves, and inner correspondences take the place of the driving subject-predicate relationship. In the first movement of the same sonata there is a preponderance of such correspondences (Example 4). Individual two-measure statements refer to one another, but they do not represent self-contained units in the sense of Koch's theory. While the second of the quoted two-measure statements further determines the tonality of the first (the sequence subdominant-dominant defines the preceding E Major as tonic and leads back to it by an "open" cadence that suggests the nature of a scaffolding), there is a lack of "definite" direction; an optional number of similar statements could follow. The two-measure units do not stand one against the other but are antithetical in an inner sense; they do not lead on, but loosely balance one another. (In the continuation of the movement, Schubert finds himself compelled to break this chain).

Example 4.

A syntax in the grammatical sense could therefore be recognized in Schubert's secondary themes only with difficulty, yet a declamatory intent nevertheless emerges with clarity from his articulation. The theme is marked to be played *portato* throughout. The marking used serves in Schubert's writing often in a dual function. It conveys articulation in the first place—an articulation related to the accents appearing in the two-measure statements—though in the combined use of the symbols the *portato* divides the two-measure units into question and answer. In the second place, it indicates inherent weight, guides the performer from mere execution into the domain of an interpretation approaching the "espressivo" (which, as such, is rare with Schubert). At times his *portato* mark underlines also a semantically defined gesture, such as the "walking" motif in the song *Der Wanderer* (D. 489) or in the Wanderer Fantasy (D. 760)—yet this leads beyond the present context.[15]

We return to the two other themes mentioned earlier. In the opening of the A Minor Piano Sonata of 1825 (D. 845), we see again a "small unit" (Example 5).

Example 5.

It leads, however, to a half close which, through the duality of leading tones—d sharp and f—would seem to negate its dominant function and rather suggest a modulation. Yet the tone d, as upbeat to measure 5, restores the tonal design (the sequence returns and gains significance in the continuation of the movement). As in the earlier A Minor Sonata, Schubert begins with a declamatory unison statement, in this case covering the entire octave rather than the fifth. Again the melodic high point is accented—marked with an accent symbol more indicative of the theme's "speaking" character than of a needed performance direction (the melodic accent, together with the broadening caused by the dotted rhythm, would supply sufficient emphasis). And again the subject requires tonal definition through a predicate, for it is limited to the tonic chord as such (whose minor mode was in this case already suggested). The chordal continuation—sixth chord on the tonic, three-four chord on the dominant, tonic root position, and sixth chord on the dominant—progresses in the manner of a definition, yet, due to its implied

---

[15]In this connection, and generally in connection with the idea of proceeding from the purely musical level of speech to its semantic meaning, see W. Dürr, "Semantische Zeichen in Schuberts Instrumentalmusik," in *IMS Kongressbericht 1987* (Torino, 1990), 781–91.

modulatory character, remains ambivalent. It provides antithesis—a "certain direction"—rather than definition. In fact, contrasts arise in all imaginable parameters: unison and chordal setting; wide melodic range (octave) and small melodic range (fourth); high and low register; rhythmic multiformity and even quarter notes; pianissimo and mezzoforte; basic tempo and "un poco ritardando"; legato and *portato*. It is not surprising that the conclusion of the theme remains "open-ended," that it drives toward development, a development that, due to the fact that all further themes are derived from the principal one, determines the entire course of the movement.

Whereas this theme is guided by tonal ambivalence, its nature suggesting a developmental rather than a thematic quality, the theme of the four-hand piano sonata, the so-called *Gran Duo* (D 812), contains such ambivalence as its very essence (Example 6).

Example 6.

At the outset the latter theme resembles the former. It shows a strictly antithetical structure: change from unison to chordal texture; change of registers; descending melodic direction in the opening statements and ascending melodic direction in the subsequent ones; and finally—though more subtly—dynamic shadings. In contrast to the previously discussed themes, however, the subject is now not oriented by an interval or chord; it is based on a melodic line that covers the interval of a seventh. The dissonant relationship of its extreme melodic points implies tonal ambivalence to begin with. The theme opens, so to speak, in C Major, but ends in A Minor (quite similar, incidentally, to the horn theme in the introduction for the great C Major Symphony). One expects that the chordal predicate will define the as yet tonally undefined theme. While in itself unambiguous, it yet obscures rather than clarifies the context: it leads to D Minor. The ensuing new unison passage seems to take up the D Minor tonality but moves gradually toward G (dominant of the opening key) and E (dominant of the subsequent A Minor). A new predicate, as if to resolve the questions left open, seems to guide to C Major (which would interpret the preceding stations as a broadly designed cadence: subject I—tonic and relative minor; predicate I—subdominant of the relative minor; subject II—subdominant of the relative minor, dominant of the original key, and its tonic). Yet it continues to modulate: the dominant progression d–d sharp in measure 7 prepares us for a half close on e (will it be a minor after all?), and the closing chord does convey the impression of a deceptive cadence. But it is a first inversion of a C Major tonic chord. The doubling of the chord's third, which Schubert as a rule carefully avoids, lends even further emphasis to the impression of a deceptive cadence. We realize that the composer is in no way concerned with tonal definition; what he wishes to convey is indeed uncertainty.

In the next measures Schubert resumes the play: C Major–a minor–d minor; and the final movement of the sonata confirms the same impression. It begins in a minor (introduced through a sustained e)[16] and gradually moves toward C Major—only to abandon this key again.

Thus the relationship of subject and predicate has undergone a change. At the time of Heinrich Christoph Koch and Kant (into whose aesthetic concepts contemporaneous musical theory had found entrance),[17] in the era of Rationalism, a musical theme was expected to present a statement analogous to the spoken phrase. It had to convey, as Koch says, "certain" (that is, definite) direction and purpose (as

---

[16]Concerning such introductory unison statements, see W. Gerstenberg, " 'Licht und Schatten' —Zur Frage des Kolorits in Schuberts Musik," in *Schubert-Kongress 1978*, ed. O. Brusatti (Graz, 1979), 72.

[17]See C. Dahlhaus, *Klassische und romantische Musikästhetik* (Laaber, 1988), 53.

understood, even with regard to semantic meaning, for vocal music). A later epoch, under the influence of literary Romanticism, saw a reversal, even though in details its departure was taken from earlier doctrines. It was now uncertainty that constituted the goal, for only uncertainty offered the desired path to further reflection. Even structures analogous to those in the grammar of language now no longer serve to provide clarity and confirmation, but rather to open manifold contradictory roads. Antithetical patterns now no longer yield fulfillment. They take the listener farther afield, introduce him—as E.T.A. Hoffmann says—to a purely poetic world, a world which "has nothing in common with the external world of the senses, yet a world which surrounds him and in which he surrenders all feelings determined by definite concepts in order to enter into that which is beyond speech."[18] The ambivalence of many a Schubertian theme can only thus be understood.

---

[18]See E.T.A. Hoffmann's famous review of Beethoven's Fifth Symphony, in *Allgemeine musikalische Zeitung* XII/40 (July 4, 1810): 630. Repr. in *Schriften zur Musik*, ed. F. Schnapp (Munich,1963), 34. English translation available in *Beethoven, Symphony No. 5 in C Minor*, ed. E. Forbes (New York, 1971), 150.

Thomas A. Denny

ARCHAIC AND CONTEMPORARY ASPECTS OF SCHUBERT'S *ALFONSO UND ESTRELLA*
Issues of Influence, Originality, and Maturation*

INTRODUCTION

Viewed as a chapter in the history of opera, Schubert's *Alfonso und Estrella* has been widely judged a rich failure. This perspective has dominated scholarly discussion of the opera, with a resulting emphasis in the literature on its dramatic and musico-dramatic shortcomings. But from another perspective, viewed as a chapter in the story of Schubert's stylistic maturation, seen as a major project from a critical period of Schubert's compositional growth, *Alfonso und Estrella* seems both more significant and more successful. The completion (noteworthy in itself) of *Alfonso und Estrella* is among the first signals that Schubert's long compositional crisis was coming to an end. The opera belongs alongside other key works of the early 1820s (the unfinished C-Minor Quartet,

---

*I would like to express my deepest gratitude to the National Endowment for the Humanities, whose generous support of my research during the Summer, 1984 and the academic year, 1986–87, enabled me to lay the foundation for the present study.

Thomas A. Denny is Associate Professor at Skidmore College, and is editing Fierrabra *for the* Neue Schubert Ausgabe.

the unfinished B-Minor Symphony, and the "Wanderer" Fantasy) through which Schubert found the path to his mature style.

The present discussion will consider *Alfonso und Estrella* from both perspectives. In examining the opera's dramatic aesthetic, it will be judged as opera *qua* opera; but in examining the nature of its musical continuity, the perspective will shift increasingly towards seeing the opera in its biographical context. Throughout, in keeping with the theme of this volume, questions of influence and originality will shape the discussion.

The three most widely cited possible influences on Schubert's operatic style are *Singspiel* and Rossini, that is, the two contemporary styles dominating Viennese operatic life, and the far more remote eighteenth-century musical style and dramatic premises of Gluck and his early nineteenth-century Viennese admirers. These influences, Gluck's in particular, will be reassessed. But the new directions Schubert was testing in composing a continuous opera reveal less indebtedness to any of these three than they do to Schubert's own originality, and to the ever more important position of Beethoven in his aesthetic stance.

Since the Gluck influence is remote, and the mechanisms for it not obvious, a brief rehearsal of Schubert's points of contact with the style and ideals of the eighteenth-century operatic reformer is appropriate. First, Schubert had considerable direct contact with Gluck's music, both in the theater and from score study.[1] Second, study of Gluck's scores formed one focal point of Schubert's study with Salieri, whose admiration for Gluck was summed up by Schubert's fellow pupil, Anselm Hüttenbrenner: "for [Salieri], music should have stopped with Gluck."[2] Third, and far more speculative, Ignaz Mosel's 1813 treatise, *Versuch einer Ästhetik des musikalischen Tonsatzes*, has provided scholars with a convenient verbal foothold from which to discuss the influence of Gluckian ideals in Schubert's Vienna. Mosel's role has been heavily emphasized in recent decades.[3] Some caution is warranted, for although

---

[1] O. E. Deutsch, ed., *Schubert: Die Erinnerungen seiner Freunde* (subsequently cited as *Erinnerungen*) (Weisbaden, 1983), 28 (Joseph von Spaun) and 68–69 (Anton Holzapfel).

[2] "Bei Gluck hätte die Musikwelt stehen bleiben sollen." *Erinnerungen*, 81.

[3] George R. Cunningham's dissertation, *Franz Schubert als Theaterkomponist* (Freiburg, 1974), was apparently the first to present this line of thinking in developed form. Speculation regarding Mosel's role has recently gained a wider audience through record liner notes written by Prof. Walther Dürr, including those for *Alfonso und Estrella* [Angel record SCL-3878 (1978)] and *Lazarus* [Orfeo, C 011101 A].

Schubert was certainly acquainted with Mosel and found him a useful patron and connection at the Court Theater, their relationship was hardly close, as the obsequious formality of Schubert's 28 February 1823 letter to Mosel attests. Schubert undoubtedly knew of Mosel's basic Gluckian orientation. To move beyond that is pure speculation, but it seems unlikely that Schubert ever discussed Mosel's ideas with him in point by point detail. Given what we generally know of Schubert's reading interests, it seems safe to speculate that Schubert never read Mosel's treatise.

DRAMATIC AESTHETIC

The dramatic aesthetic underlying *Alfonso und Estrella* differs fundamentally from that of Gluck's mature "reform" operas, and from that outlined in Mosel's treatise as well. Mosel, in writing his treatise, sought simply to function as "translator of [Gluck's] way of thinking."[4] In large part, Mosel succeeded. He provides an essentially accurate, general description of Gluck's dramatic style, which in no way offers an accurate prescription for Schubert's *Alfonso und Estrella*.

In asserting this, I am clearly taking issue with the thrust of those recent discussions of Schubert's relationship with Mosel and Salieri which have, first, asserted that Mosel and Salieri worked a strong influence on *Alfonso und Estrella* and, second, used this purported influence to explain the opera's dramatic and musical shortcomings. George R. Cunningham, apparently the first to develop this view at length, stated that "the stylistic influence of Salieri naturally entered into the stage works of Schubert, which [influence] may perhaps have played a specific role in their performance difficulties." Later, Cunningham specifically addressed the problems which resulted from "Mosel's demand for a slowly unfolding, simple plot."[5] This "demand," in Mosel's own words, was as follows:

---

[4]*Versuch einer Ästhetik des musikalischen Tonsatzes* (subsequently *Versuch*) (Vienna, 1813), 8: "Dollmetscher seiner Gesinnung."

[5]*Franz Schubert als Theaterkomponist*, 146 ("Der stilistische Einfluß Salieris ist natürlich in die Bühnenwerke Schuberts eingegangen, was vielleicht auch eine gewiße Rolle bei den Aufführungsschwierigkeiten gespielt haben mag.") and 153 ("Mosels Forderung für eine langsam sich entfaltende, einfache Handlung"). Dürr, liner notes for *Alfonso und Estrella*, echoes this on page 3: "The libretto and music of [*Alfonso und Estrella*] probably owe much to the aesthetic principles laid down by Ignaz von Mosel in 1813 in his [*Versuch*] ... Indeed, some of the weaknesses of Schubert's *Alfonso und Estrella* libretto can be traced directly to Mosel's outlook. The action is simple, almost naïve, and progresses slowly."

> Since music is the language of feeling, and a prolonging of feeling lies directly in the nature of song, [the librettist should discard all material which] demands a fast pace for the plot or which involves serious complications.... A simple tragic or heroic plot, which offers opportunities for expression of contrasting feelings and passions is the best subject for a tragic or heroic opera.[6]

Mosel cut to the heart of Gluck's style, and the themes he identified—simplicity of plot, slow pace, and the central importance of feelings—can readily guide discussion of the considerable dissimilarity between Schubert and Gluck (or Gluck-Mosel).

Every major opera of Gluck's known and admired by Schubert features the barest skeleton of a single plot line. The number of principal characters is small. All incidents relate closely to a single, emotionally rich, dramatic crisis. Although contemporaries criticized Gluck for not adhering to the Aristotelian unities, his breaches of them are in fact quite modest. Gluck avoided all that was, on the one hand, digressive, superfluous, or complicating, or, on the other hand, merely decorative or dramatically static.

The simplicity of *Alceste* is representative, if perhaps extreme. Without sacrificing too many details of importance, one can reduce the plot of *Alceste* to five sentences:

> The king is dying. The queen loves the king. The queen saves the king by arranging with the gods to die in his place. The king's joy at regaining his health turns quickly to despair when he learns of the sacrifice his queen has made. Apollo, so moved by the depth of devotion between these spouses, brings the queen back to life, to the joy of the king and the realm.

The plots of *Orfeo ed Euridice*, with just two human characters, and *Iphigenia in Tauris* are only slightly more complicated.

---

[6]Mosel, *Versuch*, 13 (in the section entitled "Von der Wahl des Stoffes"): "Da die Musik die Sprache der Empfindung ist, und ein Verweilen auf denselben schon in der Natur des Gesanges liegt,... [the librettist should discard all material which]... einen eilenden Gang der Handlung erheischt, oder welche schwere Verwicklungen hat...Eine einfache tragische oder heroische Handlung, welche Gelegenheiten zum Ausdruck von Gefühlen und Leidenschaften, und einen Contrast, zwischen derselben darbiethet, ist der schicklichste Gegenstand für die tragische oder heroische Oper."

With the exception of two works written, respectively, at the end of 1819 and the beginning of 1820, Schubert's plot lines bear scant resemblance to Gluck's characteristic type. (The two exceptional works—*Adrast*, to a text by Mayrhofer, and *Lazarus*, to a text by August Niemeyer and for many reasons an anomalous work—will be discussed below.) Any attempt to reduce *Alfonso und Estrella* (or *Fierrabras* of 1823 or *Sakontala* of late 1820) to a dramatic skeleton comparable to that of *Alceste* quickly reveals Schubert's fundamentally different approach. Consider *Alfonso und Estrella*:[7]

> An exiled king (Froila)[8] lives among adoring subjects in an idyllic and isolated mountain valley (already, the lack of emotional and dramatic dynamic is evident). The son of the king (Alfonso) chafes at the restricted life in the valley, and longs for a wider sphere of action.[9] The king counsels patience, for the time is not yet right. Meanwhile, the usurper's (Mauregato) armies have just won major victories (over unknown and irrelevant foes) and the conquering hero (Adolfo) asks

[7] No one seems previously to have noticed that the characters and events of this opera are loosely based on the succession of kings of Asturias-León in the late eighth century: Fruela (sometimes spelled Froila) (757–68), Aurelius (768–74), Silo (774–83), Mauregato (783–88), Vermudo I (788–91), and Alfonso II (791–842), of whom Mauregato and Alfonso are characters in the opera. Both in the opera and in fact, Alfonso was Froila's son. Whoever adapted history to dramatic purposes cleared away several intervening kings and sent Froila into secret exile, rather than leaving him long dead. Mauregato figures in many Spanish legends and plays (including some by Lope de Vega); he is most notorious for negotiating peace with the Moors at the annual price of 100 Asturian maidens. Ironically, Schubert and Schober's male romantic lead, Alfonso II, is known to history as Alfonso "the Chaste." (Since writing this, I have learned that Mr Hans Günter Hoke discussed similar findings in his article accompanying the c. 1983 East German release of the recording of *Alfonso und Estrella*, with Othmar Suitner as conductor. I have not seen Hoke's article.)

[8] I am indebted to Mr Till Gerrit Waidelich of Berlin for the following information.

The spelling of Schubert's character as Troila, so widespread and long entrenched in the Schubert literature, is false. Schubert spelled it Froila throughout his autograph score, as did both the poster advertising the 1854 Weimar performances and the copyist who prepared the score used for the Weimar performances (Vienna, Österreichische Nationalbibliothek: O.A. 263). That score serves as *Stichvorlage* for the *AGA* and, throughout the score, blue crayon editor's markings (almost certainly written by Johann Nepomuk Fuchs) inexplicably change Froila into Troila.

The wide dissemination of the false spelling can be traced to Fuchs's edition and Heinrich Kreissle von Hellborn's biography (Fuchs's sources), although Mr Waidelich had found a yet earlier, erroneous use of Troila in a review of the 1854 Weimar production. See also Waidelich's *Franz Schubert: Alfonso und Estrella* (Tutzing, 1991).

[9] Is it coincidence that another libretto by a close friend of Schubert's, Mayrhofer's *Adrast*, also deals with a youth who is constrained by his circumstances?

for the hand of the unwilling princess (Estrella). Mauregato uses an old prophecy to thwart this suit, saying that he who weds the princess must bring the magical chain of Eurich as gift. General confusion ensues, as the different factions react strongly to the king's proclamation.

This brings us only to the end of the first three acts, but we need go no further. The numerous characters, the multiple plot lines, and the frequent digressions all contrast sharply with Gluck's plots.

Alfonso und Estrella's complexity is typical of most early nineteenth-century dramatic genres (*Ritterdrama*, *Singspiel*, "Romantic" melodrama, etc.). This decidedly "unclassical" love of complexity contributed to the enthusiasm the age felt for Shakespeare. In no sense can these features be traced to the inspiration of Gluck's eighteenth-century dramatic aesthetic, either directly or as advocated by Mosel.[10]

Gluck's pace is slow, but never static. His plots grind onward, propelled by his relentless focus on the succession of feelings the characters experience in situations of dramatic crisis. The pace of *Alfonso und Estrella*, however, is not uniformly slow. Schubert's opera alternates between comparatively fast-paced scenes and ones of virtual stasis. This alternation stems from the dual nature of *Alfonso und Estrella*, which is really two dramatic types in one, part *Ritterdrama* (the story of Alfonso's coming of age) and part Biedermeyer "morality play" (celebrating the virtues of the saintly Froila).

Neither dramatic type derives from Gluck. Most obviously, the conventional *Ritterdrama* plot elements, which stem from a late eighteenth- and early nineteenth-century tradition,[11] are far more com-

---

[10]Mosel himself never attained Gluck's degree of simplicity, but his *Cyrus und Astyages* (1818) is far simpler than Schubert's mature dramas. According to the "Foreword" of the 1818 libretto, Mosel pressed his librettist, Matthäus von Collin, to simplify the borrowed plot, instructing him "to tighten the story and to leave out much that was superfluous." Intriguingly, Mosel in 1818 was struggling to reshape (or might we say "re-form") the same tradition with which Gluck had grappled in 1762. Mosel's opera is based on *Cyrus*, by Metastasio!

[11]A. W. Schlegel traced the *Ritterdrama* craze back to Goethe's *Götz von Berlichingen* (1773), which "pulled a great flood of Ritterschauspielen in its wake, in which nothing is historical except the names and other externalities, nothing chivalric other than the helmets, shields, and swords, nothing old-German except the supposed roughness, otherwise the sentiments are just as modern as they are ordinary." A. W. Schlegel, *Vorlesungen über dramatische Kunst und Literatur: Erster Teil*, in *Kritische Schriften und Briefe*, vol. 5 (Stuttgart, 1966), 284. "*Götz von Berlichingen* hat eine ganze

plicated and far livelier (some slow-moving parts excepted) than Gluck's plots. Schober's morality play about Froila, however, to the extent that it focuses on "feelings," does invite comparison with Gluck (and Mosel). Froila's benign, self-effacing emotions may remind one somewhat of Alceste, but they differ fundamentally from the heroic, more human feelings of Orfeo or Iphigenia.

Its dual dramatic nature lies at the heart of *Alfonso und Estrella*'s dramatic weaknesses. When morality play and *Ritterdrama* meet, Froila's goodness (which can disarm the vilest of villains) robs the *Ritterdrama* plot of an essential dramatic ingredient, tension. In fact, Froila—for whom there is no human counterpart in any of Gluck's mature operas—is the principal dramatic flaw in *Alfonso und Estrella*. Froila's virtue, too irresistible to admit suspense, flavors the whole with a didactic inevitability. As Dürr so aptly put it, "the main emphasis throughout is on the creation of a general harmony brought about through reconciliation and grace."[12] One example of this flavor will suffice. As the climax of Froila's non-dramatic story, he puts a moral platitude into action: "the sweetest victory is to forgive one's enemy!"[13] Sentimentally uplifting? Perhaps. But dramatic it is not.

The endings of Gluck's operas shed light on Froila's dramatic deficiencies. In each of Gluck's major so-called "reform" operas, the human characters, dramatically so interesting, prove unable to avert the tragedy which fate has prepared for them. In an apparent concession to eighteenth-century taste,[14] Gluck's librettos invariably allow a god to intervene, rescuing the humans from tragedy. The human drama, pressing towards its tragic close, provides the "real" drama, while the god's

---

Überschwemmung von Ritterschauspielen nach sich gezogen, in denen nichts historisch ist als die Namen und ander Äußerlichkeiten, nichts ritterlich als die Helme, Schilde und Schwerter, nichts altdeutsch als vermeintlich die Rohheit, sonst die Gesinnungen ebenso modern als gemein."

[12]*Alfonso und Estrella* [liner notes], 3.

[13]In No. 31: "der schönste Sieg ist seinen Feinden zu verzeihen." In No. 31, Froila and his old arch-enemy, Mauregato, join together in a close paraphrase of this sentiment.

[14]Ludwig Finscher ("Der verstümmelte Orpheus: über die Urgestalt und Bearbeitung von Glucks 'Orfeo,'" *Neue Zeitschrift für Musik* CXXIV (1963), 7ff, argued eloquently that the ending of *Orfeo* is in fact far more subtle and far more dramatically palatable than the *lieto fine* of more conventional eighteenth-century operas.

intervention comes at a high dramatic price. With the arrival of the god, the drama ends, and allegory begins. No gods intervene at the end of *Alfonso und Estrella*, yet their absence may be more apparent than real. Froila, although clothed as a man, is as undramatic a paragon as any of Gluck's gods, and, in fact, functions exactly like Gluck's gods, bringing about the ultimate, non-dramatic resolution. The dramatically fatal difference between Froila and the gods of Gluck's dramas is that Froila did not have the good sense to stay off stage until the human drama had run its emotional course. Instead, he threaded his god-like way through the entire "human" drama, damping its emotional resonance at virtually every entrance.

The pervasiveness of the moralizing tone in *Alfonso und Estrella* most decidedly does not stem from Gluck, nor from Gluck-Mosel. (Gluck confined this tone to the conventional allegorical happy ending. It is conspicuously absent from Mosel's own operas, the texts of which are well constructed, suspenseful theater works.) We might account for the moralizing tone of Schober's opera from various angles. First, Schubert and Schober were closely involved with a circle of idealistic young men centered in Linz. The edifying example of the noble or great man, whether found in literature or in history, was a focal point in this circle's intellectual-ethical life.[15] Second, the opera might be seen as an extreme instance of a wider Biedermeier tendency to sentimentalize bourgeois morality. Utterances similar in tone abound in Biedermeier art, including *Singspiel*, whose influence on Schubert is well established.[16] We can find fascinating parallels to *Alfonso und Estrella* along

---

[15]David Gramit in *Schubert's Songs in Schubert's Circle* (Ph.D. dissertation, Duke University, 1986) explores the intellectual premises of the Linz circle in detail. Schubert came into contact with these young men through Joseph von Spaun, whose brother Anton, along with Anton Ottenwalt, served as leader. Mayrhofer and Schober both participated actively in this group.

[16]Elizabeth Norman McKay develops these connections at length, suggesting that the naïve facets of *Singspiel* can be traced perhaps as far back as Rousseau's early *opéra comique*. See her "Schubert as a Composer of Operas," in Eva Badura-Skoda and Peter Branscombe, eds., *Schubert Studies* (Cambridge, 1982), 85–104; *The Stage-Works of Schubert, considered in the Framework of Austrian Biedermeier Society* (Ph.D. dissertation, Oxford, 1962–63), a revised version of which appeared as *Franz Schubert's Music for the Theater* (Tutzing, 1991), volume 5, Veröffentlichungen des Internationalen Franz Schubert Instituts.

the border between Biedermeier art and life, in the festivities organized for important celebrations (namedays, etc.). These parallels have apparently not been noted.

Elaborate festivities, pageants even, complete with music, poetry, and dance, commonly adorned both the domestic celebrations of namedays and the public celebrations of important professional milestones or the namedays of the imperial family. The pageants' function—to honor a socially important individual—demanded a lofty tone, a one-sided idealization of the honored individual's qualities, and platitudinous expression of the society's values as embodied by the individual. In short, such celebrations were occasions for allegory.

By the time Schubert composed *Alfonso und Estrella*, he had contributed music, and sometimes text, for many such festivities.[17] A few examples will suggest the close similarities in style, tone, and imagery between the text of *Alfonso und Estrella* and those for Schubert's real-life celebratory works. The peasants' extravagant manner of addressing Froila, "Father—Good One—Wise One!" parallels Schubert's saluting of Salieri as "Most Considerate One—Best One—Wisest One—Greatest!" Patriarchal and solar metaphors emphasize the position of the honoree at the center of society. Froila was "Father," Spendou the "Father-Man" (Vatermann), the Emperor "Vater Franz," and Salieri "Großpapa." Spendou was the "center of his own solar system, out of which pours warmth, light, and joy"; Froila and the sun rise together, and he expresses gratitude that it "pours bliss into the heart, sucks out all torments, and heals every pain."[18] Meanwhile, the

---

[17]These included: *Zur Namensfeier meines Vaters* (D. 80; 1813) for his father's nameday in 1813; as well as congratulatory pieces in honor of Salieri's 50th anniversary of life in Vienna (D. 407; 1816), in honor of Josef Spendou, the founder and director of the Widows' Institute (D. 472; 1816), and in honor of Vogl's birthday, celebrated during their travels together in Steyr during August 1819 (D. 666). In January of 1822, while in the midst of completing *Alfonso und Estrella*, Schubert composed a "Volkslied" (D. 748) for the birthday of Kaiser Franz I.

[18]Spendou: "Doch oft auch eine Sonn' im eigenen System/Ein reiches Mittelpunkt aus dem/Sich Wärm' und Licht und Freude/beseligend auf das ergiesst/womit er in Verbindung ist." Froila: "Alltäglich neue Wonne giesst du in dieses Herz. Es saugen deine Strahlen aus jeder Brust die Qualen und heilen jeden Schmerz." The solar imagery contrasts strikingly to the contemporary Romantic fascination with the "night." Also compare the prominent solar imagery in Mayrhofer's cycle "Heliopolis," dedicated to Schober. Mayrhofer dated the dedication on the manuscript copy, "Sept–Oct 1821," precisely the months when Schubert and Schober were in Niederösterreich working on *Alfonso und Estrella*.

peasants praise the "happy day" which has "brought us the Father [Froila]," a sentiment which finds nearly literal echo in the chorus for the Kaiser: "hail to you, Day, full of splendor and magnificence, you gave us Father Franz."[19] Even the godlike dramatic role suggested above for Froila finds a parallel in Schubert's references to Salieri as "Image of God" (Gottes Ebenbild) and "Angel."

Specifically, the dramatic weaknesses of the static opening to Act I can be traced to the fact that it is essentially an onstage recreation of one of these non-dramatic celebrations.[20] Sparing no detail, from the decoration of the set through the ritual passing of ceremonial horn and sword, Schubert and Schober miscalculated how much of a non-dramatic mode one could transplant into a dramatic setting. (Shorter variants of such scenes were a common *Singspiel* type.)

One wonders if there might have been a personal impulse behind this dramatic miscalculation. Vogl was planned as the first Froila. Might Schubert and Schober—consciously or unconsciously—have structured Froila's role to "honor" Vogl, without fully reckoning the dramatic costs? We can only speculate. In this connection, was it mere Romantic cliché, or some more personal allusion, which determined that Froila was a musician-king, whose subjects submitted to him because his "speech had gently overpowered them" and his "song had enchanted them?"[21]

To summarize, *Alfonso und Estrella* is, in its dramatic aspects, an early nineteenth-century work. Its dramatic failings cannot be traced to Gluck, but reflect the generally problematic dramatic aesthetic of the age, whose deficiencies were compounded by Schubert's and Schober's lack of theatrical experience.

CONTINUITY

Contrary to repeated suggestions in the literature, Schubert's decision to compose *Alfonso und Estrella* as a "continuous" opera

---

[19]Peasants: "Es kehret uns wieder/Der fröhliche Tag . . . Er hat uns ja allen/Den Vater gebracht." Kaiser: "Heil dir Tag, voll Pracht und Glanz/Du gabst uns den Vater Franz."

[20]Walther Dürr, in labelling the opening scene a cantata, may have had just this sort of Biedermeier event in mind.

[21]No. 3: "Wenn dein Wort uns sanft gemeistert/Wenn uns dein Gesang begeistert/Wurden wir dir untertan."

(without spoken dialogue) was *not* a "first" in German opera.[22] It nevertheless represents a sufficiently unusual break from both the dominant *Singspiel* tradition and Schubert's own previous operas as to cause us to ask, why? If influences were a factor, we might look for their effects at two distinct stages in the compositional process—at the moment when Schubert made the general commitment to write in this genre and, throughout the actual composition, in the countless concrete decisions by which he gave specific form to the general idea of continuity.

Because of the extremely general nature of the pre-compositional commitment, the influences which might have shaped it resist close documentation. We can posit a range of possible influences, but the evidence invariably remains inconclusive. For example, if direct musical influences led Schubert to write a continuous opera, the two most plausible (yet sharply contrasting) models would be the operas of Gluck (or his followers) and the operas of Rossini.[23] Schubert's knowledge of and admiration for both men's operas is well documented and either, or both, might have spurred him on to write *Alfonso und Estrella* without dialogue. The evidence grows even less conclusive if we look for in-

---

[22]The most immediate Viennese predecessors to Schubert's continuous opera were Mosel's *Salem* (1813) and *Cyrus und Astyages* (1818). But Schubert probably viewed even some of Gluck's operas as "German," including *Iphigenia auf/in Tauris*, which was known in Vienna only in its German version. Christian Pollack suggested recently in *Franz Schubert: Bühnenwerke* (Tutzing, 1988 [= Veröffentlichungen des Internationalen Franz Schubert Institut, vol. 3]), 197, that *Alfonso und Estrella* may in fact not even be a continuous opera (i.e., that dialogue may have been lost). Pollack's suggestion can be readily dismissed; the evidence in the autograph score—musical, dramatic, and philological—establishes beyond doubt the integrity and the intended continuity of the opera as it stands.

[23]Cunningham provides extensive documentation for Schubert's involvement in a "German opera movement" (*Franz Schubert als Theaterkomponist*, especially 111ff.), and stresses his admiration for Gluck. Regarding Schubert's reaction to Rossini, see his letter to Anselm Hüttenbrenner of 19 May 1819 (O. E. Deutsch, *Schubert: Die Dokumente seines Lebens* [Kassel, 1964], 79), and Spaun's recollections of 1858: "[Schubert]... in no way joined into the then customary attacks against Italian music and especially Rossini. He found *Il Barbiere di Siviglia* delightful and the third act of *Otello* enchanting, although he was less taken by the current operas such as *Zelmira and Elisabetta*" (translation mine, from *Erinnerungen*, 158:) "Obgleich durchaus von deutscher Richtung, stimmte er doch keineswegs dem damals gewöhnlichen Schmähen gegen italienische Musik und namentlich die Rossinischen Opern bei. Den *Barbiere di Sevilla* fand er köstlich, und der dritte Akt des *Otello* entzückte ihn.

fluence of a more theoretical or abstract nature. Conceivably, Schubert might have been converted to the "idea" of continuous opera through Salieri's teaching, or Mosel's treatise, or the views of Schubert's circle of friends. Yet of these, only Mosel's views are known in any detail. For him, continuity was a *sine qua non*, a defining characteristic of the genre of opera. (In his book, Mosel took far less interest in works using spoken dialogue, a defining characteristic of *Singspiel*.) Yet Schubert probably never adopted the precise distinctions of Mosel's terminology. Schubert's 1823 *Fierrabras*, despite its use of spoken dialogue, was labelled an "opera" in the libretto submitted to the censors.

Questions of influence (and originality) grow far more tangible as one examines Schubert's actual composition of *Alfonso und Estrella*. Schubert faced numerous concrete questions: what means to employ to create and sustain continuity? what respective functions to assign recitative and "measured" sections?[24] what, if any, models to follow? He appears to have approached these questions with an open mind, for the score reveals considerable diversity and evolution in his approach.

Unique compositional circumstances perhaps account for the extent of the evolution. As is well known, *Alfonso und Estrella* resulted from close collaboration between composer and librettist (Schubert's intimate friend, Franz Schober), mostly during their extended working vacation together in Niederösterreich. Schober's slow progress on the text forced Schubert's composition to proceed with uncharacteristic slowness.[25] Facing the novel challenge of composing a continuous opera, Schubert apparently took advantage of this enforced slowness to feel his way through a variety of solutions. Over the course of the project, the evidence of concrete modelling generally diminishes, as Schubert

---

[24] I know of no good English equivalent to the useful distinction made in French opera between "mésurée" and "recitatif." Schubert himself consciously differentiated between "recitative" and "a tempo." I consciously avoid "number" in instances where the distinction is not primarily a formal one, but rather one of rhythmic flow.

[25] Schober's letter of 4 November 1821 (*Dokumente*, 139) reports that Schubert, following behind Schober's work on the still unfinished text, had drafted less than two acts in the six weeks he had been working on *Alfonso und Estrella*. In 1823, apparently with Josef Kupelwieser's completed libretto in hand from the start, Schubert drafted the first two acts of *Fierrabras* within twelve days. (The inks in the autograph of *Fierrabras* confirm what some have long suspected, that Schubert did *not* fully score the two acts in this incredibly short time.)

found increasingly original solutions. *Alfonso und Estrella* was, for Schubert, a learning process.

Before describing what Schubert did regarding continuity, we can briefly mention one thing that he did not do: Schubert did not model his operatic continuity on Gluck's. At its most original and characteristic (for example in *Iphigenie auf Tauris*, Act I, scene 1 or Act II, scenes iii-v), Gluck's continuity was based on great formal flexibility. Heavy reliance on recitative was one key to this flexibility. Equally important was Gluck's treatment of the "measured" sections, whose brevity (the choruses are particularly brief) and formal openness (many being tonally directional) facilitated Gluck's frequent and fluid shifting between recitative and "measured" sections.

Schubert's minimal use of recitative in *Alfonso und Estrella* constitutes his most fundamental divergence from Gluck's practice. The explanation lies partly in his and Gluck's fundamentally different valuations of recitative. Gluck, typical of his age, entrusted entire scenes to recitative (for example, *Iphigenia auf Tauris*, Act II, scene v), an approach quite foreign to Schubert's instincts. Yet one should not underestimate Schober's role in the scarcity of recitative in *Alfonso und Estrella*. The amateur Schober apparently did not understand that the librettist was to control, or at least suggest, the structure of the opera by using contrasting types of versification (or even prose) to differentiate recitative from "measured" sections. Schober's libretto consists overwhelmingly of rhymed verse, a style most suitable for structured "measured" lyrical music, and contains correspondingly few passages in blank verse or prose, styles traditionally used for recitative. In contrast, M. von Collin, Mosel's librettist for *Cyrus und Astyages* (1818) and an acquaintance of Schubert's, fully understood the librettist's role, and invariably wrote blank verse for recitative and rhymed verse, with fewer feet per line, for the "measured" sections. Questions of Mosel's theoretical influence aside, Schubert and Schober apparently were not influenced by Mosel's practice.[26]

---

[26]Edward Dent (*The Rise of Romantic Opera*, Cambridge, 1976) was the first to point out that the problem with Schubert's librettos (and those of most German Romantic composers) was not limited to absurdities in plot and to their dated dramatic themes, but included metrical issues as well.

Schubert's changing treatment of continuity breaks down into three principal phases:

1. Throughout Act I, Schubert employed brief passages of transition and recitative to link the conventional closed numbers or to link the closed sections within a number. Many composers known to Schubert—including Spontini, Mosel, and Rossini (and even Gluck, at his least characteristic)—had employed this rather generic style. Later, in *Euryanthe* (1823), Weber would also rely on this style.

2. Early in Act II, in the extended first love scene between Alfonso and Estrella (Nos. 12–16), Schubert adopted a more radical approach. He composed a string of closed lyrical numbers virtually without recitative. (The recitative introducing No. 13 is the last of the scene.) In this short-lived, unique "experiment," Schubert allowed structured lyrical expression totally to dominate dramatic flexibility.

Even when the dramatic stuff called for recitative, Schober provided rhymed verse, as in the earliest moment of contact between Alfonso and Estrella (No. 12).[27] Instead of a brief recitative, Schubert responded with a through-composed number in three tempos. But Schubert himself appears disinclined to employ recitative: the autograph score reveals that Schubert had originally intended to begin No. 16 with recitative. He wrote the word, but not a single note of recitative, before opting to write a closed lyrical number.

Interestingly, despite the closed musical discreteness of each number within this unusual scene, Schubert apparently was already thinking, in ways not evident in Act I, towards a more continuous type of scene. For example, whereas Schubert normally marked the end of a number

---

[27]Est: Von Fels und Wald umrungen, wer zeigt die Pfade mir?
Alf: Was kühn das Lied gesungen seh' ich verwirklicht hier.
Est: Ein Jüngling, soll ich fliehen? Doch scheint er sanft und mild.
Alf: O wolle nicht entfliehen, du süsses Himmelsbild.
Est: Es flössen seine Züge mir Mut und Hoffnung ein.
Alf: So kann ein Traum nicht täuschen. Nein, das muss Wahrheit sein.

Est: Surrounded by rocks and woods, who will show me the way?
Alf: What the song presented, is here made real.
Est: A youth! Should I flee? Still, he looks gentle.
Alf: O don't flee, sweet, heavenly image.
Est: His features give me courage and hope.
Alf: A dream cannot deceive thus. No, this must be real.

ASPECTS OF SCHUBERT'S *ALFONSO UND ESTRELLA* 255

(or a movement within an instrumental work) with a closing notational flourish, and began the next on a fresh page, several numbers within this scene are separated only by a shared double bar. Equally suggestive, the numbering itself was a late addition, perhaps a reflection of a changed conception.

3. Beginning with the ensemble of Adolfo and his conspirators (No. 17) and throughout the remainder of Acts II and III, Schubert pushed towards more expansive (and often quite successful) approaches to continuity. He began thinking in larger units, some of which enfolded whole "numbers" which themselves lacked formal closure.

Three large "numbers" illustrate this new compositional dimension. The three share several important features—tonal closure; dramatic coherence; a multi-sectional form involving several tempos; and the same general formal pattern, consisting of an inner section of unstable or kinetic character framed by outer sections which are formally closed. Despite these similarities, Schubert's manner of "numbering" them was not consistent; sometimes he labelled them as one number (for example, No. 17), sometimes as three (Nos. 19–21, Nos. 23–26). His unified view of these latter two is nevertheless apparent in the autograph, where Nos. 19–20–21 flow into one another, separated only by a shared double bar, as do Nos. 23–24–25–26.

Similarities (and probably indebtedness) to Rossini are clearly evident in these large numbers, yet Schubert also moved in some personal and stylistically important directions which were foreign to Rossini's style. Doubtless most important among these is Schubert's emerging interest in explicit formal coherence. A few examples can suggest the range and depth of this interest in *Alfonso und Estrella*.

First, in the conspirators' ensemble (No. 17), probably the most original and successful number in the opera, Schubert generated considerable *internal* coherence, employing both motivic unity and what I call "metric continuity." Significantly, both techniques are conspicuous in the instrumental style of Schubert's early maturity. Among the several unifying motives, the two most important are the ubiquitous ascending arpeggiation of a first-inversion triad, sometimes with the scale steps filled in (see Example 1a–1d) and the more selectively used falling two-note motive with strong-weak accentuation (associated with succession of important two-syllable words: Freunde–Rache–Er *falle*–Wir *schwören*–etc.), found generally at major cadences.

Example 1.

Additional coherence results from the "metric transition" which bridges the opening *Allegro agitato* to the *Allegro assai* for Adolfo's arrival. In a "metric transition," Schubert links the two tempos with a conspicuously shared motive. Although the motive is aurally identical in both tempos, Schubert had to diminute it in the *Allegro assai* to compensate for the change in meter, from cut to common time (see Example 2).

Example 2. Metric continuity in the Conspirators' ensemble, No. 17

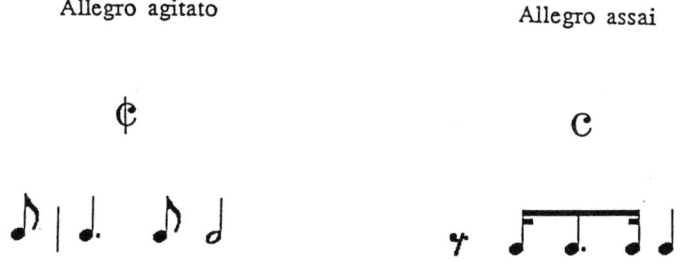

Despite the intervening fermata, the motive ensures that the new tempo is perceived to continue where the preceding one had left off. Although far less common than his use of motivic links, "metric continuity" is a central feature of Schubert's mature instrumental style, used most tellingly in the so-called "Great" C-Major Symphony (for example in the first movement, in the transition from *Andante* introduction to exposition, and in the finale, at the transition to the dominant theme group).

Second, No. 17 is not only characterized by internal links, but Schubert also used motives to connect it both to earlier and later sections of the opera. The ascending arpeggiated triad motive with which Adolfo plots revenge appeared first during Adolfo's request for Estrella's hand (Act I Finale; see Example 1e and 1f).

Example 1 (continued).

from Finale I: (e) *AGA*, p. 147; (f) *AGA*, p. 148, cf. Ex1(b)

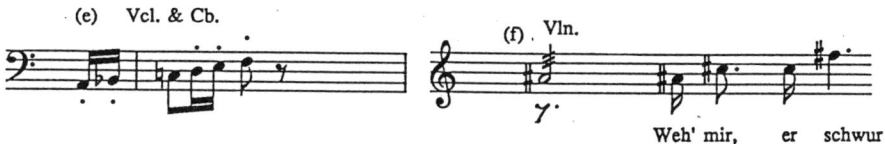

And later, in No. 22, Schubert reused two ideas from the Conspirators' ensemble—the falling strong-weak motive associated with "Rache" plus an important melody from Adolfo's oration[28]—at the arrival of Adolfo's troops at the gates of Leon. Given the symphonic treatment of these motives within No. 17, these external links transcend what is normally meant by a "reminiscence motive."

Third, Schubert forged Nos. 17–22 into a single large musical-dramatic unit, using a combination of motivic relationships, tonal closure, and even a large-scale plan of tonal symmetry as follows:

---

[28]The cadential melody appears in No. 22 at the words, "Adolfo ist ihr Haupt" (*AGA*, p. 332) and twice in No. 17 at the words "deinen Scepter will ich tragen in dieser *starker Siegerhand*" and "bis ich zu seinem *Heil erscheinen*" (*AGA*, 254, 265, respectively). In No. 17, the harmonic progression both times is a deceptive cadence; in No. 22, the melodic arrival on the tonic is unharmonized.

Figure 1. Tonal symmetry, *Alfonso und Estrella*, Act II/17–22

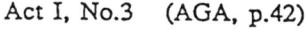

In so doing, Schubert ignored the disunifying and disruptive force of the scene change after No. 17, choosing instead to emphasize a deeper dramatic unity, namely, that the attack (No. 22) fulfills the promise of the conspiracy (No. 17).

Finally, at one of the most important formal junctures within the Act III Finale, that is, at the first arrival in E major, the key in which the opera will ends (*AGA*, p. 517), Schubert reprises a melodic phrase first heard early in the opening act (No. 3; melody originally in E flat) (see example 3).

Example 3.

Act I, No.3   (AGA, p.42)

Act III, Finale   (AGA, p.153)

Although a seemingly conventional reminiscence technique—the peasants gave Froila gifts of gratitude in No. 3 while in Finale III they express their fears that Froila will leave them—the tonal function and consequent articulative weight link even this small event to elements in Schubert's maturing instrumental style.

Alfonso und Estrella is the first work in which these concerns surface to such a considerable extent. From the opera, it was but a short step to the extreme coherence of the "Wanderer" Fantasy, and the numerous less obsessively unified works from 1822 on through the composition of the C-major symphony in 1825–26. In short, the stylistic concerns emerging in *Alfonso und Estrella*—and here lies the opera's pivotal biographical significance—are among those most prominent during the next period of Schubert's *instrumental* works.

CONCLUSIONS: THE BIOGRAPHICAL PERSPECTIVE

Alfonso und Estrella is contemporary, not archaic, in style. Dramatically and musically, it represents the Viennese theater of the early 1820s.

Others among Schubert's dramatic works, however, reflect considerable influence from eighteenth-century styles, an influence which seems to have peaked shortly before *Alfonso und Estrella*, during late 1819 and early 1820, with his work on *Adrast* and *Lazarus*. *Adrast* reveals an interesting mixture of archaic and contemporary features. Mayrhofer's simple, classical libretto (written specifically for Schubert) is quite different from the complicated *Ritterdrama* mode of *Alfonso und Estrella* and *Fierrabras*. Perhaps this simplicity reflects Gluck's ideals in action, or it may merely reflect Mayrhofer's own old-fashioned tendencies. Regardless, Schubert's approach to the text was non-Gluckian, for he employed spoken dialogue (now lost).

Lazarus, its many beauties notwithstanding, is, on the other hand, an unabashedly archaic piece, employing an antique libretto (1778) and openly adopting the old-fashioned style of the *azione sacra*. Stylistic aspects of *Lazarus* which differ sharply from Schubert's other works of the period include the unusually heavy reliance on recitative, the use of the extended scene (containing several numbers and much intervening recitative) as the main formal unit, and his handling of the orchestration (strings overwhelmingly predominant in the recitatives and, in the numbers, the use only of selected woodwinds, rather than the full woodwinds which had become his norm). Schubert's description of

Salieri's *Gesu al limbo*—"a Gluck-like creation"—could well fit his own *Lazarus*.[29]

Schubert's switch from the archaic dramatic style (of *Lazarus* in particular) to the clearly contemporary idiom of *Alfonso und Estrella* is perhaps best understood from a longer biographical perspective. Theatrical projects comprise an important aspect of an extended period of artistic exploration and maturation (1817–1824), during which Schubert's large-scale works revealed an increasingly personal style. As he matured, Schubert's external points of professional reference (role models, heroes, and rivals) changed. Broadly speaking, his orientation shifted from Salieri (and eighteenth-century masters in general, including Gluck) to Beethoven.

A journal entry (16 June 1816) and a letter to Leopold Kupelwieser (31 March 1824) mark the rough chronological limits of this transformation.[30] Whereas, in 1816, Schubert explicitly praised the values and style of Salieri (and Salieri's model, Gluck) and obliquely condemned certain of Beethoven's tendencies, by 1824, Schubert made no mention of either Salieri or Gluck. Instead, Beethoven has emerged clearly as Schubert's professional role model, if not unspoken rival.

The precise nature and timing of the intervening changes are elusive, but some general observations can be made. In September, 1819, Salieri, still Schubert's mentor although no longer his teacher, wrote a reference letter which emphasized Schubert's competence as a composer of sacred and theater music, the two traditional areas of work for a *Kapellmeister*. It would be tempting to dismiss this as a wholly conventional document, if Schubert had not seemed to take it so fully to heart. For a full fifteen months following Salieri's letter, Schubert's compositional energies were consumed in vigorous (if scattered and ultimately fruitless) attempts to write music for the church and theater. *Adrast*, the *Kyrie* of the A-flat Major Mass, and *Lazarus* (could this archaic project have even been suggested by Salieri?) were the earliest projects during this period. But in late 1820 or early 1821, Schubert abruptly abandoned what we might speculate was the pursuit of Salieri's *Kapellmeister* ideal, breaking off work on a theater piece, *Sakontala*,

---

[29]"Gluckisch gearbeitet" (*Dokumente*, 45).
[30]*Dokumente*, 45 and 235.

and a sacred work, the Mass (having drafted it to the end).[31] Although Schubert would remain loyal to Salieri and occasionally ask him for help,[32] Salieri's influence would never again be of central importance.

Schubert's growing enthusiasm for Beethoven's work can be traced back at least to late winter, 1820, when he set out to copy Beethoven's Fourth Symphony.[33] Probably the first compositional fruits of this interest come with the burst of instrumental composition between December 1820 and August 1821 (a string quartet and two symphonies, all unfinished). From late 1821 on, Schubert's growing fascination with motivic unity, first evident in *Alfonso und Estrella* and intensifying in the "Wanderer" Fantasy, suggests increasing engagement with Beethoven's style. Just two years later, Schubert found himself on the "path to a grand symphony," and there can be no doubt that, in Schubert's mind, he was following Beethoven's path.

Alfonso und Estrella was the first completed work of Schubert's maturity. Following its completion, Schubert experienced a palpable surge in self-confidence and compositional momentum. During the eighteen months after completing the opera, Schubert quickly completed the long-dormant A-flat Mass, made major stylistic breakthroughs in the unfinished B-minor Symphony and the "Wanderer" Fantasy, and sustained a high level of productivity through 1823, foreshadowing the even more remarkable output of 1824.

From this perspective, the "failure" of the opera dwindles into insignificance. The "success" of the opera rests on the stylistic discoveries Schubert made while composing it, and on its position as central biographical turning point. *Alfonso und Estrella* ushered in a period of growing artistic confidence, of greater engagement with the works of Beethoven, of increasing orientation toward instrumental composition, of liberation from the tutelage of the eighteenth-century ideals of Salieri, and of accelerating stylistic maturation. In short, *Alfonso und Estrella* was an important milestone along Schubert's "path to a grand symphony."

---

[31]Handwriting and watermarks enable us to sort out the chronology of the period, including Schubert's progress on the Mass. Cf. the author's article, "The Years of Schubert's A-flat Major Mass, First Version: Chronological and Biographical Issues," *Acta Musicologica*, cxiii (1991), 73–97.

[32]Salieri (and Mosel) apparently wrote letters recommending *Alfonso und Estrella* (*Dokumente*, 168).

[33]Handwriting (with bass clefs underscored by two diagonal strokes and the non-interlocking natural sign) establishes that Schubert made this copy between mid-February and mid-March 1820. See "The Years of Schubert's A-flat Major Mass," 82 and 95.

Percy M. Young

THE TRANSITION FROM BAROQUE TO ROMANTIC
A Study in English Provincial Music-Making

Born during the lifetime of Handel and only two years after the death of Bach, John Marsh, gentleman—whose lifetime surrounded that of Mozart—outlived Beethoven. By any kind of reckoning, that comprehended a period of previously unparalleled change in the structure and the nature of European music. Unlike in the period of even more dramatic change a century later, however, it was relatively comfortable to live through the climate of music as the eighteenth century turned into the nineteenth, for principles of musical composition and performance were still related to the understanding of the cultivated amateur. In Marsh's time the territory of music was still undivided: folk-music, not yet pinned down by the omnivorous collector nor emotionally and intellectually distanced from art music, still existed in a real sense. At the same time—partly on account of the coming-of-age of the pianoforte, partly on account of the development of the music publishing industry—it was possible for the keen music-lover to have a greater awareness of happenings in the area of classical music, and beyond.

John Marsh had every qualification to observe what was happening in the period under notice. He was a reasonable performer (for which his own evaluation is the only guide) on several instruments, and

---

Percy M. Young has published widely, especially on the music of Handel and Elgar. He has recently completed a reconstruction of Elgar's unfinished opera The Spanish Lady.

ready at any time to take charge of vocal or instrumental ensembles. He was, while largely self-taught, a knowledgeable and enterprising of church music and secular music. He was a constant diarist, commentator and critic, and a lively observer of the general English musical scene. So far as Europe was concerned, living in the south-eastern corner of England, from time to time he directly experienced that sense of anxiety once often aroused in the British by continental politico-military ambitions. Like many men of his time he was fascinated by the possibilities exposed by an expanding knowledge of science. He published in 1806 *The Astrarium improved, or Views of the principal fixt Stars and Constellations...*, and in 1809 *A Short Introduction to the Theory of Harmonics, or the Philosophy of Musical Sounds*. Mechanically adept, he applied himself to instrumental construction. In a professional sense Marsh was a small-town lawyer, whose inheritance of property in due course enabled him to retire from office routine and pursue his many enthusiasms.

Marsh was a diligent diarist and his Journal,[1] running from 1768—when he was articled to a lawyer in the small town of Gosport, near Portsmouth—until within the year of his death is a significant document for many reasons. Although heavily weighted in the direction of music it is a general record of life in critical times, so that what concerns music becomes the more significant when set within the pattern of daily activity. On arriving in Gosport, Marsh almost at once plunged into musical activity. His landlady's spinet tempted him to learn to play the instrument, "but, meeting unfortunately with an erroneous book of instruction it put me in an improper mode of fingering, from which I have scarcely ever since been able to recover." Through early tuition, however, he was a more than competent violinist and was immediately eager to explore local opportunities for chamber and orchestral playing. Soon he had the chance to play second fiddle in a "grand crash, there being sixteen performers" in Portsmouth. Next, at a country house at Winterslow, near Salisbury, he heard a "good band" from that city, "who played some of [J. C.] Bach's opera overtures, which I had not then heard, and which gave me some new musical ideas in respect of style, particularly in the horn-parts, which instrument I had before not met

---

[1] Cambridge University Library Add MS 7757; there is a gap between 1794 and 1800.

with at [the] Portsmouth Concert, where I was too much occupied with my own part to attend to their particular effect."

Very soon Marsh was in demand as a violinist, and, on one occasion, engaged to play in Southampton, he optimistically took parts of two of his own works—a symphony and a concerto—in the hope that they might be played through. They were, at a "general crash by the whole band. . . in the great room of the Coach and Horses [Inn]." In three hours of practice on that occasion the players read through the "third set of Abel's Symphonies, then lately published, which were tried nearly all through without any intermixture of soloes [*sic*], or more than one duet or trio."

In 1770 a new schoolmaster, a Mr. Watson, came to Romsey. Described as a "capital old-style player upon the violin," he was at once invited to play with Marsh, who commented: "He excelled me in the ancient music [of Corelli] which he had formerly practised at Oxford. With regard, however, to the more modern music of Bach, Abel, Stamitz etc. which he was unacquainted with I found the superiority of performance to be on my side, as having been for some years out of the habit of playing in concert, he was become inexpert at reading music or playing at sight, and had an awkward manner of bowing many modern passages." Watson, it seems, had not yet caught up with Geminiani's *Art of Playing on the Violin* (1751). But, having played the cello when a student at Oxford, he was able to give Marsh an introductory lesson on that instrument.

Marsh was energetic in stimulating local effort in every direction. He composed, or arranged, tunes for the church bells; took the church singers through their parts; and quickly learned the social credentials of a glee singer. By the beginning of 1772 a regular music-meeting was established at the Bell in Romsey—the inn was a vital centre of English music-making in the eighteenth century—with an ensemble of five fiddles, two hautboys, flute, violoncello, and bassoon, on which kind of ensemble much of English music of the period was founded. After some initial uncertainty, the Romsey music-meeting (i.e. society) continued to Marsh's satisfaction, and "as an amusement for many a leisure-hour at home" he arranged works "adapted to the abilities of the respective performers," and composed "new hautboy, flute and ripieno bass parts to many of the modern overtures, symphonies etc."

There were annual Musical Festivals in the cathedral cities of Winchester and Salisbury at which Marsh became a regular attender. For some considerable time the Festival mainstay was excerpts from the oratorios of Handel. On account of the patronage of James Harris, Member of Parliament, amateur philosopher and musician, and friend of Handel, the Salisbury Festival was the more enterprising. In 1773 Marsh took full advantage of the social and musical opportunities offered by this Festival. Well pleased by a performance of *Samson* (after which he danced the night through with the lady who was soon to become his wife), he was totally captivated by a miscellaneous evening concert. The principals were J. C. Bach, harpsichord; G. B. Cervetto, violoncello; J. C. Fischer, oboe—whom Marsh particularly admired; and Anna Storace, "then quite a girl, who danced away afterwards with great spirit."

Three years later, on account of his profession, Marsh went to live in Salisbury in which—being already known to the musicians of the city—he found a more secure cultural environment than in Romsey. There was a particularly well-organized annual series of subscription concerts which prospered under the musical as well as the general control of James Harris. At that time, except for a few well-known virtuosi, the best amateur performers in England were seldom noticeably inferior to rank-and-file professionals, and Harris authoritatively directed concerts from the harpsichord, while another wealthy citizen and amateur composer, W. B. Earle, played the organ when needed. Dr. Stephens, the cathedral organist, happily played the cello. In Salisbury, where there was wealth and leisure, Marsh, whose entry to the musical fraternity was ensured by his all-round ability, received regular invitations to musical houses. On 5 August 1776, he visited a Miss Mary Hancock, at her invitation, to hear "her new grand piano, the first of these instruments I had then seen, and which I was most pleased with." Shortly afterwards he attended a party at Harris's house, where a musical play—*Cimon*—with songs set either by Dr. Stephens or to tunes taken by Harris from 'old Italian music', was performed. The orchestra of two violins, viola, cello, flute, oboe, and French horn, was led by Harris from the pianoforte. "I was," Marsh noted with satisfaction at this time, "now indeed got into a new world, as it were, and as well and happily situated as I could wish, being where there was a cathedral, a subscription concert throughout the year, and catch club in the winter...."

Next year Marsh broke new ground. In March 1777 he was able to persuade his orchestral colleagues to "try through" his fifth symphony in F, composed in February 1775. He was well satisfied with the result. At this time he was, when possible, playing the viola, the least regarded of all instruments at the time. The deficiency of the viola, according to Marsh, was that, corresponding to the counter-tenor rather than the tenor compass, it did not "fill up the gradation of instruments." Accordingly he invented and built a new instrument, a *basso viola*. "As I was now rather proud of my new instrument and wished to play it in concert in addition to the other tenors in full pieces, I now transposed the tenor parts of many of the pieces commonly selected by Mr. Harris, and altered them so as to suit the basso viola, on which I sometimes took an obbligato fagotto part, or fagotto or violoncello obbligato accompaniment to a song and on the nineteenth [April?] I played my new quartetto or conversation piece for the violin, tenor, basso viola, and violoncello at the concert, of which I played the basso viola."

At the Music Festival in September of that year Marsh first heard "concertantes, or concertoes for more than one instrument [concerted symphonies, as for the Bach-Abel Hanover Square concerts], of which on Wednesday every one of Abel's was performed for the violin, hautboy and violoncello, and in the evening one of Bach's for violin, hautboy, tenor, and violoncello with ripieno parts to each in both which were cadences [cadenzas] for the principal instruments together, which were most admirably executed by Cramer, Fischer, Stamitz, and Cervetto." At a private concert in October, Joseph Corfe, one of the cathedral lay clerks, with his daughter played one of Burney's recently published duets for harpsichord or pianoforte "upon the plan of some he had heard in Germany." A few days later Marsh, considering the benefits that might accrue to other works, especially 'concert overtures', went to work on the overture to *Astarte*, which—being heartily approved by his sister (who played the piano)—was followed by those to *Artaxerxes* and *Otho*. Since he often played the organ at the cathedral or one of the parish churches, the duet principle was applied to favourite works, such as the "Hallelujah" chorus and the first Coronation Anthem, to supply new voluntaries for the annual procession of judges.

Against all this demonstration of musical interest and invention there needs to be said something of those fears that were the natural concomitant to life at that time. During the summer of 1777 smallpox was rife in Salisbury. Marsh was advised to take his family out of the city into the clearer air of the country, and to have them inoculated (a remarkably early example of this treatment). And on the international scene, in spite of his brother Edward's promotion to lieutenant while serving in American waters, ominous news was reaching Marsh from across the Atlantic: "This being about the height of the American war, people were continually anxious to hear details from America; whence on the third of December news arrived of Lord Howe's having defeated general Washington, though with great slaughter on both sides. This however was in a day or two succeeded by a melancholy reverse, when news arrived of general Burgoyne's being surrounded and taken prisoner with about seven thousand men and sent to Boston."

In time of international tension during the eighteenth century the British Government emphasized the significance of the auxiliary defense force of the locally organized militia. Exactly when Marsh was concerned with the state of affairs in America he was also much taken with the robust sounds produced by the wind players of the Salisbury militia band, which tumbled him into a state of mental tumult. "My mind," he wrote, "was so haunted with musical ideas, that I got no sleep the whole night afterwards, during which I composed my overture for two orchestras,[2] afterwards published, which has always pleased me as much as any piece I ever wrote. This I the next day sketched out in score, for which I luckily had the opportunity of Mr. Slater's being from home on business the whole day, and had myself no thing particularly to employ me at the office."

In 1781 Marsh was delivered from the necessity of working in an office by the inheritance of property near Canterbury, which city became the centre of his interests for the next six years. In spite of the fact that this was the seat of the Primate of the Church of England, music in the cathedral was indifferently administered, according to Marsh, by the then organist, Samuel Porter. It is a sign of the inferior status of a

---

[2]On the cover of the Conversation Symphony ("No 35" added by hand to title in copy in Manchester Central Library) is a diagram showing "Arrangement of the parts of the Sinfonie, in order to produce its intended effect."

professional musician of the period that it was Marsh who took the lead in having a new organ built by Samuel Green for the cathedral. For the occasion of its opening in 1784 (after it had been used in Westminster Abbey for the Handel Commemoration) Marsh composed his anthem "O praise God in his holiness."

Having arrived in Canterbury, Marsh quickly became aware of a deplorable situation in respect of orchestral music. Subscription concerts were ill attended and there was no overall sense of purpose. Not surprisingly, perhaps, it was not long before the whole management was gratefully put into Marsh's hands. Having assessed the qualities (and defects) of his gentlemen players and of the available wind from the East Kent Militia, he set out "to new-model the orchestra which was quite upon the old-fashioned plan, the principal first and second fiddle standing each out in front, and the rest of the fiddles and basses and tenor behind on the same level with the wind-instruments raised above them at the back of the orchestra, which, being fixed to the room I let remain, but had the front and lower part altered into two stages of different heights, in the front or lowest of which I now meant to place the harpsichord, principal violoncelloes and tenors with the singers, and in the other or middle row of the orchestra the fiddles, all in a line. As to the wind-instruments, those I allotted to the back or uppermost row, as before. According to this plan the leader would be exactly in the centre of the orchestra with the principal second fiddle next to him, and the principal violoncello and singer just under him."[3]

The orchestra consisted of four first (Marsh being leader), and four second violins, two clarinets, two horns, three cellos, two violas, double bass, and harpsichord. Five of the players were lay clerks from the cathedral and Porter, the organist, was at the harpsichord. The principal singer, Mrs. Goodban, wife of the landlord of the Prince of Orange (also a violinist), was "a not very tasty singer, but with a powerful voice," who joined the badly trained cathedral boys and the lay clerks in singing glees. The *pièce de résistance* at this first concert was Marsh's latest symphony, "with chasse royale," a Haydn-derived kind of entertainment to which Marsh was particularly addicted.

---

[3]*Cf.* below.

Not long afterwards he began compiling a treatise on thorough bass, based on Niccolo Pasquali's *Thorough bass made easy* (1757), while, in the same week, finishing a new bottom to the pond by his house, and planting there willows and poplars. These tasks accomplished he went to a "private concert" in Canterbury, where he could try his double-orchestra overture, as well as the second of the *Symphonies concertantes* of Jean-Baptiste Davaux, and the overture to [Bononcini's?] *Astarte*. All of this was a rehearsal for the next public concert, "which plan," noted Marsh, "I meant in future to adopt with regard to all new pieces."

About this time Marsh became acquainted with Francis Broderip, music-dealer and publisher, and it was with Broderip that in November 1783 he dined before going for the first time to a meeting of the Anacreontic Society. Here, at the Crown and Anchor, he was particularly gratified with the concert before supper, "at which Cramer and Garriboldi [sic] played; in the course of which two or three symphonies of Haydn were most admirably performed." Necessarily glees were part of the evening. The jovial side of official City life is indulgently recollected in Marsh's comic, and gluttonous, glee (with instrumental accompaniment) *The City Feast or Man of True Taste* (c. 1790), centred on a gavotte motif that suggests Gilbert and Sullivan.

Example 1.

THE TRANSITION FROM BAROQUE TO ROMANTIC 271

In the next year, considering whether or not he might wish to practise as a barrister, Marsh began visiting London more frequently in order to qualify through attendance at the Inner Temple. Being in London in May he was able to obtain tickets for the Handel Commemoration at Westminster Abbey and the Pantheon. His account of the opening music, which colourfully complements that of Burney, gives an idea of the impression made on an experienced musician by the forces then used.

> Their majesties being at length settled and the signal given by the principal director, the grand coronation anthem struck off, led by the celebrated Mr Hay. The first movement of this or introductory symphony I had always before thought for want ot a sufficient body of harmony to support the arpeggios of the fiddles, to be rather tedious, and after the first ten or twelve bars uninteresting and monotonous. But with the band now engaged in it I thought nothing could exceed the grandeur of the effect. This symphony with its beautiful modulations having continued sometime, at length the whole force of the orchestra with all the voices, full organ, trumpets, trombones, double drums etc. burst upon us all at once in the words—'Zadok the Priest'—the force and effect of which almost took me off my legs, and caused the blood to forsake my cheeks.

In 1787 Marsh moved once more, to Chichester, where once again much of the musical life of a little city depended on the professional musicians of the cathedral, the more prosperous of the citizens, and wealthier patrons of the neighbourhood. His reputation as musician and orchestral director being well established, at the news of his intended coming to Chichester Marsh was promptly invited to undertake the Subscription concerts. Just before assuming this responsibility he had been able to look in at the end of a concert, "as they were playing the last piece, a symphony of Vanhalls, the band consisting of three fiddles, led by old Payne, one violoncello. Mr. Toghill, a bassoon and two horns from the Sussex militia band, one tenor, Mr. Moore, and two flutes, Humphrey, the bookseller and another. The band however, though small, was fully sufficient for the company, which consisted of only two ladies."

By the end of August 1787 Marsh felt that the concerts, under his supervision, had established themselves. He then felt impelled to "settle a plan for a winter catch club at the old concert room." It was decided by Marsh and a number of lay clerks from the cathedral "to meet together for twelve nights on every other Friday at the old Concert Room, but so as not to interfere with the subscription-concert nights, and amuse ourselves with some instrumental music from half-past six till half-past eight, at which time we were to sit down to a supper, consisting of oysters and Welch rabbits, to be provided for us by Mr. Triggs, sergeant at mace, and afterwards to sing catches, glees etc., round the fire, wetting our whistles with punch wine, etc. as agreed by the members present." It was a condition that only those able to perform instrumentally or vocally should be present.

On 5 July 1790 the Assembly of Common Council of the Mayor, Aldermen and Citizens of Chichester ordered "that John Marsh, esq. be allowed to erect an organ at the upper end of the new Council Chamber without expense to the corporation."[4] In more ways than one a public benefactor, Marsh lived in Chichester for forty years, during a period in which the successive crises in European affairs were paralleled by those developments in musical style and expression that inaugurated a new era, in which Classical surrendered to Romantic. During these years, with an awareness of the needs of and dangers to the community, Marsh set down his thoughts often against a background of confusion.

In 1792, "there being... a great spirit of republicanism and levelling prevalent all over the kingdom... here were great apprehensions of riots and tumults in London; on which account the tower [of London] was fortified, and the guard at the bank [of England] doubled. Ships were also put in commission and the militia in the eastern counties ordered to be embodied; on which account the friends to good order and government all now met in several places, to form associations for supporting the constitution; a meeting of which kind was on the fourth held at the town hall Chichester, where some resolutions against sedition were drawn up and signed." In 1793, on 25 January, "we first heard of the execution, or murder, of the king of France on the Monday preceding"; 1 February "was rendered lamentably memorable by being that on which war was declared at Paris against this Kingdom." When the Journal resumes in 1800 the evidences of mismanaged national finances, poor harvests, and the strains of conducting a continental war

---

[4]Minute Book of the Common Council of the City of Chichester 1783–1826, Sussex Record Society 1963, Resolution No 60.

are apparent. In June Marsh noted: "At this time bread was raised to seventeen pence the quartern loaf, mutton and lamb to ninepence a pound, and beef so scarce as hardly to be got at all on Monday the twenty-third, we had some beef for the first time [in] three four or five weeks." With other responsible citizens of Chichester, he was now engaged in raising funds for the relief of poverty.

Early in the year Marsh was entertained in Bath by the Piozzis, at whose house he met the celebrated glee composer Dr. Henry Harrington, and heard some excellent pianoforte playing. At Oxford, where his son Edward was a scholar, he met Joseph Reinagle at a private tea-party, and enjoyed an afternoon of chamber music—several quartets of Pleyel, an unpublished trio of Reinagle, and one of his own (in B flat) composed in the previous autumn. He also sat in the organ-loft of St. Mary's Church with William Crotch, Professor of Music in the University, who gratifyingly chose to play Marsh's first Fugue in C as a voluntary.[5] Afterwards, at Christchurch Cathedral, at Marsh's request, Crotch played the "Hailstone" chorus from *Israel in Egypt*. Proceeding next to St. John's College, after hearing an anthem by Crotch, Marsh accepted the invitation to play a voluntary—part of his own Concerto in G. Next year Marsh was able to attend some lectures by Crotch, delivered as part of his Professorial duties, "and was much pleased at the manner of their delivery." Thus was Crotch nudging the University into modern times. In the same year Marsh composed two glees and three sacred items for Crotch's Oxford Harmonic Society.

At a morning rehearsal during the Festival at Salisbury in 1800 Marsh for the first time heard some of Haydn's *Creation* (which had only a few months previously been first heard in London), selections from which were to be performed in the Cathedral the next day. Other works were Handel's Funeral Anthem and a Mass by Jommelli. Marsh was already acquainted with J. P. Salomon, to whom he had recommended a young friend of his own as a pupil, and on 31 May 1802 was delighted to be able to be in London and to attend Salomon's benefit Concert at Willis's Rooms. He was "much entertained with a fine concert in which Mrs. Billington and Braham were the chief singers. The instrumental part was also exceedingly good, as besides Haydn's grand symphony with

[5]Probably *Twenty Voluntaries*, 1795, XX.

the military movement, and Mozart's overture to the Magic Flute, both of which were admirably performed, Salomon played a violin concerto with much taste." (The 'Military' Symphony Marsh had heard in a Hanover Square concert in 1794.) But the novelty of the evening was from "the Mess. Petrides two new French-horn players, who played a concerto together with much execution, and in the second act played a piece, in which the echo-passages were played so very pianissimo and delicately, that I was at first myself deceived, and thought they were played by another pair of horns in a room behind the orchestra."

There was a charming interlude in December 1802: "On Tuesday, the twenty-first, our son, Henry, returned to us from London, in order to meet his brother John, and his bride, who on the next day came to us from Oxford with Edward, whom they had prevailed upon contrary to his former intention to be a third in their post-chaise and join our family-party at Christmas, so that our three sons after having been dispersed for upward of eight years at length all joined us again. As with my brother, William, we now made up five performers in one family, we after tea played some quintettoes and quartettoes together in the drawing-room. The next day being that of the third private concert Miss Poole came over and dined with us, and accompanied us all to it, at which by way of a curiosity I with my brother and three sons played my own quintetto in B flat. The flute part being played by Henry, my brother took the first fiddle, John the second, Edward the tenor, and myself the violoncello."

In October 1803 Marsh was brought back to the difficulties of the times in a curious manner. He was a friend and neighbour of William Hayley, patron of William Blake—to become famous as poet, artist, and mystic. A laconic comment in the Journal noted, "Mr. Blake of Felpham [near Chichester], the engraver, accused by 2 soldiers of having spoken seditious words." Blake was taken to court, but acquitted, his principal accuser having been a drunken soldier whom Blake had evicted from his garden. Two years later Marsh noticed how there were again preparations on the French side of the English Channel for invasion, which necessitated the harvest workers being required to assemble with the volunteer militia (in which Marsh was actively engaged as a major). The invasion did not take place. A year later, inflation being rampant, "the great rise in my rents, since I first came into possession seems scarcely more than adequate to the great diminution of the value of money, or increase in the price of articles, taxes etc. . . ." In 1806, however, Marsh was put in good spirits by the academic success of his son Edward, now a Fellow at Oriel College who had been offered an attractive appointment as tutor to the sons of Sir John Wrottesley. In May Marsh went to London to visit Edward and one evening he was a guest at Sir John Wrottesley's London house, where "I met the two Miss Wrottesleys, his sisters, and a Miss Gardiner, staying with them. As we were to have some music in the evening we were then joined by a Sign. Spagnoletti, a very good violin from the opera band, and a tenor, who came with him. These with Sir John Wrottesley, who played the violoncello, accompanied Miss Wrottesley in a piece of Beethoven's which she played in a very good style; after which I played the second fiddle in one of Haydn's quintetto symphonies, and Miss Gardiner played a piece on the harp."

On 8 June Marsh received from Clementi proofs of the plates to his *Hints to young Composers* and from Broderip a collection of his organ pieces.[6] His extraordinary energy and unflagging receptiveness to new places, people and ideas, took him—somewhat breathlessly at times, past the first quarter of the nineteenth century. Remarkably, for long distance coach travel over indifferent roads entailed much discomfort, Marsh visited much of England, and his closing volumes review the state of music in some of the distant counties. Not infrequently he stands still in a Wordsworthian reverie, to capture an impression. In 1809 he arrived in Lincoln in the late afternoon of an October day: "The appearance of the city under and on the side of a hill with its majestic cathedral at the top had an extraordinary effect. I immediately marched up the hill to the cathedral, and was saluted, just when I came to the west-end, with great Tom [the heaviest of the bells] striking five." As usual he went immediately to the organist. Conducted round the cathedral, given an opportunity to play the organ, shown the ruins of a royal palace, he finally came to view the new county jail. Marsh was concerned for penal reform and in 1808,

---

[6]Compositions of the Harmonic Society of Oxford III, 1800, Bodleian Library, Tenbury MS 600; "Come cheerfulness" (p. 8), "Blow, blow thou winter wind" (p. 16), "Lord have mercy" (p. 36), "I will arise" (p. 58)—see Example 4, p. 282—and (2nd version) "Lord have mercy" (p. 62); "I will arise" here is in D major, for C[anto] ATB a capella, and entitled "Motett," Marsh signing himself as "Hon. Member of the Society."

at Gloucester, had missed a *Messiah* performance ("which we had so often heard") in order to visit John Howard's new model prison in that city.

From Lincoln, Marsh travelled to Newark to examine the organ built there five years previously by George Pike England on Marsh's recommendation. Thence he went to the neighbouring city of Nottingham, to hear performances of familiar works by Handel and Haydn to raise funds for the support of widows and orphans of the clergy. Two years later he went to the rapidly growing industrial city of Birmingham, for the Music Festival. The conductor was Samuel Wesley, architect of the English Bach movement. Marsh was here impressed by the sheer size of the forces employed—200 singers and instrumentalists. A Beethoven symphony gave the Birmingham audience its first opportunity to hear a work of this master.

In 1813, in honor of the victory of the allies at Leipzig, "there were great rejoicings all over England, and on the fifth [of November] Chichester Cross was illuminated in the evening, and there being no wind, exhibited a most elegant and beautiful appearance." In June 1815, came "the glorious news of the defeat of Bonaparte by Lord Wellington and Marshall Blu[e]cher." But account needed to be taken of the distresses caused by the long years of war. Marsh was among the citizens of Chichester who, in 1815, aimed to set up an evening school for adults, and, two years later, he was one of those called to a meeting by the Mayor "to take into consideration the numerous poor now out of employment."

In July Marsh was in London and became aware of other changes that had taken place during the long and arduous times of war. There was, indeed, a new kind of music, as Marsh came to understand: ". . . I played at a concert of amateurs and professors at Forster's in the Strand, where we tried Beethoven's pastoral symphony, which we were puzzled to get through." The comment impresses by its taciturnity. Next day he went to the English Opera House (the former Lyceum Theatre in the Strand), where C. E. Horn's *The Persian Hunters* was being played, and was amazed to find the theatre now lit by gas. Next day he went to see the great Apollonicon, a masterpiece of organ-builder's skill, if not discretion—a five-manuel organ from the workshop of Flight and Robson which could be played either in the normal way, or, mechanically, with barrels. These Marsh cheerfully activated to produce the overtures to Cherubini's *Anacréon* and Mozart's *La clemenza di Tito*.

There was in the immediate post-war years a notable increase in every form of musical activity in England, and even after the death of his wife in 1818 Marsh continued his activities with undiminished determination and curiosity. In 1819 a tour of northern cathedrals enabled him to discover that one or two of his church compositions were in the general repertory. He once again attended the Three Choirs Festival, which this year was at Hereford. In 1823 he went to a large-scale Festival in York Minster. The programme of the three day event included, as well as *Messiah*, the first Act of Haydn's *Creation*, and Beethoven's *Eroica* symphony and *Egmont* overture; but what he especially noted were the skills of the orchestra, as displayed when "Catalani chose to sing the opening of the Messiah 'Comfort ye' etc. in D instead of E, which not only obliged the band to transpose the accompaniments, but to transpose the overture also to D minor, which (Dr. Camidge [the Minster organist] said) they did much better than might have been expected; and she also sang 'I heard that my redeemer liveth' in E flat." (It would seem likely that Marsh was the 'Correspondent' who wrote about this to *The Harmonicon* of 1823.) From York Marsh went to Liverpool, where also there was a Musical Festival, directed by Sir George Smart—one of the great conductors of the nineteenth century, and the leading exponent of Beethoven in England. It is characteristic of Marsh, that while he applauded the "fine and striking parts" of *The Mount of Olives* (which he was hearing for the first time), he was especially affected by a visit to the blind asylum, where a choir of blind inmates—"above twenty female and several tenor, alto and bass voices, very well accompanied by a blind man on the fine organ [built by the firm of Gray] I had heard the day before"—sang a Service, with an anthem from Pergolesi.

In 1827 it was time again for the Three Choirs Festival at Worcester. This was to be the last such event attended by Marsh, with a programme going still further, beyond Beethoven, into a future represented by Meyerbeer and Rossini. On the way to Worcester Marsh went to Southwell, where his son Edward was a prebendary of the Minster church. For the evening of 31 August Edward had arranged a concert, which began between 7.30 and 8 o'clock:

We began with the third of my printed symphonies in D,[7] in which the Rev Robert Fowler Junr. and Mr Hutchinson played the flute-parts, Mr Pheasant of the choir the violoncello, Mr Thompson of the choir, and another the two horns, there being with the second fiddle and the tenor, played by Mr Heathcote's assistant, and pianoforte played by Mr Heathcote, nine instruments, which were placed in the bow at the further end of the drawing-room. The concert bill consisted of eighteen pieces, viz. two of my overtures, that to Lodoiska, and Kammell's third notturno, three of mine, and three other glees, three songs by Mr. Robert Fowler, Messrs Pheasant and Thompson, two piano-forte duets, and one for the piano and flute, the whole concluding with my vocal finale—'Happy are we met,' in the repetition of the parts of which we mustered ten voices, which with the pianoforte and my fiddle made a grand concluding crash; after which was a supper in the dining-room, and one for the choirmen and musicians in another room, the whole assembled, including the performers, being about forty-two persons, all of whom seemed much pleased, and dispersed before twelve o'clock.

Marsh touched both life and music at many points, and it was a broad-based concern both for the health of his community and also of music in the community that gives him a particular claim to continuing respect. During his lifetime London, on account of its prosperity able to attract many virtuoso performers and notable composers from abroad, became a major European center of music. Other cities in Britain, however, were for the most part dependent on their local resources of skill and enthusiasm. Happily the distinction between amateur and professional was not so great that an amateur, whose talents were balanced by disposable means and leisure, could not contribute significantly to musical well-being. It was to Marsh's advantage that he belonged to the provinces.

In that formal musical education (outside of cathedral choir-schools) only began in England in 1822, with the foundation of the Royal Academy of Music of which William Crotch was principal, Marsh's versatility and practical skills well qualified him to exert influence on education, to which, by his example and his publications, he may be seen to have made a notable contribution, both regionally and nationally.

---

[7]Published by Smart, advertised in "A Catalogue of / Vocal and Instrumental Music / Compos'd & Publish'd by J. Marsh, Esqr, Chichester," cover of Sinfonia V.

He was in every way a practical man, in whom common sense was allowed to prevail. His essential qualities are revealed in his account of his part in the appointment of a new cathedral organist in Chichester in 1803. During the process of selection candidates were sensibly and informally tested not only in the skills required in the cathedral but also in respect of the social musicianship—in this case a glee party—in which the successful candidate would be expected in due course to play a leading role. One candidate, a young man from Windsor named Salmon, was accompanied to Chichester by his father (also apparently a musician). This is Marsh's report: "Had it, however, not been for Mr Salmon the elder, who sang the upper part in some glees, we could have had no singing at all, as the young man could only sing bass which we did not want, and that he did in a glee or two we tried in a mawkish manner, neither did he choose to take a fiddle in a duet or quartet, or seem disposed to play anything upon the pianoforte...."

Another candidate, Holland, from Oxford, had a good tenor voice, but was unable to sing "an alto or upper part in an anthem or a glee, or a middle part, and at the same time accompany the whole." Nor, so far as Marsh was concerned, was this all. For he failed to show "any great degree of judgment as in playing the thorough bass to one of Corelli's concertoes he took the chords quite in the upper part of the instrument, and sometimes amongst the additional keys, his principal aim seeming to be to make himself heard and distinguished beyond the other instruments. He also sang 'Pious orgies'—of Handel without much taste, or attempting any shake." The place was given to Thomas Bennett, a former chorister at Salisbury who, at the time of the vacancy at the cathedral, was organist of St. John's Chapel in Chichester.

Marsh anticipated those who have been generally allowed credit for the reform of church music in England in the nineteenth century. An energetic composer of services and anthems at a time when the repertory required enlargement, he also took a lead in respect of the singing of the psalms (in the Church of England a daily obligation) by proposing that organists should come to an agreement on a rational and general method of pointing.[8] As a boy he had once been taken by his father to Holland, where the experience of hearing the organ in the

---

[8]*Cathedral Chant Book*, c. 1810.

Grote Kerk in Haarlem left a lasting impression; he became particularly sensitive to the range of tonal colours available to the organist. In his most active years there was a great demand for organs in English churches and he saw the popularity of the instrument as a means of broadening the general experience of music. The organ voluntary for many became the most immediate focus of musical appreciation.

Discovering without difficulty that more bad voluntaries than good were generally played, Marsh set out to remedy the situation. Towards the end of the eighteenth century he published three volumes of *Voluntaries for ... Young Practitioners*,[9] consisting of some original pieces but mostly of arrangements. In an extensive Preface to the first set Marsh examines in some detail the nature, function and viability of the organ in its normal ecclesiastical setting. He describes a fair-sized three manual instrument—without pedals—not very different from Green's Salisbury instrument of 1792, and goes in some detail into possibilities of registration. He suggests appropriate combinations of stops to accompany, on the one hand, services and anthems sung by the cathedral choir, and, on the other, congregational singing of psalms and hymns. Concerning the organist's repertory Marsh counselled prudence, so that—with the gluttonous text of his *City Feast* gavotte style in mind—"gavots or tempo di gavotta" should be avoided. For Marsh himself, not surprisingly, the familiar English Voluntary of the eighteenth century was a convenient and congenial launching pad. However, his resonant fugues for two performers of around 1778 having clearly given some general satisfaction, he moved with other English composers of organ music towards the increasingly accepted rigors of fugal structure. There is an Adagio and Fugue in C major (Vol. 1, 20) and a more ambitious Adagio with double fugue in A minor (Vol. II, 12). The latter fugue, preceded by a movement akin to an extemporized interlude to a metrical psalm (Example 2), is adventurous in its development of the changing tonal movements suggested by the exposition (Example 3):

---

[9] c. 1791, 1795, 1800.

Example 2.

Example 3.

The third set, more utilitarian, includes 23 Preludes or Short Introductions for Verse Anthems, for those unable readily to extemporize suitable material. As well as these books of Voluntaries, Marsh published during the last twenty years of his life six books of Select Movements, mostly arrangements of items taken from a wide range of composers. The first book contains movements from concertos by Corelli; the second, "select airs and chorusses" from Handel's oratorios ("the particular ideas conveyed by the words to which they have been usually sung, are very likely to be excited by the Music alone"). The following volumes range widely. Tartini, Sacchini, Geminiani and Martini, and the English composers Avison, Stanley, and Felton (as well as some less well known) are represented in the third collection, with Arne and Abel, Jommelli and Pergolesi prominent in the fourth. The fifth set introduces Haydn, Pleyel, and Mozart, while the *Andante cantabile con variazioni* of Beethoven's Op. 1 no. 3, which Marsh had heard on an evening in Sir John Wrottesley's house in 1806, brought the collection up to date. Concerning the respective claims of John Stanley and James Worgan, the most celebrated organists of their day, Marsh praised the 'simplicity and intelligibility' of the first, while of the second, when he played, "the effect [was] as it were of a grand Orchestra, interspersed with solo passages for trumpets, hautboys, flutes, bassoons, &c."

Of Marsh's anthems "I will arise" illustrates the points he makes about the virtues of simplicity, but—in its revised published form—through detailed dynamic gradations it also shows a subtle feeling for, in this case, choral color. An introduction of ten measures is based on the opening passage:

Example 4.

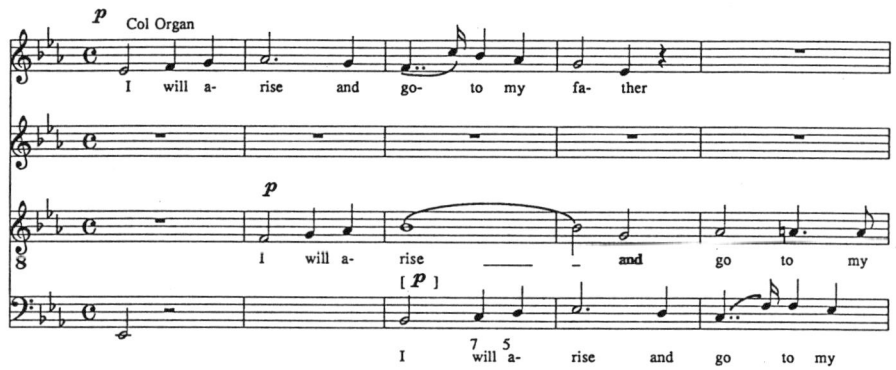

Making ad hoc arrangements for whatever combinations of instruments might be available at any time was a major part of Marsh's practical experience. Since he was versatile in being able to play a number of instruments he was well placed to influence attitudes towards orchestration. This he did through *Hints to Young Composers of Instrumental Music* (1805?), a friendly introduction to the art of composition, with descriptions of modern instruments and two examples of "how to orchestrate" specially composed for the purpose. These little pieces were set out in full score (he insisted that orchestral music could only thus be learned) and usefully annotated. Commenting on the dearth of good oboists outside of London, Marsh drew attention to the fact that in the provinces, more often than not, oboe parts were undertaken by the abler clarinettists who were avilable in military bands. Given to the cultivation of epigrams, Marsh nicely advises that, "Composers. . . in general cannot do better than conform to the example of Handel, in making but sparing use of the more powerful instruments."

While retaining a firm belief in the inviolability of Handelian and English Baroque style, as a composer Marsh placed his confidence fully in the initiatives undertaken by the genial trio of Abel, the English Bach, and Haydn. In respect of the two former composers Marsh was not uncritical. In an extended essay in which he compared "ancient" and "modern," he placed before the composition student the disadvantages of standardization of design:

> There is however in general so great a uniformity in the style and plan of their symphonies, and so great a sameness in them, that it has been

said of them, particularly of Bach's (considering them as opera Overtures, or theatrical pieces) that the first or principal movements seem to be calculated for the meridian of the pit, (where the critics generally assemble) the middle strain for that of the boxes, (where people of a more refined taste usually sit) and the last strain for that of the galleries.[10]

For Marsh himself an admirable sense of melody, texture, and tonal variety was not quite matched by a capacity for a symphonic extension of ideas, which is not altogether surprising. He was above all an occasional composer, an early exemplar of the principle of *Gebrauchsmusik*. He wrote music for particular conditions, and certainly without an ear on posthumous fame. As was fitting in Napoleon's *nation de boutiquiers* he usefully supplied a growing demand.

It was in emulation of Haydn that Marsh wrote his "celebrated" Overture/Symphony *La Chasse*, which lacks nothing in graphic definition. After an *Andante* passage of alternating horn and oboe summons against the assembly of the hunt, an engaging rural theme (derived from the previous section) describes at some length the "setting out from home":

Example 5.

Dispersed through several keys (in C minor an original point of colour comes from flute and cello in octaves), this alternates with an illustrative pattern of triplets. The fox discovered, *La chasse* begins and ends.

---

[10]*A Comparison / between the / Ancient and Modern Styles of Music, / in which the / Merits and Demerits of each are respectively pointed out*, anonymously printed in a supplement to *The Monthly Magazine* II (1796): 981; published, with Introduction by C. L. Cudworth, *Music and Letters* XXXVI (1955): 155.

Of his chamber music Marsh's Quartetto in B flat "in imitation of Haydn's Opera prima" shows a fine control of textures and a properly Haydnesque "conversational" interchange of thematic material. The *Conversation Sinfonia* for two orchestras which is, perhaps, Marsh's best-known but rarely (if ever) performed work, was undertaken with J. C. Bach's Opus 18, number 1 in mind. That he was keen on experiment in regard to the placing of players has already been shown. On the cover of the *Conversation Symphony* the exact lay-out proposed is illustrated. The orchestra is shown on three levels, from the front as follows: center, violoncello Principale e Cembalo; 1st orch. l., violino secondo, violino primo / 2nd orch. r., viola prima, viola seconda; 1st orch. l., basso Primo e Fagotto, Oboes; centre, timpani; orch. r., Corni, Basso Secondo e Contra Bassa. Below the plan was the notice, "In large Concert Rooms, each Tenor part should always be doubled as well as the Fiddle parts, each of which may very properly be trebled, that the latter (if either) may be predominant."[11]

The slow movement of this symphony is distinguished by the opportunity offered to the viola:

Example 6.

[11]Parts of the Conversation Symphony, as well as of Symphonies 106, "La Chasse" (no. 7), "A Favorite Overture in Parts for a Large or Small Band / Publish'd by Subscription Quarterly / for the use of / Country Concerts, and Three Finales, or short concluding Pieces for Concerts," all marked "Chichester Concert", probably by Marsh himself, are in the Cambridge University Library (MR310.a.75.3 -).

Example 6 (continued)

The progress made by the viola was accelerated by Marsh's concern for the instrument's acoustical qualities, his experiments with his bassa viola, and by the fact that often in the orchestra with which he was most associated there was always the possibility that there would only be one player to this part.

The circumstances of Marsh's music-making did not encourage too frequent exposition of darker thoughts. The last item in a book of miscellaneous church music, a funeral hymn, did however suggest an unusually scored work—"with a part for the Great Bell of a Church." One movement in the third book of Voluntaries exploits the dark key of D minor, but it is in the introduction to his sixth symphony that (through Haydn) the Romantic tendency most expressively appears:

However enthusiastic he was for the music of the 'Moderns', Marsh never became indifferent to the virtues of the 'Ancients'. One of his last works, of which a copy was presented by him to the Music Room

Example 7.

in Oxford on 16 November 1826, was *Three Overtures... composed after the manner of the ancient masters*. In this way he addressed himself to the Directors of the Antient Music:

> ... according to the rules of the Concert of *Ancient Music* they have a legitimate claim to come under that denomination [as being 30 years old]; if indeed the purpose of the Directors of that concert be to encourage the composition of music in their favorite style, I humbly submit that, instead of the age of the composition, it would be better to make the *style* of it their criterion of admission.

Alfred Mann

A EUROPEAN AT HOME ABROAD
An Autobiographical Sketch

THE CONFLICTS

1

The other day, I read an autobiographical essay by a twentieth-century German writer who, like myself, was driven out of Germany during the time of its greatest disgrace and granted freedom in America. It is an arresting account of a hardship characteristic of its period, a hardship seemingly insignificant in comparison with the unspeakable hardships of the World Wars: the hardship of abiding isolation. What struck me was that it was described as generally forgotten and that I, who had lived through it, had all but forgotten it as well, because in the end I was spared its effects. Autobiography, whose value I had always viewed as somewhat equivocal, suddenly took on a new meaning, as a measure of saving such lessons of history from oblivion, and as an expression of pervading gratitude.

Communication throughout the world has become instant in our time. Events are witnessed on the screen as they happen, and a written document is transmitted with the same immediacy as a call on the telephone. Yet remnants of less enlightened times persist. At the dawn of the approaching century, the screen still shows prisoners and hostages with whom all outside communication had ceased. A similar disruption was the rule at midpoint of the waning century. In 1945 the war was over, destruction had stopped, and Europe was liberated, though still largely separated from the rest of the world. For years the only messages exchanged in families divided over warring territories were the merciful Red Cross letters—a few words covering no more than one or two lines that had been allowed to go through enemy lines. I once received such a letter from my father who lived through the war in my native town of Hamburg. It said that my grandfather had died in 1942 but that the rest of the family was all right. The year had to suffice by way of a date, for no one knew how long the letter would travel.

When the hostilities ceased, communications were not resumed. The occupied countries, divided into Allied military zones, remained excluded from the international mail and telephone service and from all international travel that was not on official military or diplomatic business. Under the circumstances, an unofficial system developed. Mail to the occupation troops was used to carry messages to German civilians, in hopes that a connection might be found through some fortunate coincidence or relay. Conversely, German civilians sought out American soldiers willing to act as intermediaries when writing home. It was often the very first indication that a relative or friend abroad had indeed survived, when such a "contraband" message succeeded in reaching its destination.

For illegal it was. Relatively late in the war, thought had been given to what would happen when the American soldier would find himself face to face with the German civilian. Henry Morgenthau, Jr., Secretary of the Treasury under Roosevelt, and in many respects his closest adviser, had established the formula to be applied, a stern rule of "non-fraternization." By and large, it failed. When the shooting ends, the anonymous enemy becomes a distinct human being again. In time, "frat'nizin'" was, in the disobedient soldier's language, adopted as a household word for a new aspect of his social life. Yet if any kindly gesture caught the attention of higher authorities, disciplinary action was apt to result, and the enforced severance made the less sense to either side the longer it extended into the hard-won peace.

2

It was on my twentieth birthday, in 1937, that I first realized that I must leave my homeland. What loomed as a desperate conflict then became in retrospect my future's blessing, but it took time to arrive at such understanding. I had spent a happy childhood in Germany, filled with rich and formative impressions. While my parents' marriage was dissolved early, I was too young to sense the grief the separation must have caused. My mother was a musician and my father a portrait painter, and the two artistic temperaments were too contrary to be reconciled. But I remember vividly the genuine regard and affection they maintained for each other throughout their lives; both of them remarried, though under very different circumstances. In early adolescence, I, though living with my mother, was devoted to the profession of my father, in whose studio I found myself every week. When I was thirteen I completed, with his help, a self-portrait which has retained its place on the wall. But after that—my first autobiographical statement—my interests turned, and I became absorbed in my mother's profession.

She had been entrusted with the piano class that the Hamburg University curriculum had established for teachers. Drawn into the class, the University's Collegium Musicum transformed the instrumental instruction into a chamber music situation that fascinated me. By my mother's wise decision—which helped me greatly in my later experience as a conductor—I was trained as a string player, and my violin study was enhanced when, in a competition, I won the coveted prize of a fine instrument, a viola. One day, the bass player of the Collegium asked if, for the sake of convenience, he could leave his bass at our home. I could not keep my fingers off it, and before long, I found myself also under the tutelage of the Philharmonic Orchestra's principal of the bass section. (History repeated itself; when my oldest son was fifteen, he took the bass out of my hand to devote himself to the study and profession of that instrument.)

Under the influence of Wanda Landowska, my mother became one of Germany's earliest twentieth-century harpsichordists, and she established a Baroque ensemble, then still a novelty. Friends brought from Arnold Dolmetsch's Festivals in England what was then a newly rediscovered instrument, the recorder. I became deeply involved in the study and performance of Baroque music, and it had a bearing upon my wish to pursue the profession of my mother's students; its revival had, in turn, revitalized music instruction in the schools.

But I was barred from it. I belonged to what the National Socialist regime had categorized, in a curious pseudo-scientific manner, as different classes of "cross-breed." According to one's percentages of "aryan" blood, one was admitted to, or denied, various walks of life. My father's family came from Silesian and Frisian peasant stock—my father's father was a sea-faring man—but my mother's was that of an old Jewish merchant's family. Thus my life had become subject to the judgement of two halves: one, which closed opportunity after opportunity for my future and livelihood, and one which presented me on my twentieth birthday with the notice of draft into the German Army.

3

I was drafted. Through the kind intervention of my teacher, I did receive a student's deferment of a year, but the single day I spent in the German Army—the crudeness of its physical examination, its Prussian regimentation—remains a jarring memory. The teacher to whom I owed my lease on life was the head of the viola class at the Berlin Academy of Music, where I had enrolled as a student earlier that year—one of the fortunate turns in my life that arose from denials imposed.

University study, which would have led to a teaching career, having become inaccessible through the prevailing regulations, I had probed the alternate possibility of training as an orchestra musician. Professor Fritz Stein, Director of the Academy and an eminent conductor and scholar, was one of the—largely forgotten—Germans in high office who, to the extent possible, resisted the strictures of the regime. He saw to it that I was accepted, and an unsuspected range of opportunities opened to the entering student. I had three major subjects: viola, composition, and conducting. By a happy coincidence one of the first modern specialized recorder players taught at the school, so that I could perfect my technique on that instrument, and I also received my first formal instruction in musicology. The resources were ample, and within a short time they provided me with a sure professional foundation; yet in the background remained the unalterable verdict that none of this could lead to any professional future in Germany.

What held my particular interest was the instruction in composition. My earlier school days had prepared me well for the wealth of new impressions, and for a number of years I had studied theory with a local organist well-known and respected for his published organ chorales. Now I became acquainted with strict counterpoint, and it re-introduced me to a name I had only vaguely known: Johann Joseph Fux, the Viennese court composer and Master of the Imperial Chapel in the age of Bach and Handel. I found a copy of his famed counterpoint manual, *Gradus ad Parnassum*, in the school's library, and with a measure of reverence I looked at the book and the former owner's signature in the volume—Joseph Joachim who, I knew, had been Director of the Academy when my mother had studied there thirty years earlier. What followed was one of those discoveries that lent direction to my life. I realized that this was the book which had served Haydn, Mozart, and Beethoven—in fact, in some way, all the great masters from Bach to the composers of the twentieth century—for study and instruction, but that its complete text had survived only in rare copies—and its language was Latin. Suddenly, the nine years of Latin lessons every day, the norm of my secondary school curriculum, appeared to me in a new light, and I decided to make a translation.

The school I had attended was founded at St. John's in Hamburg by a friend of Luther, and when I was in the seventh grade, it celebrated its four hundredth anniversary. Its principal subjects through the ages had been Latin and Greek, but its musical tradition was strong. I remember seeing, whenever I entered the building, the two plaques showing Telemann and C. P. E. Bach, because they had been the music teachers there in their time. And it seemed to me as if they were looking over my shoulder as I excitedly set about my task—Telemann had been the first to plan a German translation, but it never appeared; later J. S. Bach had one of his students carry it out, but, like the original text, it was never reprinted. What was clearly needed was a new, modern and annotated translation.

I had the good luck to find a courageous publisher. For issuing a book from the hand of one in my precarious situation was not without obstacles and dangers, and it was a severe blow for the young translator to see his name removed from the title page in proofs. But the publisher, whose caution was well founded, had enough ingenuity and character to place it in small print on its reverse page. And most important, he had the vision to send review copies to a large array of the major newspapers and journals of Europe. It met with a surprising reaction. Reviews were streaming in from Berlin, Vienna, Basel, Milan and Budapest, and Ernest Newman devoted an editorial to it in the London *Times*.

4

I was no longer in Germany when all of this happened. I had had a year to prepare my emigration—except it could not be known that it would be that, for I was now under military rule. I was caught three ways. A soldier could not leave; a German with a passport handsomely adorned with a swastika was not too welcome across borders; and, should it become apparent that the bearer of the passport was in a conflict with the law of the swastika that might make a return difficult or impossible, the visitor was doubly unwelcome, and the borders would tightly close. This prompted the choice of Italy, then a Fascist country. Yet Italy was also the legendary land of art and music which had attracted my countrymen over the centuries. It held promise beyond mere rescue, but, foremost in my deliberations, it was the only country in which I would find a relative. My mother's younger sister, Gertrud Weiss, a scientist, had been called to a Milan firm early in her career. She had become enamored with the country and eventually decided to make it her permanent home.

But how different is the abrupt process of uprooting. As the train took me south, I clung to the idea that upon leaving Germany, I would still enter a country where German was spoken, for crossing the Rhine at the southern border of Germany, the traveler finds himself in the Swiss city of Basel. It was late at night when I arrived at the border station. Basel, an international city, has a central Swiss terminal, a French terminal, and a German terminal. At the latter, torn by divergent emotions, I showed the passport that, I hoped, would grant exit and entry to the one who had not wanted to leave in the first place. But the German border guard was only interested in the fact that I had two weeks' military leave, and the Swiss border guard merely checked how much German currency I had—it was precious little.

I found a small hotel, and the next morning I could not believe the opulence on the Swiss breakfast table, nor the Hitler caricatures in the newspapers. I was reminded of the Swiss border gendarme's concern when, a few hours later, I called on the Director of the Schola Cantorum Basiliensis, the distinguished conductor Paul Sacher. His institution was famed as a center, as a veritable Mecca, for research and performance of early music. He told me I could study and work there if independent financial means would guarantee my stay. The next evening I crossed the Italian border.

5

The beauty of Italy's scene, the brightness of its sky, are somehow reflected in the nature of its people. I was not only warmly received by my own relative, but by the people whose language I had a hard time understanding. Yet no sooner had I tried my first timid "buon giorno," than I was told "Ma come parla!—Come si spiega!" ("How you speak!—How you express yourself!"). Some of this grace seemed to have rubbed off on the German consular officials. Without much ado, my two-weeks' leave was changed to a student's permit for two years, which opened to me the doors of the venerable Royal Conservatory. Yet to piece together an existence in a foreign country remained a formidable charge, and I remember with abiding gratitude how the ties of family and friendship helped to guide me through my two student years in Italy.

I met with congenial company among German immigrants. Their means were often hardly more ample than mine, but they held to what in European society was in those days still a cherished custom: whenever possible, one gathered for evenings of playing string quartets or devoted to literature and art. I gave some violin and viola lessons—aside from German lessons to young Italian business people—and even some drawing lessons. A chamber music group formed, and we were engaged for private concerts at the more affluent Milanese homes, among them that of the American consul. The rediscovery of early music and instruments had just begun to find interest in Italy. Before long a publisher entrusted me with the preparation of an instruction book for the recorder; and a small music school, the *Scuola Musicale di Milano*, asked for my services as a performer and teacher.

It all came to a halt when, late in 1938, Mussolini announced, in pathetic compliance with his German fellow-dictator, that all non-aryan immigrants must leave the country within six months. Though the clouds of the approaching war were all too evident, no one took time to reflect that the edict might mean eventual salvation. Only the panic of impending arrest, deportation, and concentration camp governed the day. Where to turn? No European country was willing to grant entrance to stranded Germans unable to return to their homeland. Immigration to the United States was ruled by a strict—and overcrowded—quota system which required, in addition, an affidavit for the immigrant's indefinite support. The rumor spread quickly that the one country open without any restrictions was China, and my old passport's Chinese visa, a curiously ornate affair, serves as a reminder of the turmoil of those days.

There was in my chamber music group a young couple, professional musicians also recently escaped from Germany, whose widespread family included a distant cousin managing a small concert agency in America. They drew me into an ingenious, desperate plan. We would join in a Baroque ensemble offering programs of little known early music and wire their cousin, asking for a pro-forma American concert engagement which we would then submit to the consul, in whose house we had performed, asking for the required temporary entrance visa. Their relative, who knew his business, grasped the novelty, was intrigued by its genuine potential, and complied.

6

We were saved—or so it seemed. In reality, the panic continued. How bold are the hopes of the fugitive! The consul greeted us as old friends, but this did not alter the fact that, in accordance with proper office procedure, he referred us to a young colleague in charge of temporary visas. I will never lose the memory of the courtesy and conscientiousness with which this young man went about his assignment. There was no mention of the fact that all documents, such as we had, were suspect under the circumstances. But a new complication had entered emigré travel. German governmental offices had called in all passports to stamp the ones of Jewish passport holders with a "J"—an especially insidious cruelty in the case of those who had already crossed the German border and would merely find it harder to move between other borders. It denied my friends the temporary entry to the United States, but our official explained that if I (whose passport had not been defaced) were to obtain a separate contract specifying only my involvement, it could be honored. He obviously regretted not being able to do more, though our exchange remained entirely formal.

One is naturally unwilling to accept such a decision, no matter from what logic it may be derived. Among the Americans we had met at the consul's home was the vice-consul, a young lady of unusual charm who was subsequently transferred to the consular office in Lugano, Switzerland. We remembered her well, for it had taken us by surprise that, rather than any domestic help, she had done the serving at the reception following our concert—a first glimpse into unfamiliar American customs. The futile thought occurred to us that she and the smaller office staff in Lugano might judge our case differently. Commuter travel between Milan and Lugano, on a day's permit, was still possible, and the attempt had to be made.

She received and recognized us graciously, but disappeared with our papers into an adjoining office. Minutes of anxious waiting; then she breezed in again. "Ci deve essere uno sbaglio" ("There must be a mistake")—our case had to be handled at the office in Milan, where we lived; she would unfortunately be unable to be of help. Nor was it of any help to remind ourselves that it could not have been otherwise. Forty years later, almost to the day, I met with the company of friends in the Saucon Valley Country Club, Pennsylvania, at a reception following a performance of the B Minor Mass I had conducted at the Bethlehem Bach Festival. Among the guests was a lady whose very beautiful features belied her seventy-some years. In the course of the conversation it was mentioned that she had been in the consular service at Milan in the months preceding the Second World War. "I was in Milan at that time"—as I said the words, there seemed to be a sudden flash of recognition. Yet the recollection of those years had grown too hazy. I wondered if she realized that I was once among those to whom she had had to deny entry to the United States, but our talk drifted to other things closer at hand.

7

Another plan was needed. My friends did ask their cousin to send me a separate contract. But for their own rescue, they adopted a new scheme. England, whose upper class was beginning to feel the stringencies of a new social era, offered at that time visas to immigrants entering under contract as domestic servants. For the search of such a contract they pleaded with close relatives who had found refuge in London. It was the next-of-kin and the fellow sufferer in the turbulent circumstances who were invariably the emigré's surest help. The search succeeded; my friends left, and I was to see them again in the roles of cook and butler during one day's reunion in England.

What mattered in these frantic days was always the visa, not its consequences. We had arranged that, should my contract arrive and produce the American visa, I would try to use it to obtain an English visa. By a complicated procedure, an English transit visa would be granted for the purpose of sailing on an English boat and from an English port, provided the visa was accompanied by proof of paid passage. The desperately needed financial help came from my parents.

In Germany, the life of the persecuted had meanwhile turned into a nightmare—a nightmare organized by a punctilious bureaucracy. Yet much of its detail was safely kept within the German borders. The bold idea by which my mother eventually escaped from Germany could not be communicated by censored mail or censored telephone conversation. Her passport, too, had been called in to be stamped—and thus to be rendered utterly useless —but she never followed the order to pick it up again. Through one of her students, who had business friends in nearby Denmark, she resolved to find a Danish citizen, an idealist, who could agree to a passport marriage, so that as a Danish citizen herself, she would be able to recover her freedom. Jens Jørgen Grau, the dealer in plants and seeds from a small town near Copenhagen whom she married, was about my age, but I knew nothing about him, nor did I ever meet him. (The marriage was dissolved after the war by a document signed, as Danish etiquette requires, by the ruling king.)

My mother did not wish to enter this marriage without my knowledge, and the problems of severed communication—that began long before the war, as they continued long after it—had become so pressing that my father decided to use his unencumbered passport to travel to Milan, so that we could speak with one another and see one another again before the uncertain months and years that would lie ahead.

My father had remarried not long after my parents' divorce, and a daughter from his second marriage, trained as a weaver, came with her family in later years to America on an affidavit given by myself and my wife. My father's second wife was a dancer, but her profession, like my father's, had begun to disintegrate in the period preceding the war. She took a position, which in time developed into a key administrative assignment, with the Art Museum in Altona, Hamburg's neighboring town, and it was thus from remarkably composite sources that my father brought with him the money to pay for my emigration, together with the salient news of which I had not been aware.

The confirmation of my individual concert engagement had arrived, and it was an unforgettable moment when the young official from the American consulate passed through the waiting room in which I had joined the many who were uneasily anticipating their various verdicts, smiled at me, and said: "Did you receive the contract?" He stamped into my passport the large rectangular entry, a relic I have preserved, that said "SEEN For the journey to the United States."

8

I obtained the hoped-for English visa. It read very specifically "TRANSIT. Mr. Alfred Mann. Embarking at Liverpool on 22nd April 1939 on s/s Britannic," but it is astounding how nebulous this wording was to the mind of one who had only a vague concept of another, far, continent and who now clung to Europe the way he had clung to Germany before. We had arranged that my mother would meet me in London, and my Milan friends and I held out the vain hope that, together with her, we would realize our project of a Baroque Ensemble in England.

In order to travel from Milan to London, one has to cross France, and with my assembled papers I presented myself to the French consul. It was the shortest of all such visits. His outstretched arm and finger pointed dramatically to the door. He had noticed that it was only a token down-payment that held my passage on s/s Britannic to New York. Did I know, he demanded in a thunderous voice, what "Balance to pay" meant?—"Saldo da pagare!" And he added as an emphatic parting message: "Ho parlato italiano!," the Italian equivalent for "I have expressed myself unmistakably!"—which, in spite of the grim moment, struck me as funny, for his Italian was no more free of mistakes than mine.

The only route open now was by air—then still a fairly unusual mode of travel. I had shied away from it, not only because of the higher cost, but because I had never been in an airplane. There was also no service from Milan. The only connection was from Zurich, and by now I was apprehensive about crossing the border to Switzerland. With greatly mixed emotions I got on the train with my few belongings and took leave of Italy. But the journey to Zurich and the departure from there by air were uneventful. It was a beautiful sunny spring day. As we crossed over the bend of the Rhine at Basel there was a moment when, far below, a few huge banners appeared, proudly displaying the symbol of the Third Reich. By the time I had recognized them, we were flying over French territory, and I reflected upon the strange travel route that took me over two countries into which I could not enter—one of them my own and the other its traditional enemy—while I was headed for a third one, for which I had an entrance permit for one day. But surely, this could be extended . . .

Hüttenbach was the name of my friends from Milan, Otto and Trude Hüttenbach. And it is curious how the ring of the name, which suggests the world of German Romanticism, of such artists as Anselm Hüttenbrenner and Anselm Feuerbach, vanishes in foreign surroundings. The Italians had dropped the name's initial letter, which they could not pronounce; and the umlaut, which gave the name its characteristic sound, had disappeared like a last vestige of the past. Otto's sister Beatrice, an actress, had dealt with the matter directly and abandoned the name. As Bea Hutten, she had begun a new career; her fashionable London flat offered a brief first gesture of warm hospitality. Otto's brother Alfred, a sculptor, had moved into a rambling place on the outskirts of London, and in a kind of annex to his studio, my mother, who had arrived a few days earlier, and I found temporary refuge. Still overwhelmed by the moments of reunion, and by the fact that people I had never met had given the transient guests a home, I set about my portentous task of facing British authorities. But the name of the agency to which I had to report, Home Office, lent only elusive reassurance to my mission.

It was due merely to the relative politeness of the British that my visit lasted a few moments longer than that at the French consulate. The official raised his eyebrows: a special musical undertaking? Very interesting. But it had no bearing on immigration matters. He was sorry not to be able to oblige. Before I knew it—such figures of speech have indeed their validity—I was aboard the s/s Britannic and on the Atlantic ocean.

DEPARTURE AND RETURN

1

The old mode of transatlantic travel bestows a kind gift upon the traveler: a week's enforced vacation, a span of time apt to be of great benefit to one reflecting upon the thought of sailing toward a new continent where one is expected by nobody in particular. Through early smaller voyages on the North Sea and the Baltic, I had taken a liking to life aboard ship. I enjoyed small talk on deck and in the dining room, though I quickly found out that my school English would be in need of a basic overhaul. But when a young American asked me, with shining eyes, "Are you a refugee?" I said no. The word still held a totally negative connotation in my vocabulary. While I had not wanted to leave Europe, now that European territory had become confined for me to the space of a medium-sized vessel, I did not want to be sent back upon arrival.

I had a plan. At the Milan Conservatory I had found in the wealth of its library the compositions of the classic violist Alessandro Rolla, the mentor of Paganini, who at the beginning of the nineteenth century had established the Conservatory's string classes; and I had copied many of his unknown manuscript scores. In the course of her work as a music critic, my mother used to send reports to the *Musical Courier*, a New York journal; and I remembered that once the viola professor of the Curtis Institute of Music on Philadelphia's Rittenhouse Square—all rather strange names to me—had corresponded with her about a modern viola work she had reviewed. America appeared to me as the land of the virtuoso, eager for new works. And I decided that I would use the time of travel between the Old and the New Worlds to learn one of the Italian master's viola concertos in order to present myself with it at the Curtis Institute. Thus, for most of the hours of ocean days, I remained locked in my cabin, practicing; and when a fellow passenger inquired about my participation in a program of impromptu entertainment he was organizing, I declined. I had a long concerto to memorize.

Everybody was leaning over the railing the morning we arrived in New York harbor, absorbed in gazing at the Statue of Liberty whose beckoning welcome so eloquently speaks to the new immigrant. But when I inadvertently turned around, it was as if a mighty chord had suddenly been struck, and my awed upward glance took in for the first time the imposing silhouette of Manhattan. A new life had begun.

I had made friends with a young man from my hometown on the boat. He was received by a cousin, a lady who, though born in the States, spoke flawless German. In an unceremonious way that was new to me, she took charge, and as she drove us up the Henry Hudson Parkway (did American traffic move on the left or the right side of the road?), I vaguely began to sense the novel spirit of a country in which everyone is an immigrant. Broadway—my eyes wandered down the endless avenue of so many generations of newly-arrived. She took us to an apartment house of indefinite age and, to my surprise, spoke in German, after a first few words of English, to the elderly manager who took us up in the elevator. She had spotted his accent—he had gotten off the boat not so long ago.

My Hamburg friend and I took a room together and set about our first excursions into unknown territory. By good fortune, I found friends from Milan in the same house, the family of a German businessman with whom I had played string quartet and who had taken violin lessons from me. Also freshly arrived, they had moved into the room above ours, and the man had found temporary work with a construction company. His wife said "Now, we all are without any means to speak of, but you need a point of departure. For the time being, we expect the two of you at noon every day for a very simple lunch in our room."

Some distant relatives of mine lived on 98th Street, and here I was to have a taste of the reverse side of immigrant camaraderie. I called on them and was invited for dinner a week or two later. The meal was accompanied by rather stiff conversation, and after coffee there was a highly amusing moment. The matriarch of the family, a great-aunt of mine, asked me: "Rauchst Du?" ("Do you smoke?"). Freudian psychology led me to hear her words as "Brauchst Du?"—a colloquial way of saying "Do you need any cash?" For a minute, the conversation, somewhat strained, moved on two levels, until I understood. No, thank you, I didn't smoke (not at that time as yet). I departed with a bag of things meant to be useful for two bachelors who had set up improvised housekeeping, among which we discovered a broken, old-fashioned toaster; we resolved to use its two sides for incoming and outgoing mail.

2

Meanwhile I pursued the scheme of finding my way to the Curtis Institute. One met many graduates of the Institute among New York musicians. It turned out that one of them was a friend from childhood days—son of a Russian violinist whose family had lived next to us in the Hamburg apartment house but moved to America before he and I had reached grade school age. A touching reunion, but in all its joy and warmth also strange. Brilliantly gifted, he had followed his father's profession, and upon graduation had been offered a position in the Pittsburgh Symphony by its conductor, Fritz Reiner, then in charge of the Curtis Institute's orchestra. But he had other goals. He had changed his name—Kurt Polnarioff—to Paul Nero, and taken up a career of "the hottest fiddling since Rome burned." Well do I remember his New York debut in which he brought the house down with his jazz arrangements of Paganini's *Caprices*, and with such hits as the "Town Hall Blues" and "Pizzicats."

Kurt volunteered to take me to Philadelphia ("Two to Philly," he said, to my surprise, to the man at the ticket counter.) He told me that the viola professor I had named was much too old-fashioned; he would introduce me to his young successor. Thus I met my future teacher, Max Aronoff—who had also founded his own school, the New School of Music in Philadelphia, which ultimately my two older sons were to attend. That he was a remarkably perceptive pedagogue became immediately apparent from his reaction when I told him my story. "Look, your book will be much more helpful to you than your concerto; let me give it to our new director and have you meet him."

It was one of the most fortunate coincidences in the extended course of my emigration. The composer Randall Thompson, having just been appointed to succeed Josef Hofmann, the celebrated pianist, as director of the Curtis Institute, was dissatisfied with the school's sole orientation to virtuosity. A characteristic impression had caught his eye upon first entering the building of whose function he was to take charge. At the immediate right there were huge double doors behind which was housed one of the finest libraries of books and manuscripts in the country. These doors were closed. A lending library of performance editions for the use of faculty and students was in the basement. The thought had not left him that he wanted these doors opened; but a new staff member would be needed to guard the valuable collection—preferably a staff member close in age to the students, who might be suited to aid them in the use of the unfamiliar literature and guide them in the understanding that it contained treasures that were in the first place gathered for *them*.

I met Randall Thompson in the Harvard Club of New York (he was a graduate of Harvard University, to which he eventually returned as Chairman of Music). My book was in his hand and, as a pleasant conversation developed, he expressed surprise at my as yet rather halting English. I explained that I had learned English in school, but that it had largely disintegrated because for the past two years my language had been Italian. And unexpectedly, he said: "Allora parliamo italiano"—for several years he had held a fellowship at the American Academy in Rome.

By way of comment on the more fluent exchange that followed, it must be said that, in principle, there was no difficulty about a penniless immigrant taking up studies at the Institute—all its admissions were on scholarship basis only—but that my thoughts were prompted by a different idea. My entry into the United States was based on a visa for a concert performance that did not take place. I did not have a student's visa, and my presence in the country would soon be illegal. It struck me as indicative of an American liberal attitude that there were lawyers quite openly recognized for their specialty of "legalizing illegal immigration status," but it seemed preferable to avoid that status to begin with. Among the very few categories to which non-quota immigration could be granted was that of "instructors at higher institutions of learning in foreign countries upon the offer of a contract by a comparable institution in the United States." While I had not been able to take up my assigned tasks, I had both a contract from the *Scuola Musicale di Milano* and one from the Berlin Academy for School and Church Music. It had been issued, for the establishment of recorder classes for teachers, in ignorance of my non-aryan descent which, however, was disclosed when it came to the moment of counter-signing. There negotiations ceased, though I had the contract in my possession.

It took Randall Thompson naturally by some surprise when I unravelled this state of affairs and explained that, for obvious reasons, my primary interest was not so much in admission as a student but in an appointment to the faculty. I had brought a non-commercial recording, then still a complete novelty, of my recorder performance at a Milan studio, which I left with him. In answer to my involved tale, he said he would "have to think for a moment." From that moment grew a friendship for life.

3

My translation of Fux's *Gradus ad Parnassum* had struck a responsive chord with Randall Thompson, because from his own early studies had developed the wish that a modern translation might be made of the counterpoint treatise by Padre Giambattista Martini, the teacher of Bach's youngest son and Mozart. The thought had now come to him that such a translation would be a suitable task for the librarian he wanted to appoint (an excerpt appeared as part of my *Study of Fugue* published some years later). In the end I received both the appointment and a scholarship in viola and composition.

And now a veritable paradise opened. All that I had been denied in Germany became reality, and I found myself in the company of gifted young artists and the most celebrated teachers. Elisabeth Schumann was there, the great soprano; Emmanuel Feuermann, the cellist (later succeeded by Gregor Piatigorsky); and Rudolf Serkin, who became a dear friend. Mine was a dual appointment. I entered upon my duties in the library, and I was entrusted with a course of recorder instruction for the flute class of William Kincaid, famed member of the Philadelphia Orchestra, but himself intrigued with the Baroque predecessor of the modern instrument. It also caught the interest of Eugene Ormandy, then recently appointed as conductor of the Philadelphia Orchestra, who engaged my recorder ensemble for one of the Orchestra's youth concerts. With one of my new students and the Institute's chamber orchestra, I recorded Bach's Brandenburg Concerto No. 4 as the first American issue in the original orchestration.

Baroque music and performance practice saw at that time their first flourishing on the American scene. One day, there appeared a group dressed in Austrian costume at the Institute. They were members of the von Trapp family, then the only Baroque ensemble that had widely toured in the country. They had completed several highly successful concert seasons and had decided on a "sabbatical" with concentrated further studies in singing and recorder playing, on which they sought advice. The family had been given a temporary home in one of the suburbs of Philadelphia by Henry S. Drinker, distinguished lawyer, philanthropist and Bach enthusiast. There I found one of the most congenial teaching assignments I have ever had—and how deeply did the young German refugee appreciate the weekly invitation to stay, when the afternoon's work was completed, for supper in the German-speaking tableround. But there, we also experienced the shock that our country had unleashed a new World War.

Yet two more precious years of freedom in a country still at peace were to follow. My mother had come to the United States shortly after my arrival and had taken, together with an immigrant cousin of ours, a small apartment in New York, where I could visit on weekends. Now close to sixty, she had bravely faced a new career. The original concert tour—with half of the ensemble delayed in England—had never come to fruition. But she did find in New York a concert agent who arranged tours for her, often with myself, friends from Curtis, and Suzanne Bloch, the daughter of the composer and the country's first widely known lutenist. At the Institute, I had taken on the translation of Padre Martini's treatise as well as an English translation from Fux's work, and for both of them I had the greatly valued help of John Edmunds, a young composer at the Institute, who guided me in mastering literary English. The latter translation introduced me to my future publisher, W. W. Norton, and their musical adviser, Paul Henry Lang, later my teacher at Columbia University, and my mentor in all subsequent publishing projects. My arrival in the country had indeed brought a rich harvest.

4

Randall Thompson's tenure at the Curtis Institute of Music was to be unfortunately brief. The school, committed to conservative ideals, could not adjust to a change from a purely professional to a humanistic orientation. After three years, Director and Institute parted ways; Randall Thompson assumed the chairmanship of music at the venerable University of Virginia, founded by Thomas Jefferson, and his career led him from there to Princeton University and Harvard University.

Before leaving, he had introduced me to those Philadelphia circles that represent the city's most admirable legacy, the Quakers, or Society of Friends. At the northern edge of Philadelphia, yet still within the city limits, are the old communities of Germantown and Chestnut Hill where some of the country's finest secondary schools are situated, the Germantown Friends School, Germantown Academy, and Chestnut Hill Academy. The Germantown Friends School was involved in a new educational program. By tradition, the Quakers had been averse to music in their service of worship and in their schools. But in time, music had assumed an important part in Quaker society. A group of Germantown Friends School parents had gathered for the purpose of establishing a program that would make music "as important a major subject as English and History," as was stated in the publication mentioned below. While the school had a reputable choir and a small orchestra, they wished to establish a chamber music curriculum to strengthen the department, and they had turned to Randall Thompson for advice. A writer, at that time the leader of the group, published in the *Atlantic Monthly* an article entitled "Our School's New Music Teacher."

The new music teacher was the young Curtis instructor Randall Thompson had recommended. I graduated from the Institute, and as my functions on the faculty and staff ended with Randall Thompson's departure, I took up the work in school music that had been the dream of my German student days. Over the years, both the Curtis Institute and the Germantown Friends School retained a role of alma mater for me and my family. My wife taught at the Germantown Friends School for a period during which our two older sons attended the school, and I returned to the Institute, when Rudolf Serkin had become its director, to audition and select soloists for the Festivals of the Bach Choir of Bethlehem.

Choral conducting had soon become a part of my Germantown Friends School duties; I met with congenial and generous colleagues. I played string quartets with the students, instructed them in recorder ensembles, and guided the orchestra members in the task—new to them—of providing a sensitive accompaniment to the choir.

Yet the wonderful days at Germantown Friends were clouded by the grim news of a world at war, and it rendered all the more scary the fact that the time for a last extension of my temporary visa threatened to run out. I now became acquainted with another aspect of Quaker society, the American Friends Service Committee whose beneficial and knowledgeable protection saved the fate of many a refugee throughout two World Wars. By United States immigration laws it is decreed that a temporary visa cannot be converted to a permanent one within the borders of the country, but that the immigrant must leave again in order to apply for a proper immigration visa at a consular office in a foreign country. It was a formidable prospect both my mother and I had to confront. The Friends Service Committee worked in cooperation with other agencies and with consular officers, and in the end, my mother was advised to go to Canada, where quota numbers for Danish citizens had become available, and I was advised to go to Cuba.

5

It was to the Cuba of the days before Castro's reign that my journey took me (and I regret to this day that at the time I had not yet learned the art of smoking cigars). Once again I packed my belongings, my instruments, and the music and books that would aid me in a new start should I fail to obtain re-entry into the United States. Once again I concerned myself with the rudiments of a new language (which offered a welcome affinity to Italian). It was still travel by boat, and thus an unexpected spell of luxury.

During the three days on the Atlantic I found the company of several young Germans and of the family of an elderly German professor. As can be imagined, our purpose of travel was the same, and together we moved into a modest boarding house upon arrival.

I realized that by now I was an experienced traveler, ready to savor the novelty of unfamiliar surroundings as well as their occasional hardships. One of my new young companions sounded an alarm in the middle of the first night: something was crawling in his bed. But I tried to calm him down, as we ousted the unwelcome guest, with the reminiscence of my Milanese landlady's classical remark in a similar situation, "Allora prendo la medicina" ("I'll go get the 'medicine' ").

Still vivid in memory is the figure of our little Cuban waiter at meals. He always had a large, not-quite-white serviette slung over his arm, and as he politely seated us, he wiped off with it our chair and our plate, in that order. The professor's wife tried discreetly to rush with her plate to a nearby sink before the serving; but the timing didn't always work, and I suggested that it might be best to relax. Gradually we all did. Havanna is a beautiful city, and promenading its avenues in the evenings, sampling the refreshing varieties of *jugo de piña* (pineapple juice) was a genuine tourist's pleasure. I even heard a concert of Havanna's Symphony Orchestra and met an old acquaintance—the concertmaster had given his debut in Milan.

Yet we were not tourists, and each of us uneasily anticipated the appointment at the American Consulate. Our cases were all different, as we had found out in conversation, despite their basic similarity. I no longer had a contract with an institution of higher learning, and I lacked a basic requirement —an affidavit of support from a relative in the United States. The American Friends Service Committee had been aware of this, and Natalie Kimber, the unforgettable old Quaker lady who had prepared my documents, had decided to give me the affidavit herself. I must digress here for a moment, to a point ahead in my narration, in recording her equally unforgettable answer to a representative of the federal agency who questioned her about my reliability upon my application to join the American Counter-Intelligence Service: "He has the key to my house"—it had been her touching farewell gesture, when I set out on a next portentous voyage.

Our little colony of visa petitioners had reported to the American Consulate en masse and been given separate appointments. My thoughts went back to Lugano, and I was very conscious of the fact that my fate depended upon the individual review and interpretation of a very complex set of papers by a person totally unknown to me. But my fears were unfounded. It proved to be a very sympathetic interview, and it almost amused me that the consular officer very patiently asked to be enlightened on the intricacies of the National Socialist interpretation of non-aryan status and its various degrees (it was to be my last conversation on the subject). He gave a delightful answer to my explanations: "You mean, it's like the British boy who said: ‹My father is English, but my mother and I are Irish.›)"

6

I returned with an immigration visa that entitled me, in a keenly realized moment, to take out the so-called first papers—the "declaration of intention to become a United States citizen." It normally takes five years until the issue of "second papers"—the confirmation of citizenship. During this time, the immigrant retains the old passport and original nationality. Thus, before the first of the five years had passed, at the thunder clap of Pearl Harbor, I became an "enemy alien," having to give regular account to authorities of my whereabouts—a status that my mother, safely returned from Canada, was spared. But my first papers averted the danger of internment, and I soon realized that my existence could continue in normal course and without further restrictions.

I had even acquired a second-hand car, a small Model A Ford—for $25 (it was sold, with much regret, after ten years, for parts and at the price of $35). It had character; its reverse gear was more powerful than any of the others, and its former owner was said to have turned it around in charging up the steep hill at 125th Street and Riverside Drive (which did not change the appearance of its travel, because it looked the same from front and back).

Despite its indomitable spirit, the car had a weak battery that required constant recharging. I had gotten into the habit of parking it by the wayside on pleasant summer afternoons when I returned from teaching in the suburbs, locking it up while the engine was going strong in neutral, and taking a brief walk as the battery was gathering new strength. When I returned on one of those occasions, a state trooper was standing next to the car; and I thought, "This is the end." An uneasy explanation followed when I was asked to produce my papers: I was an enemy alien—in fact, one who had but recently gotten over the Prussian notion that you stand at attention when facing an officer of the law. A remnant of this attitude must have stirred the policeman to leniency—or was it the looks of my car? After a rather lengthy exchange, and much shaking of his head, came the verdict: "Well, Alfred, good luck."

Yet the role of the enemy alien who aspired to United States citizenship was in time to be more sharply defined and his five years of candidacy drastically reduced. History curiously repeated itself. Having taken out first papers, I was liable to the draft. The strange reversal came almost as a relief, for the new life I had been granted in the New World had unfolded against the awesome background of a war that was ever close—agonizingly so day by day. As its tides had begun to turn, the bombs had destroyed London—the London where the friends who had helped me to escape were caught; the bombs had destroyed Hamburg in one of the worst raids of the war; Milan was in German hands. The act of conscription, now so differently presented in the traditional Greetings of the President, seemed so infinitely right, the new upheaval and uncertainty so deeply justified that the only reaction to it could be the wish to serve.

The transition it brought about was aided by much kind help. I was assured of a government allowance for the support of my mother, of my room in Philadelphia, my position at the school—whatever the span of time until I might safely return—even of a garage where my car and its battery could rest. Yet however gratifying its circumstances and deeply felt its motivation, it was not an altogether easy new departure. About ten years later, when a family conversation happened to touch upon my bewildering turns of fortune, our six-year-old asked, "Daddy, was you with the good guys?"—"Yes, and I barely made it."

7

The division to which I was eventually assigned reached Normandy a few months after the Allied invasion. We were well supplied, carrying ample baggage. "Most of this," said an old sergeant, "we'll leave at our basic camp." The basic camp turned out to be a well-soaked meadow, and it continued to rain for most of the thirty days that we camped on it. At some distance rose a small church steeple and the roofs of a few houses, and one day, when the rain briefly stopped, two of my comrades set out on an unauthorized exploratory expedition. "Lemme know if they got a drugstore," said a third one.

But I rejoiced at being in Europe again—surrounded by country that seemed dearly familiar, though I had never been there. My army experience had varied a good deal. Still expecting some of the rigid and senseless regimentation of the Old World military, I was pleasantly surprised at the more liberal treatment and the lavish care the American soldier received; yet much of the basic training—extended during my term of duty from four to seventeen weeks—was necessarily grim. It had taken place under the hot sun of Georgia, and before it ended, I was sworn in as an American citizen (who still points with pride to his Southern legacy).

From the outset I had hoped that I might be assigned to interpreter's duty, and I succeeded in getting into the specialized training program—but only into a unit waiting to be assigned; the wait was long and the program was discontinued before any assignment had occurred. I learned that military personnel decisions work with highly varying speeds; from one day to the next, I was an infantry man in a tank division headed for combat. I succeeded in presenting to my commanding officer the question whether any chance for interpreting duties remained, but since the destination of the division was unknown—and would be secret anyway—it was a moot point.

I now did something that so far had been excluded from my thoughts. While the division was still in camp, I probed the possibility of being transferred to the division band. And once more—now where I had least expected it—I found a sympathetic fellow-musician. Richard Zoller, the young band leader with whom my correspondence has continued to this day, took an interest in what there was I had to tell, and his band had not reached its full quota of members. It was a very new experience to be a violinist in a jazz ensemble and to supplant my recorder with flute and piccolo, but after much hard practice the latter experienced, on a rare sunny afternoon, its European debut in the little market square by the church steeple at the edge of the rain-drenched field.

Suddenly, the division was on the move. It had become part of the army of General Patton (of whose dynamic double-pistoled appearance

I got a close-up, because the band had to be there when he first talked to the troops). Patton's goals were to tear through France and drive a wedge into German territory. He succeeded in the first of these but came to a halt at the Rhine as winter—the winter of 1944-45—set in. It was the Battle of the Bulge, the Führer's "Christmas present to his people," that broke the winter stalemate and rushed our division from Lorrain to Luxembourg and its German border.

Although I tried to dismiss it as foolish emotion, it seemed as if the landscape had begun to speak to me, to the one who now after seven, the legendary number of years, had made such a strange return. Yet reflection was given little time. From one day to the next, German interrogators were needed in the front lines. What I had wanted took on stark reality, and I had to say good-bye to my friends from the band. The experienced old-timers had been good to the novice, and—although the band's duties, ever since our arrival overseas, had strayed far from musical concerns—I had learned a great deal from them. I was to see some of them again when, toward the end of the campaign, everything had veritably turned into front lines and action.

8

It was not to the interrogation of prisoners-of-war that I was assigned—the combat units had had to find ways to deal with this matter from the beginning of the invasion—but to the more involved exchange with the civilian population and its potentially dangerous elements. This was to be carried out by detachments of the Counter-Intelligence Corps, and my rank changed from "private" to the more interesting but somewhat ominous "special agent," while my own credentials for the assignment were investigated by a government agency in the States. We were given officers' insignia, though without rank, and the title "Mr.," so that in a sudden problematic civilian situation we would be able to advise and direct any superior officer. In reality this rather scary prerogative led to a fairly innocuous, and more often than not pathetic, routine. Face to face with a first group of civilians that was lined up in a house for interrogation, I found myself talking to bewildered farm people whose land was now as devastated as that of their enemies. Absorbed in my task, I was all but unaware of a captain's hasty entrance and warning, "You had better put on your helmet. The Germans are shelling the town." Subsequently, I received a citation for the incident, but my wife's interpretation, given to the story years later ("The bravery was because you didn't know what was going on") was not far off the mark.

I now worked with new companions, several of whom were recent immigrants like myself. One of them, very young and easy-going, had such a thick German accent that he was repeatedly taken prisoner by the American troops who suspected him to be a German spy, and we had to work hard to free him day by day. I had given thought to what I would do if I should fall into the hands of German troops and decided that I would stick to English and pretend not to understand anything else—my scheme was fortunately never put to the test.

The following weeks brought more dramatic encounters, such as the arrest of the fugitive Hungarian prime minister, one of the principal German "collaborators." But my most dramatic encounter, dramatic in quite a different sense, occurred at the end of the war. Having passed through Oberammergau, home of the traditional Passion plays, by night, my unit stopped at the small Bavarian resort town of Garmisch. We were told we would move on again in ten minutes. But the ten minutes grew into a year—hostilities had ceased.

The town was spared destruction; its officials had fled into the mountains, their sorry group was brought back under arrest with the help of local police, and a provisional order restored. Within the first few days of the American occupation, however, I was to meet Garmisch's most eminent resident, the composer Richard Strauss. In the most unexpected manner, my official duties merged for once with the most intense personal and professional interest. When the tall, imposing figure of the eighty-year-old appeared in the door frame, it seemed to me as if a chapter from music history were opening before my eyes. Yet my exchange with this last of the great classic-romantic masters, which extended through the course of several months and of which I have given accounts elsewhere, differed strikingly from one related by a distinguished namesake. Two weeks later, Klaus Mann, the eldest son of Thomas Mann, interviewed Strauss for the American Army newspaper. His report, preserved in the form of a letter to his famous father, portrays merely the naive egocentric oblivious to the events into which his long life had carried him. There is justification in both approaches, though the conflict of opinions served me as a timely warning of the weighty challenges of judgement that lay ahead at the point of victory.

It was with unaccustomed freedom that we carried out the many assignments inherent in assisting the establishment of a military government. To my pleasant surprise, with travel by rail and boat precariously restored, furloughs were granted after a few months to either France or England. I seized a suddenly available opportunity of a trip to London for a long-anticipated reunion with my Milanese friends who, in their enforced wait, had survived the ordeals of the past years. But shortly thereafter, an adventurous jeep ride which, as a special agent, I was able to authorize myself, carried me and a friend from my detachment through British-occupied territory to my home town.

Forever unforgettable will be this arrival in a changed Hamburg, tracing familiar roads that defied recognition, for what they lined was all but leveled to the ground. In the bizarre site of the city's center, the Art Gallery was one of the few undamaged buildings, and there I tried to find information in my bewildered search. What I finally did receive was a totally unfamiliar address in a distant part of town.

What remains to be told seems as if taken from the pages of a novel. Yet no novel can vie with reality, and both the horrors and miracles of our century may not differ so much from those of others. We had been given some hospitality and badly needed fuel at an Allied headquarters and braced ourselves for the final part of our journey. It led to a street whose houses were for the most part destroyed, but with eerie fastidiousness, house numbers were marked on the ruins. In the last block only one house seemed unharmed; it proved to be the one for which we were looking. On close approach, we saw that one side of it was gone, too, but we found a door to what was left standing. I entered and embraced my father.

RECONCILIATION

1

In Hamburg I was able to search, in rushed moments, for traces of friends from student days. The fates of war had led them to French-occupied territory where I found them, not far from where my unit was stationed, in some unharmed farm buildings that had become their strangely idyllic shelter. One of them stands out in especially fond memories, an abandoned cottage—its stone walls seemingly built for eternity—which its grateful temporary inhabitants christened their *palazzo vecchio*, though its variously patched-up roof tended to provide glimpses of the stars.

The return to Europe, I keenly felt, remained incomplete without a return to Italy. On a three-day pass, a lonesome drive across the Alps took me back to Milan whose streets I recognized more easily than those of my home town. It was again an adventuresome journey, on which I passed the stations whose gradual change from German to Italian names recalled the account in Goethe's Italian journey. And I reflected upon the greater adventures that the classical landscape had so serenely endured over the centuries.

It would have been futile to look for the familiar surroundings, whatever their condition. They had become illegal residences for the erstwhile immigrants long before the German armies swept through the city. I remembered, however, one name—one figure in Milanese intellectual life who might have been lifted above the turmoil of the past years. Lavinia Mazzuchetti, the distinguished writer and translator of Thomas Mann's works, would—if she had survived Fascism and the bombs—have retained her residence. In the moments of desperate dissolution she had offered to store my aunt's belongings, and she might have word.

The house was still standing, and I presented my inquiries to the *portinaia*—that marvelous source of ever-present security, assistance and gossip, whose guardianship rules autocratically over the entrance to many an old-fashioned apartment building in major European cities. "La professoressa Mazzuchetti?" No, she was not home. "La dottoressa Weiss?" Yes, staying here. "Here?!" "Si, di qui."

In a dark hour, as SS columns were already streaming into the streets of Milan—I learned at this miraculous reunion—my aunt had yielded to the advice of friends and put herself in the hands of "un bravo contrabandiere"—"a reliable smuggler." Then in her sixties, and throughout her life having suffered from acrophobia, she had crossed under his guidance, taking with her only a shopping bag, the mountain passes that led by a secret way to the Swiss border. She was welcomed by immediate internment—Swiss traditional neutrality does not extend to the impoverished fugitive. When the war ended, Italian authorities rolled out the red carpet and gave her Italian citizenship.

Yet the days of intense fear, relief, danger, and indescribable elation were nearing their end. The return was awaiting another return, for I had become at home abroad, and the words "at home" and "abroad" were beginning to merge in widened meaning. There were to be many returns, east and west, in the half century to follow, and what has become more and more clearly perceptible over the years, and in their great moments, is the blessing of reconciliation.

2

On the voyage back in the troop ship I had leisure to speak with a fellow soldier, who was a fine musician, about American academic life of which I knew still very little. Professor Paul Henry Lang had introduced me to the staff at the publishing firm of W. W. Norton as "Dr. Mann," and when I explained that I had as yet not arrived at that station in my career, had remarked: "Well, that can be mended." These words had remained in my mind, and I decided that, once back in the United States, I would enroll at Columbia University where Lang was teaching. I had received professional training in three countries, but the time had come to take up the university studies to which I had aspired as an eighteen-year-old, and the so-called G.I. Bill of Rights offered the needed financial support, as it was to offer my oldest son again when he reached draft age and served in the United States Marine Band's "White House Strings."

I returned to my school in Germantown and was warmly received. In the years since, though, its admirable headmaster had retired and turned over his duties to a successor whose considerable reputation rested on being an "educator"—a concept whose potentially problematic nature I was to encounter again in later years. As such, he had formulated ideas about music education which were as definite as his knowledge of the field was scant. This did not affect the school's choral program as much as it did the instrumental ensemble instruction—my particular assignment—and it was eventually agreed with my colleagues that I would train as my successor a gifted graduate of the school. In the following spring I took on the new task of establishing a music department at a college newly incorporated as part of Rutgers University, on whose faculty I served for the next three decades. But my affection for Germantown Friends has never faded, and much appreciated visits have taken me back to the school in my role as a parent.

During the summer between my changing appointments I crossed the continent for the first time. I had been invited to teach a course in counterpoint at a newly founded conservatory, later to become part of Whitworth College, in Spokane, Washington.

My Milan friends had been able to leave England and come to the United States on an affidavit from their next-of-kin, Hans Moldenhauer, the director of the school and a remarkable figure in post-war American life. We had met during my early days in the country, and I had witnessed a rare case of absorbed pioneer spirit. Moldenhauer, a curious mixture of Romantic dreamer and astute businessman, had immediately found a position in New York City, but he was not content with the thought of building a modest existence in the East. A passionate mountaineer, he longed for the West, and there he wanted to devote himself wholly to his avocation, music, in which he had considerable skill. From a private piano studio in Spokane, he developed within a short time a professional music school. He quickly expanded its staff and built the Spokane Conservatory into a flourishing institution. But in middle years his activity was halted by an affliction that eventually led to blindness, and with astounding ingenuity he turned to another interest as a collector of music autographs. The Moldenhauer Archives, at the time of his death the most formidable manuscript collection of its kind in the country, are, according to his carefully laid out plan, now distributed over a number of major music libraries in the Western world, and the Library of Congress has in recent days involved my help in the publication of a catalogue.

3

One of the students in my summer course was Carolyn Owens, daughter of a retired Air Force general in whose home I became a kindly welcomed guest. Though the general, a wonderful man, had his reservations about a "flute player," she and I were married a year later, and as I write these lines, our lives have moved close to the time of our golden wedding anniversary. She has borne me three beautiful sons, all of whom turned to the profession of music. With her gift in writing, she became the author of many plays and director of a youth theater, and for many years she edited every page of my own writing.

I found myself in the somewhat baffling situation of starting an academic career at the same time I started graduate studies—a situation that has become less imaginable today, though it was then not too unusual. I learned of what great value it is for the teacher not to cease being student; but I encountered another aspect of early academic life that ever since has struck me as perplexing. It is summarized in the dictum "Publish or Perish." The lot of the harrassed young scholar is a well-known modern phenomenon, and publication prepared under threat and pressure has become an all-too-realistic predicament. But I have never made peace with the distortion of values implied—and over the years I have witnessed many moments of wonder and excitement at the discovery of something that a graduate student wanted to—not had to—publish.

While patience was naturally imposed on my labors to acquire a literary skill in the English language, I was impatient about the needs I saw for the issue of music publications. What interested me were two lacunae in the available literature: reliable editions of little-known classical works suitable for modest means of performance, and editions of works from the great heritage of choral music written originally on English texts. Thus I seized an opportunity to turn the situation around: the young instructor tried to convince his University that it must concern itself with new projects of publication. I had been introduced to the University's Research Council which regularly funded faculty projects but so far had not allotted any funds for the publication of music.

With its help, I established a University series of music editions, and along with choral works by Gibbons and Purcell and with instrumental works by Salomone Rossi, Johann Christian Bach, and my favorite Alessandro Rolla, I presented some unpublished instrumental and vocal works by Handel. The uncovering of the latter emanated from a bold plan, conceived early in the venture, to issue a performance edition of Handel's personal conducting score of *Messiah*.

I had formed a small choir at the college, and before long we faced the well-familiar challenge of any such organization, the challenge of entering into the incomparable masterpiece of English choral music. It puzzled me that there was no full score of the work published for the American market, and I became intrigued with the fact that the stated goals for the publication of instrumental and choral music in my series so obviously converged in a conducting score that would reflect Handel's own.

Messiah performances were at that time customarily conducted from a piano-vocal reduction, not from an orchestral score. Respectable organists had published organ accompaniments, and the conductor of the average choral group was intimidated by the budgetary and professional demands of the orchestral score. Professional conductors and symphony orchestras, on the other hand, availed themselves of the nineteenth-century editions in which the orchestra was grossly enlarged.

What was overlooked was that the orchestral accompaniment for *Messiah* forms an exception in Handel's work. Designed for the Dublin orchestra, with which the composer was not familiar, it is unusually modest. Choral and orchestral practice in school and civic organizations, as yet not reconciled but going their separate ways, had not been aware of the score's unique texture.

About ten years after I had entered upon my University duties, a Guggenheim Fellowship enabled me to go to England to explore the sources. In the process I realized that sketches for *Messiah* were innately connected with manuscripts intended for Handel's use in the instruction of composition. A wealth of unpublished autographs was opened to me, and unexpectedly I was led back to my studies in contrapuntal pedagogy.

4

It has been the good fortune of my career that in all its phases it combined scholarship with performance, theory with practice. When Otto Klemperer, in the late 1940s, scheduled a performance of Bach's Brandenburg Concertos at New York's New School of Social Research, he decided (as the first of the eminent symphony conductors on the American scene to take on this issue) to use harpsichord and recorders in his orchestra. The novelty this still represented is well illustrated by a playful inquiry from a distinguished member of the audience. Arthur

Mendel, conductor of New York's Cantata Singers and in later years America's leading Bach scholar, expressed his surprise at the fact that the recorders in the fourth Brandenburg Concerto (which a Curtis student and friend, Anton Winkler, and I had played) were in tune: did this have anything to do with the ivory mouthpieces on our instruments?

From this exchange and its charming conjecture developed a friendship of many years. Recorders were now regularly used in the Cantata Singers' performances. But in time, Mendel consulted with me on a problem of greater concern. He had been unable to find a double bass player sufficiently interested in the intricacies of small-scaled continuo accompaniment. For his Schütz recordings (the earliest in the country) I became his contrabassist, and in 1952, when he was called to take the chairmanship of music at Princeton University, his associate conductor and eventual successor.

This latter prestigious assignment I owed both to the relative paucity of promising candidates and to a somewhat ambitious three-day Bach Festival for which, at the occasion of the Bach anniversary of 1950, my young Rutgers department had persuaded the University to allot the necessary funds.

The cultivation of Bach's work had traditionally been limited to isolated organizations in smaller towns of the country. The large cities, with their symphony orchestras and recitals promoted by the concert industry, favored a repertoire of works from the nineteenth, and increasingly also the twentieth, centuries. Thus New York's Cantata Singers, a chamber chorus devoted to conscientious principles of Baroque performance and founded in 1934 by the Swiss conductor Paul Boepple, represented an exception greatly welcomed by a faithful audience of *conoscenti*. When Boepple was invited after three years to take over the direction of the more prominent Dessoff Choirs, established in 1924 by the Viennese conductor Margarethe Dessoff, Mendel, who had been his assistant, succeeded him, and the Cantata Singers became during the next two decades a "laboratory" for the rising modern Bach scholarship in America. It was in consultation with him that I suggested the organization might also become a testing ground for American Handel scholarship.

5

The 1950 Bach Festival at Rutgers University was the occasion of some of my mother's last concert appearances. A recording from the period was completed at her apartment, and she died a year later after a long illness. She had lived to know her oldest grandson who, then less than two years old, never lost the impression of her personality; and the shock of the passing of generations prompted my wish to take the members of my young family to Europe. At a renewed visit to Hamburg they met—for the only time—my father.

The new journey to the old continent stirred fresh incentives. There was a memorable visit and discussion of Bach performance with the aged Albert Schweitzer, whom I had known through my mother's work. I met again with my German publisher and friends from school days, but I became aware that totally new challenges lay ahead—questions for which the answers might rest in libraries and archives which now we could merely pass along the road. A half dozen years later I was able to return for the first study trip, to be followed by many.

In the intervening years a foremost task was to provide the New York audience with choral programs that had new ideas to offer. I was fascinated with the problem that American choral organizations wrestled with the compromise of singing Bach's works in translation (the Cantata Singers' presentations in the original language were still a rarity), whereas Handel's works on English texts remained, with the exception of *Messiah*, unknown. But before reorienting the programs of my choir, I wanted to concern myself with its traditional task of presenting some of the (as yet "unknown") works of Bach. We performed the motets, then still largely viewed from the perspective of nineteenth-century Caecilianism, using instruments with the voices (while seemingly a fresh departure, dealt with as early as in Schweitzer's Bach biography), and, with a program of Magnificat settings ranging from Monteverdi to Bach, approached the issue of placing Bach's work in a historical context. Yet soon we turned to the Anglican texts in the works of Handel, and with my group at the University and support from the University Research Council, I eventually recorded the earliest set of Handel's English Psalms.

It was curious. Much of this still needed to be done from handwritten performance material, and when the recording was completed, no American publisher dared to take on the risk of issuing such obscure works. An enterprising German recording firm finally placed them on the market, and only then an American representative took over the distribution in the New World. I learned a lesson from this, and much of my subsequent publishing was done on the other side of the ocean, to return, often in two languages, to this side in its finished form.

6

Someone informed me in those years that I had become a well-known Handel scholar—a matter of which neither I nor the world of Handel scholarship was aware. Yet reputations, whatever their nature and degree of deservedness, travelled fast in an age where advance publicity had assumed a fashionable role. True, I had given many "first" Handel performances, but the charge of Handel scholarship was yet to be approached.

My dissertation had led me in another direction. In my German and English translations of the famed *Gradus ad Parnassum*, I had dealt only with the author's treatment of counterpoint, and for the use of my own students I had meanwhile added a translation of subsequent chapters concerned with the discussion of fugue. This, in turn, invited an investigation of the entire history of fugal theory, which was to become the subject of my thesis. It was published as *The Study of Fugue* by Rutgers University Press and, like *The Study of Counterpoint*, also in England. A few years later it returned to the imprint of my faithful publisher, W. W. Norton, in paperback, and it has since been re-issued under further imprints. But while the book embarked on its own life, its subject did not rest. My hope was to turn to its ramifications in the didactic work of Haydn, Mozart and Beethoven, and archival studies, not yet clearly envisioned and formulated, were needed.

In 1961, the International Musicological Society held its Eighth Congress in New York—and those who attended have preserved a vivid memory of the extraordinary September heat wave that found neither guests nor hosts prepared. Extraordinary, in every respect, was the entire event. Wilting in their unaccustomed shirt-sleeve sessions, eminent scholars from all over the world formed a gathering that introduced me to the quilted pattern of international musicology, and much that emanated from those ninety-some degree days guided me for the next thirty years.

One of my own teachers at Columbia, Erich Hertzmann, expert in the research concerned with Mozart and Beethoven manuscripts, presented at the meeting a report about the influence of contrapuntal studies upon Mozart's style. He was then preparing an edition of Thomas Attwood's studies with Mozart, the most comprehensive document of classical pedagogy in composition. It was to appear in the *Neue Mozart-Ausgabe*, the new publication of Mozart's complete works begun only five years earlier, and the president of the firm Bärenreiter, its publisher, was present. Hertzmann did not live to complete his edition, and the task fell later to me in collaboration with two colleagues.

Chairman of the session was the Danish scholar Jens Peter Larsen, then the leading figure in Haydn and Handel research. He took an interest in my plans for a *Messiah* edition, and he urged me to attend the yearly Handel Festivals in Halle, Handel's birthplace, as well as in Göttingen, where the twentieth-century revival of Handel's dramatic works had originated. I followed his advice and, meeting regularly from then on in this country and abroad, we became the closest friends.

I was equally drawn to Larsen's personality, kind but totally uncompromising, and his impeccable scholarship. A key word in his work has been *Überlieferung*—the manner in which the great works were handed down—and his studies gave me invaluable new insight in dealing with my own chosen tasks.

7

Halle was at that time a city behind the Iron Curtain, and not without apprehension did I embark upon journeys to a Germany once again under totalitarian rule. My wife feared, as she said, the absentminded faux pas that would land me in Siberia and the salt mines for good; but we gained gratifying reassurance in the new ventures since, almost invariably, I travelled with a fellow Handelian from Princeton, Merrill Knapp, whose authoritative appearance and unquestionably American German worked wonders on the intimidating, arrogant border guards.

A remarkable role awaited the Americans, soon members of the Board of Directors of the *Georg-Friedrich-Händel-Gesellschaft* and its editorial board for the *Hallische Händel-Ausgabe*, in what were international meetings in an isolated state that reflected a strange mixture of Totalitarian and Wilhelminian eras. (Official life abounded with titles and decorations, and the more prominent among the ranks of their vocal soloists were still given the title "Kammersänger," though emphatically there were no longer any princely chambers to which to be appointed.) More than once the delegates from overseas found themselves faced with the charge of mediation in quarrels of a small family of experts all devoted to the same cause. With equal justification, the British and the Germans claimed Handel as their own, West Germans clashed with East Germans, and there were tense moments when the speeches got a little too political.

The fact remains that the musical events of the Cold War years were the only ones that had a truly international language to offer, and they did bring about the very first formal rapproachment of East and West.

My repeated European voyages brought to fruition major working plans, at first often vaguely conceived, that had continued to generate one another. A more clearly defined picture arose not only of Handel the composer and the conductor, but also of Handel the teacher. I was able to explore the traditionally controversial student-teacher relationship of Beethoven and Haydn. And through the startling discovery of a large number of unknown Schubert autographs by the brilliant scholar Christa Landon I obtained clarity about the story of Schubert's lifelong pursuit of the questions of theory.

One basic critical phase was as yet neglected in my studies: a focused inquiry into the performance and research of Bach's work. This realization emerged at an instant when, past my fiftieth year, I was entrusted with the direction of the Bach Choir of Bethlehem. This venerable institution, the "American Bayreuth," had originated in the latter part of the nineteenth century and, in following the tradition of the large nineteenth-century amateur choir, stood as the very antithesis of New York's Cantata Singers. Yet America had owed to it many of its premieres of major Bach works. Rooted in classical Moravian music practice, it had a solid ancestry, honored and perpetuated as a civic heritage; and its board of directors had taken a particular interest in my Cantata Singers programs that placed Bach's music variously in historical perspective. Nevertheless, by its statutes the organization was committed to the exclusive performance of Bach's works, a stipulation of great benefit to the design of their programs and a welcome challenge of concentration imposed upon the one responsible for this design.

With post-war Germany divided into unequal halves, the *Neue Bachgesellschaft*, founded as an international association in Leipzig, Bach's town, at the beginning of the century, saw itself obliged to safeguard its legitimacy by establishing separate chapters in East and West. This scheme, in turn, rendered representation in chapters outside the two German countries desirable, and in succeeding years it became a most valuable enrichment of my tenure as Bach Choir conductor that I could offer the international Society the Bethlehem office (housed in one of the city's historical buildings) as headquarters for an American chapter. The chapter has since grown into an American Bach Society, but its ties with international Bach scholarship remain.

8

As Chapter Secretary, whose office did not change from term to term, I worked with different boards of the Chapter and the Society over a span of twenty years. One of the Chapter chairmen during this period was Robert Freeman—director of the Eastman School of Music and himself trained in Bach scholarship under Mendel at Princeton—who, in the course of our shared duties, rather unexpectedly invited me to join the faculty of his school. Among my qualifying factors, I learned later, was ripe age (most of the members of Eastman's Musicology Department, though distinguished, were quite young)—whereas I lacked the typical qualification for the Rutgers medal awarded to me by my old institution at the parting: it was normally reserved for recipients not directly connected with the University. And I felt equally proud of my success and failure to conform to the specified criteria.

I had by that time reached retirement age and had no longer contemplated a move. But "retirement" had always struck me as a strange thought for one who, by definition, professed to the calling of his work. The old-type *professor emeritus* used to remain actively connected with his institution, and somehow I had harbored a vision that I might follow this outmoded practice in my career. It seemed too unrealistic in the circumstances of a modern society, but for years to follow, I returned to Rutgers University to chair the meetings of the editorial board for my University series of music editions, just as I returned to Bethlehem and its Bach performances as conductor emeritus. When the time came for mandatory retirement, the University of Rochester, parent institution of the Eastman School of Music, allowed me generously to continue teaching individual courses as a retired member of the School's faculty. In deep appreciation, I realized that the retiree's vague dream had come true.

The new environment to which Robert Freeman introduced me represented the fulfillment of many dreams. For the first time since Curtis days, I returned to a professional music school. I had appeared in concerts there thirty years earlier, and I found as my new colleagues fellow students from Curtis and Columbia. For Eastman, known for its eminent performing faculty, had also one of the best musicology departments in the country, and its library (whose history antedates that of the school) is justly famed for its extraordinary resources.

The old-age present I was thus given is manifold. Once, during my earliest days in Milan, on a forlorn hour's walk through the park surrounding the medieval fortress of the Sforzas, I had constructed a picture in vivid daydreaming. I liked the quiet foot paths where the noise of the city was silenced and the only sound heard was that of playing children. To my surprise, it was occasionally interrupted by some German words and calls coming from their guardians who, in old-fashioned governess dress and by old-fashioned custom, served the aristocratic families of the internationally-oriented city. Nostalgia guided me back to my German student days, and suddenly I saw myself in front of my choir (which I was not to have for quite a few years hence), rehearsing Bach's motet "Singet dem Herrn ein neues Lied", a work which had always struck me as one of Bach's most wondrous. "Sing Ye to the Lord a New Song"—a prophetic reminiscence.

I thought then that never again would I sing and hear this work performed in German, for the fact that Bach's music had travelled, in its original setting, through all the world, was then still unknown to me. It was to be among the first that I so performed in New York, in

Bethlehem, and also at my new school in Rochester. A year after my own appointment followed that of a new choral director, Donald Neuen, and together we planned a Bach conference to be held at Eastman the following year. We subsequently joined in a recording project using my *Messiah* edition during a semester in which Jens Peter Larsen came to the school as a visiting professor; and a unique working association has bound our work together ever since.

But my new title was Professor of Musicology—a title that, so formulated, I had not held before and that impressed upon me the unification of the professions of scholarship and performance I had found in formers years so often at odds.

Scholarship, in its most enlightened moments, is borne of performance, as instruction is of scholarship. And those instructed are the teachers and the students. My students have become my colleagues and editors, and my thoughts return to cherished moments in which I similarly joined my teachers. Kurt Thomas, the mentor to whom I owe the origins of my work in Berlin student days, and in later, troubled years one of the successors to Bach's office, came to New York thirty-five years ago to conduct my choir. Nostalgia has given way to grateful memories—my own performances in Carnegie Hall, Philadelphia's Academy of Music, Boston's Symphony Hall, Berlin's Philharmonie, and St. Thomas's; those where I conducted orchestras of which my sons were members; those, more recently, in which I played quartets with my grandsons; public lectures at international conferences; honorary membership in Handel and Bach Societies.

Hölderlin speaks of the tender glow in which the light and the dark of bygone days merge. What remains is gratitude and challenge.

Michael R. Dodds

AN ALFRED MANN BIBLIOGRAPHY

It has been difficult to select and categorize the titles compiled in this listing and extending over sixty years of Alfred Mann's publishing activity. With his contributions to the *Hallische Händel–Ausgabe* and *Neue Schubert–Ausgabe*, he introduced a format that departed from that generally adopted in the sets of Critical Editions. The volumes were planned as books in which the musical text was interspersed rather than presented separately. A comparable plan was followed in his *The Study of Fugue* and *Theory and Practice*, where monograph and critical edition are merged. A series of small volumes that appeared under his editorship as special issues of the *American Choral Review* during the past thirty years, such as Handel studies by Jens Peter Larsen and Bach studies by Alfred Dürr and Wilhelm Ehmann, reviews in American and German periodicals, and notes for recordings, have not been included. Omitted, as well, was a list of American and European recordings of works by Bach, Buxtehude, Handel, Schütz, and other Baroque masters on which he appeared variously as recorder soloist, contrabassist, or conductor.

Michael R. Dodds is a candidate for the degree of PhD in musicology at the Eastman School of Music.

CRITICAL EDITIONS AND MONOGRAPHS

Die Lehre vom Kontrapunkt: Johann Joseph Fux, Gradus ad Parnassum, 2. Buch, 1.–3. Uebung, Celle: Moeck, 1938; 2nd ed. 1951, annotated German translation. English editions as: *Johann Joseph Fux: Steps to Parnassus. The Study of Counterpoint*, translated and edited with the collaboration of John St Edmunds. New York: Norton, 1943; London: Dent, 1944; in paperback: *The Study of Counterpoint*. New York: Norton, 1965, and Toronto: McLeod, 1965.

Johann Joseph Fux: Gradus ad Parnassum, in *Sämtliche Werke*, Serie VII, Band I. Kassel: Bärenreiter, and Graz: Akademische Druck u. Verlagsanstalt, 1967 (facsimile edition of the original text with German and English commentary).

Johann Joseph Fux: Singfundament, in *Sämtliche Werke*, Serie VII, Band II, with Eva Badura–Skoda. Kassel: Bärenreiter, and Graz: Akademische Druck u. Verlagsanstalt, 1992.

Georg Friedrich Händel: Aufzeichnungen zur Kompositionlehre/Composition Lessons, in *Hallische Händel-Ausgabe*, Supplement, Band I. Kassel: Bärenreiter, and Leipzig: Deutscher Verlag für Musik, 1978 (German and English text).

Thomas Attwoods Theorie- und Kompositionsstudien bei Mozart, in *Neue Mozart–Ausgabe*, Serie X, Band 30/1, with Erich Hertzmann, Cecil B. Oldman, and Daniel Heartz. Kassel, etc.: Bärenreiter, 1965; Kritischer Bericht, with Daniel Heartz, 1969.

Barbara Ployers und Franz Jakob Freystädtlers Theorie- und Kompositionstudien bei Mozart, in *Neue Mozart–Ausgabe*, Serie X, Band 30/2, with Hellmut Federhofer. Kassel: Bärenreiter, 1989.

Schuberts Studien, in *Neue Schubert–Ausgabe*, Serie VIII, Band 2. Kassel: Bärenreiter, 1986.

The Study of Fugue. New Brunswick: Rutgers, 1958; London: Faber, [1959]; Westport, Connecticut: Greenwood, 1981; in paperback: New York: Norton, 1965; Toronto: McLeod, 1965; New York: Dover, 1987.

Bethlehem Bach Studies. Bethlehem, Pennsylvania: Moravian Book Shop, 1985.

Theory and Practice: The Great Composers as Teachers and Students. New York and London: Norton, 1987; New York: Dover, 1994.

Bach and Handel: Choral Performance Practice. Chapel Hill, North Carolina: Hinshaw, 1992; 2nd edition, 1994.

Handel's Orchestral Music. New York: Schirmer Books, in press.

ARTICLES

"The Riddle of Mephistopheles." *The Germanic Review* 24, no. 4 (1949):265–68.

"The Artistic Testament of Richard Strauss." *The Musical Quarterly* 36, no. 1 (1950):1–8.

"Records in the Classroom." *Notes* 8, no. 3 (1951):471–75.

"Baroque Music in the College." *Proceedings of the College Music Association* (December 1955).

"Music Theory in College Teaching," with William Mitchell and Robert Trotter. *Proceedings of the College Music Association* (December 1959).

"Georg Philipp Telemann." In *Collier's Encyclopedia*, Louis Shores, ed. in chief. New York: MacMillan Educational Corporation, 1960.

"Sources of the Classical Idiom." In *Report of the Eighth Congress, New York 1961*, edited by Jan La Rue, International Society for Musicology, 2:135–39. Kassel: Bärenreiter, 1962.

"Händels Fugenlehre—ein unveröffentlichtes Manuskript." In *Bericht über den internationalen musikwissenschaftlichen Kongreß Kassel 1962*, edited by Georg Reichert and Martin Just, 172–74. Kassel: Bärenreiter, 1963.

"Zum Concertistenprinzip bei Händel." In *Musik als Lobgesang, Festschrift für Wilhelm Ehmann*, edited by Gerhard Mittring and Gerhard Rödding, 72–82. Darmstadt: Merseburger, 1964.

"Eine Kompositionslehre von Händel." *Händel-Jahrbuch* 1964/65:35–57.

"Report from Salzburg: The Present State of Mozart Research." *Current Musicology* 1 (1965):92–94.

"Zur Aufführungspraxis Händelscher Vokalmusik." *Händel-Jahrbuch* 1966:38–44.

"Eine Textrevision von der Hand Joseph Haydns." In *Musik und Verlag: Karl Vötterle zum 65. Geburtstag*, edited by Richard Baum and Wolfgang Rehm, 433–37. Kassel: Bärenreiter, 1968.

"Artist and Teacher." In *Eighteenth-Century Studies in Honor of Paul Henry Lang, Current Musicology* 9 (1969):141–46.

"Handelian Rehearsal and Performance Practice." *College Music Symposium* 9 (1969):97–100.

"The Present State of Handel Research," with J. Merrill Knapp. *Acta Musicologia* 41, nos. 1–2 (1969):4–26.

"Beethoven's Contrapuntal Studies with Haydn." *Musical Quarterly* 56, no. 4 (1970):711–26; reprinted in *The Creative World of Beethoven*, edited by Paul Henry Lang. New York: Norton, 1971.

"Haydn as Student and Critic of Fux." In *Studies in Eighteenth-Century Music: A Tribute to Karl Geiringer on His Seventieth Birthday*, edited by H. C. Robbins Landon with Roger E. Chapman, 323–32. London: George Allen & Unwin, 1970.

"Zum deutschen Erbe Händels." *Neue Zeitschrift für Musik* 125, no. 9 (1964):3–7. Reprinted in *Festschrift: 50 Jahre Göttinger Händel-Festspiele*, edited by Walter Meyerhoff, 48–56. Kassel: Bärenreiter, 1970.

"Haydns Kontrapunktlehre und Beethovens Studien." In *Bericht über den internationalen musikwissenschaftlichen Kongreß Bonn 1970*, edited by Carl Dahlhaus, Hans Joachim Marx, Magda Marx-Weber, and Günther Massenkeil, 70–74. Kassel: Bärenreiter, 1972.

"*Messiah*: The Verbal Text." In *Festskrift Jens Peter Larsen*, edited by Nils Schiørring, Henrik Glahn, and Carsten E. Hatting, 181–88. Copenhagen: Wilhelm Hansen Musik-Forlag, 1972.

"Haydn's Elementarbuch: A Document of Classic Counterpoint Instruction." In *The Music Forum*, edited by William J. Mitchell and Felix Salzer, 3:197–237. New York: Columbia, 1973.

"Padre Martini und Fux." In *Festschrift für Ernst Hermann Meyer*, edited by Georg Knepler, 253–55. Leipzig: Deutscher Verlag für Musik, 1973.

"Bass Problems in *Messiah*." In *Studies in Renaissance and Baroque Music in Honor of Arthur Mendel*, edited by Robert L. Marshall, 359–62. . Kassel: Bärenreiter, and Hackensack, New Jersey: Joseph Boonin, 1974.

"Zur Kontrapunktlehre Haydns und Mozart." *Mozart-Jahrbuch* 1978/79:195–9.

"The Opening of *Messiah*: A Problem of Performance Practice." *American Choral Review* 21, no. 3 (1979):9–13.

"Zu Schuberts Studien im strengen Satz." In *Schubert-Kongreß Wien 1978: Bericht*, edited by Otto Brusatti, 127–39. Graz: Akademische Druck und Verlaganstalt, 1979.

"Canon," with J. Kenneth Wilson. In *The New Grove Dictionary of Music and Musicians*, Stanley Sadie, ed., London: Macmillan Publishers Ltd., 1980.

"Zur Frage der Datierung durch Wasserzeichen: Mit einem Brief von Frederick Hudson." *Händel-Jahrbuch* 1980:123–28.

"Bach's A Major Mass—A Nativity Mass?" In *Essays on the Music of J.S. Bach: A Tribute to Gerhard Herz*, edited by Robert L. Weaver, 43–47. New York: Pendragon, 1981. Reprinted as *"Missa Brevis and Historia: Bach's A Major Mass." Bach* 16, no. 1 (1985):6–11.

"Haydn's Relationship to the *stile antico*." In *Haydn Studies: Proceedings of the International Haydn Conference, Washington, D.C., 1975*, edited by Jens Peter Larsen, Howard Serwer and James Webster, 374–76. . New York & London: Norton, 1981.

"Ist Komponieren lehrbar?: Zur klassischen Fugenlehre." *Musica* 30, no. 4 (1981):335–39.

"Vorwort zu den Referaten des Händel-Symposiums New York 1979." *Händel-Jahrbuch* 1981:37.

"Schubert's Lesson with Sechter." *Nineteenth Century Music* 6, no. 2 (1982):159–65.

"Handel's Successor: Notes on John Christopher Smith the Younger." In *Music in Eighteenth-Century England: Essays in Memory of Charles Cudworth*, edited by Christopher Hogwood and Richard Luckett, 135–45. Cambridge University Press, 1983.

"Mattheson as Biographer of Handel." In *New Mattheson Studies*, edited by George J. Buelow and Hans Joachim Marx, 345–52. Cambridge University Press, 1983.

"Problems with Handel Oratorio." *Händel-Jahrbuch* 1983:39–41.

"Zur mährischen Bachpflege in Amerika." In *Bachiana et Alia Musicologica: Festschrift Alfred Dürr zum 65. Geburtstag*, edited by Wolfgang Rehm, 178–82. Kassel: Bärenreiter, 1983.

"Das Kammerduett im englischen Schaffen Händels." In *Göttinger Händel-Beiträge* I (1984):59–69.

"Tchaikovsky as Teacher." In *Music and Civilization: Essays in Honor of Paul Henry Lang*, edited by Edmond Strainchamps and Maria Rika Maniates with Christopher Hatch, 279–96. New York: Norton, 1984.

"Zum Salzburger Studienbuch." *Mozart-Jahrbuch* 1984/85: 71–75

"Bach and Handel as Teachers of Thorough Bass." In *Bach, Handel, Scarlatti: Tercentenary Essays*, edited by Peter Williams, 245–57. Cambridge University Press, 1985.

"Bach und die Fuxsche Lehre: Theorie und Kompositionspraxis." In *Johann Sebastian Bach und Johann Joseph Fux: Bericht über das Symposium anläßlich des 58. Bachfestes der Neuen Bachgesellschaft in Graz*, edited by Johann Trummer and Rudolf Flotzinger, 82–86. Kassel: Bärenreiter, 1985.

"Eine unbekannte Notiz zur Händel-Biographie." *Händel-Jahrbuch* 1985:61–62.

"An Unknown Detail of Handel Biography." *Bach* 16, no. 2 (1985):3–5.

"Handel the Organist." *American Organist* 19 (1985):68–70.

"Zur Generalbaßlehre Bachs und Händels." In *Basler Jahrbuch für historische Musikpraxis* 9 (1985):25–38.

"Handel's English Duets." In *George Frideric Handel's Chamber Duets*, 19–43. Los Angeles: William Andrews Clark Memorial Library, University of California, 1987.

"Zur Problematik des Händelbildes." In *Alte Musik als ästhetische Gegenwart: Bach, Händel, Schütz; Bericht über den internationalen musikwissenschaftlichen Kongreß, Stuttgart 1985* edited by Dietrich Berke and Dorothee Hanemann, 1:27–35. Kassel: Bärenreiter, 1987.

"Englische Formen in Händels Werk. Bermerkungen zur Gattungstypologie und Aufführungspraxis." In *Händel auf dem Theater, Conference Report, Karlsruhe 1985*, 39–45. Stuttgart: Laaber, 1988.

"Bach's Parody Technique and its Frontiers." In *Bach Studies*, edited by Don O. Franklin, 115–24. Cambridge University Press, 1989.

"A Document from the Hand of Arthur Mendel: Introduction and Commentary." *Bach* 20, no. 3 (1989):4–14.

"*Gradus* und *Singfundament*: Quellenstudien zur Lehrweise von Johann Joseph Fux." In *Festschrift Wolfgang Rehm zum 60. Geburtstag*, edited by Dietrich Berke and Harald Heckmann, 25–30. Kassel: Bärenreiter, 1989.

"In Memoriam: Karl Geiringer." *Bach* 20, no. 1 (1989):5.

"Leopold Mozart als Lehrer seines Sohnes." *Mozart-Jahrbuch* 1989/90:31–35.

"Johann Joseph Fux's Theoretical Writings: A Classical Legacy." In *Johann Joseph Fux and the Music of the Austro-Italian Baroque*, edited by Harry White, 57–71. Aldershot, Hants: Scolar Press, 1992.

"*Missa* and *Messiah*." In *A Bach Tribute: Essays in Honor of William H. Scheide*, edited by Paul Brainard and Ray Robinson. Kassel: Bärenreiter, and Chapel Hill, N.C.: Hinshaw, 1994.

"German Organ Tablature in Handel's Autographs." In *The Organist as Scholar: Essays in Honor of Russell Saunders*, edited by Kerala J. Snyder, 151–64. Stuyvesant, NY: Pendragon, 1994.

AMERICAN CHORAL REVIEW EDITORIALS

"New Sacred Drama: The Nativity According to St. Luke," 4, no. 2, 1962.

"On a First American Tour: Bach's St. John Passion," 4, no. 3, 1962.

"Choral Music in Germany: Bach's Heritage," 5, no. 4, 1963.

"The Play of Herod," 6, no. 2, 1964.

"An International Heinrich Schütz Festival," 7, no. 3, 1965.

"New Choral Drama: The Passion According to St. Luke," 7, no. 4, 1965.

"Handel and Haydn Society: Legacy of a Pioneer," 8, no. 1, 1965.

"Albert Schweitzer on Bach's Motets," 8, no. 2, 1965.

"A Fresh View of Handel," 9, no. 3, 1967.

"A Tribute to Leonard Bernstein," 10, no. 4, 1968.

"A Choral Conductor Steps In," 20, no. 1, 1978.

"Performing Bach's Cantatas: Harnoncourt versus Rilling," 20, no. 4, 1978.

"The Opening of *Messiah*: A Problem of Performance Practice," 21, no. 3, 1979.

"De Rossi Singers," 22, no. 4, 1980.

"Salute to Robert Shaw," 23, no. 4, 1981.

"A Tribute to Hugo Distler," 26, no. 1, 1984.

"In Memoriam: Irving Lowens," 26, no. 3, 1984.

"A Document from the Organ Renaissance: In Memory of Rudolph Maack," 28 no. 1, 1986.

"Reflections on the Anniversary Year: A Report," 28, no. 2, 1986.

"Handel and Haydn: American Choral History," 28, no. 4, 1986.

"The Show Choir: A Conductor's Challenge and Defense," 29, no. 1, 1987.

"In Memoriam: Ifor Jones," 31, no. 1, 1989.

"'Handel & Haydn': A Salute at the 175th," 32, no. 1–2, 1990.

"A New Phase," 33, no. 2, 1991.

"In Memoriam: Paul Henry Lang," 34, no. 1, 1992.

EDITIONS OF BOOKS

Kurt Thomas: The Choral Conductor. New York: Associated Music Publishers, 1971. English adaptation with William H. Reese of Kurt Thomas, *Lehrbuch der Chorleitung.*

Randall Thompson: A Choral Legacy. Boston: E.C. Schirmer, 1974, 1980, 1983.

Bach in Bethlehem Today: A Conference Report. Bethlehem, Pennsylvania: Moravian Book Shop, 1979.

Modern Music Librarianship: Essays in Honor of Ruth Watanabe. Stuyvesant, New York: Pendragon, and Kassel: Bärenreiter, 1989.

Paul Henry Lang: Musicology and Performance—Collected Essays, edited by Alfred Mann and George J. Buelow. Lincoln, Nebraska: University of Nebraska Press, in press.

INTRODUCTIONS FOR REPRINTS

Jens Peter Larsen. *Handel's Messiah: Origins, Composition, Sources*, 2nd ed. New York: Norton, 1989.

Knud Jeppesen. *Counterpoint: The Polyphonic Vocal Style of the Sixteenth Century.* Glen Haydon, trans. New York: Dover, 1992.

EDITIONS OF MUSIC

Maurice Greene. *Anthem for Christmas Day.* Glen Rock, New Jersey: J. Fischer & Bro., 1961.

Jean Baptiste Loeillet. *Trio–Sonata in D Minor, Op. 2, No. 4.* New York: Music Press, 1947.

Johann Christoph Pepusch. *Sonata VIII*, in Erna Dancker-Langer, ed., *Johann Christoph Pepusch: Zwei Sonaten.* Celle: Moeck, 1939.

Alessandro Rolla. *Sonata for Viola and Piano.* San Antonio, Texas: Southern Music Co., 1991.

Heinrich Schütz. *The Annunciation* (from *Kleine Geistliche Konzerte* II, 1639). Glen Rock, New Jersey: J. Fischer & Bro., 1956.

Rutgers University Documents of Music. New Brunswick: Rutgers, 1953–1990, distributed by Jerona Music Corporation, Hackensack, New Jersey.

In this series:

No. 1. Johann Christian Bach, *Piano Concerto, Op. 1, No. 4 in G Major*, 1953.

No. 2. Henry Purcell, *Christmas Anthem: Behold, I Bring You Glad Tidings*, 1953.

No. 3. Orlando Gibbons, *Concerted Anthems* ("This is the Record of John" and "Behold, Thou hast made my Days"), with Melvin Strauss, 1958.

No. 4. Salomone Rossi, *Trio Sonatas for Two Violins and Basso Continuo*, with Fritz Rikko, 1965.

No. 5. Alessandro Rolla, *Concertino for Viola, Violoncello and Bassoon*, 1987.

No. 6. George Frideric Handel, *Messiah*, 1959–65.

No. 9. George Frideric Handel, *Ten Small Keyboard Fugues: Lessons in Composition / Zehn kleine Klavierfugen: Lehrbeispiele zur Komposition*, [1979].

No. 10. George Frideric Handel, *Two Sacred Arias / Zwei geistliche Arien*, [1990].

Separate re-issue:

G. F. Handel: *Messiah*, in full score. New York: Dover, 1989.

SCHOOL MUSIC

Zweistimmige Spielstücke. Celle: Moeck, 1934.

Deutsche Volkstänze, with Joachim Stave. Celle: Moeck, 1934/35.

Kleine Schulmusik. Celle: Moeck, 1937.

Jakob Regnart, *Lively Airs* (selection of vilanellas from *Kurtzweilige Teutsche Lieder*, Nürnburg 1576). New York: Clark & Way, 1940.

English Duets (eighteenth-century arrangements of works by Henry Purcell and his English contemporaries). New York: Hargail, 1942.

Orange School Music (published for the Public Schools of Orange, New Jersey). New York: McGinnis & Marx, 1956–1961.